A CITIZEN'S GUIDE TO
ECONOMICS

THIRD EDITION

MIKEL W. COHICK | JAMES R. RICHARDS | GIAN ARYANI

Kendall Hunt
publishing company

Kendall Hunt
publishing company

www.kendallhunt.com
Send all inquiries to:
4050 Westmark Drive
Dubuque, IA 52004-1840

Copyright © 2022 by Kendall Hunt Publishing Company

PAK ISBN: 979-8-7657-0096-9
Text Alone ISBN: 979-8-7657-0095-2

Published in the United States of America

Contents

Preface

In this edition, we added business decision making in oligopoly, expanded our discussion of the tools of the Federal Reserve, included the economic results of the 2017 to 2018 tax and regulatory cuts and of the government responses to the COVID-19 pandemic, and showed how the results of these responses triggered increase in inflation.

The purpose of this text is to help people understand the economics that affects them as they go about their daily lives—training and learning, working and earning, providing for their family, planning for the future, starting up and running a business, and being good citizens.

Economics, contrary to conventional wisdom, is not just about money, or about the stock market, or what Congress and the President do. It is not, as Thomas Carlyle said, "the dismal science."

The very essence of understanding economics is the ability to describe why and how economic participants—and that includes everyone—must make decisions, as they strive to improve themselves.

People want to be better off after they take an action than before. Because of this, we start off with the basic ideas of economics. They are based on the decision-making techniques of people who rationally choose to do things that will make them better off and will improve their quality of life.

These basic ideas show how each sector of the economy—consumers, businesses, government, international participants, employers, employees, and resource owners—put them to use for the betterment of themselves and for the betterment of society in general.

We show how an economic society can be set up to insure the greatest possible betterment for its citizens. In 1776, Adam Smith wrote that a necessary requirement for someone to end up better off is to make someone else better off, too. We show how specialization, competition, and trade accomplish exactly that. We show how free trade, unfettered by intrusive government prohibitions and restrictions, is the clearest way to maximize a society's standard of living.

To describe the nation's economy, we concentrate on **the two most significant macroeconomic variables: the inflation rate and the unemployment rate.** We want to be able to track what has happened in the past, what is happening in the present, and what we can expect to happen in the future when the Federal Reserve, the President, and Congress take action to intervene in the economy.

We hope you, the reader, will be much more capable of understanding and deciphering what the news media and the politicians are saying about the economy, much more informed about what is happening in the world, much more aware of the options you have in dealing with your individual economic world, and much more capable of exercising your important responsibility of citizenship.

We welcome Gian Aryani to our team as a new author. We would also like to express our appreciation to Collin College professors Clay Randall, Laura Hicks, and Mohammed Tahiro for providing valuable comments and insightful suggestions to improve the Third Edition of our textbook.

1 The Basic Ideas of Economics

Economics studies the actions of people as they conduct their daily lives. Every day, your life is filled with decisions. Many are not very significant, but they must be made. Many are repetitive. You made them before and now you must make them again, like deciding whether to brush your teeth or choosing which clothes to wear. Many are significant and require a lot of preparation before you decide. Many must be made without complete information.

These decisions all must be made because nobody can have everything they want, including you. Someone must choose which of the available alternatives will be accepted and which will be foregone. Economics analyzes the many ways that making decisions can be accomplished in the modern world. This is why economics is the science of decision-making.

In this chapter, we introduce the basic concepts and ideas of economics. These basic concepts and ideas apply not only to each of us as individuals going about our daily activities, but also to societies in general as they organize for the welfare of the people living in that society.

After studying this chapter, you should be able to:

1. Tell how individuals, consumers, producers, and governments make decisions.
2. Tell why the existence of scarcity forces us to make decisions.
3. Describe how goods and services are produced.
4. Tell why there is always a cost in making decisions, even if no money changes hands.
5. Describe what alternative organizing mechanisms exist for a society.
6. Describe how these alternative organizing mechanisms differ in answering vital economic questions.
7. Describe what payoff exists when there is state protection of private property rights.
8. Outline what the production possibilities curve (PPC) shows us.
9. Tell why we want economic growth.

How Do People Normally Act?

The principal assumption made in this book is that **people act rationally**, that is, **they think before they act.** In the real world, some people occasionally perform irrational acts, do crazy things, and act before they think. But most of the rest of the time, people will be **rational**.

Being rational means people plan ahead. They think things through before performing a particular act. They gather information and ask their friends what they think. They recall their past experiences and remember if performing a particular act in the past was worthwhile.

Why do people do this? **They want to better themselves**. They want to improve their net worth, to be better off after they complete the act than they were before. The reason people do what they do is to obtain satisfaction, that is, to fulfill previously unfilled wants and needs. Their goal is to increase their happiness. Satisfaction, fulfillment, and happiness all connote the same result.

People have unfilled wants and needs. Some are large; some are small, almost trivial. Some are urgent and must be taken care of as soon as possible; some can be delayed. Therefore, each unfilled want or need has a priority status. Rational people try to satisfy their highest priority wants and needs first. You are a prime example of such a rational person.

Where Do the Things We Use Every Day Come From?

In economics, we divide the things that satisfy our wants and needs into two categories:

(i) Goods and

(II) Services

Goods are things produced. Examples are cars, hamburgers, pecan pies, and ear pods. Goods can be produced ahead of time and placed on the shelf waiting for the customer.

Services are actions produced. Examples are oil changes, trash collection, classroom teaching, and hair styling. Services cannot be produced ahead of time. The customer must wait while the service is carried out. Both categories are produced in a process where resources are transformed into satisfying goods and services.

Resources are the inputs into a production process. There are four categories of resources: land, labor, capital, and entrepreneurship. As is true in any discipline, words are defined specifically for the discipline, even though the very same word may be used more casually in everyday life. The resource categories are an excellent example of this. **Caution!** Do not try to get by in economics, or any other discipline, using the casual, everyday definition of a term when the discipline uses a specific definition.

Land includes all natural resources. These are the gifts of Mother Nature, including everything received from the earth, from the sea, and from the air. The payment for a land resource is **rent**. This comes from the French word *rente*, used by them to identify the payment for an agricultural good. We casually use the word "rent" to describe the payment for anything we wish to use for a limited amount of time.

Labor includes all humans at work, from the factory worker to the manager, both at a job and at home. All humans have some capacity to perform labor. The **wage** is, collectively, the reward for labor. For a firm, the wage includes not only take-home pay but also the value of the benefits package that comes with the job and the administrative costs to the company of hiring a worker, including payroll taxes levied on the company. Each human has only 24 hours available in each day to do all the things he or she wants to do, including work. Thus, time itself is the basis for the labor resource. There is manual labor, such as mechanics, assembly line workers, construction workers, and technicians. Also, there is mental labor, such as engineers, graphic designers, teachers, and computer software developers.

Capital consists of human-made goods that are used to produce other goods and services. This category includes all tools and equipment, vehicles, and buildings. Business enterprises are the owners of capital since it is here where most production takes place. Karl Marx, one of the founders of communism, called the owners of capital "capitalists."

In casual talk in the real world, capital describes money, as in "I need to raise capital to start up a business." Money is indeed a tool. It makes the process of exchanging goods and services so much easier. We work around this situation by calling money **financial** and the tools and equipment that money buys **physical capital.** A collective term is **capital goods.** Since businesses finance most of the purchases they make of capital goods by borrowing the money to do so, the payment for the capital resource is **interest.** The cost of borrowing the money and the return from investing the money in capital goods are both expressed as a rate of interest. This makes the comparison of benefits and costs easy.

Entrepreneurship is human action to create goods and services and to set up and operate the process to do just that. The entrepreneur takes an invention or a new idea and brings it to commercial success. Not all humans have entrepreneurial ability, since being entrepreneurial requires one to take risks and many of us are risk avoiders.

The principal risks faced by entrepreneurs are failure to accurately predict the market for their good or service, failure to develop a process to produce the good or service at a profit, and failure to generate an acceptable return on the investment for the firm's shareholders. **Profit is the reward for successful entrepreneurship**. In a later chapter, we shall see how the achievement of profit energizes the entrepreneur to expand while the reality of **losses** (negative profit) causes the entrepreneur to curtail operations or shift to other activities.

All of the resource categories must be paid for. Highly valued resources come at a high price and resources that have little value command a low price. This is one reason a skilled surgeon will be paid more than an unskilled day laborer.

How Are Goods and Services Produced?

The entrepreneur selects resources and combines them as **inputs** into some **process** which will transform them into **outputs.** Think of the process as a recipe, a list of steps to take to make something. The entrepreneur designs the outputs of production to satisfy a particular want or need of potential customers. The entrepreneur wants to do this as efficiently as possible within the current state of technology. **Figure 1-1** shows the production process that transforms resource inputs into satisfying outputs. We strive for efficiency and for improvement by implementing new **technology.**

Efficiency is defined as getting the maximum salable output produced at the lowest possible cost of the inputs used, while minimizing the waste. In this way, the entrepreneur can maximize sales revenue and minimize costs of acquiring the resources and operating the process. Increasing sales revenue and reducing costs add to profit.

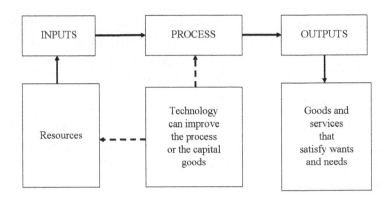

FIGURE 1-1. The Production Process

Resources (land, labor, capital goods, and entrepreneurship) are inputs converted by the entrepreneur's process into outputs that satisfy consumers' wants and needs. An inefficient process will also produce waste products which, if disposed of improperly, cause pollution.

Source: Mikel Cohick.

Waste products are the inevitable by-product of an inefficient process. They cost money to dispose of. If disposed of improperly, they cause pollution. Also, the resources used that result in waste products represent added costs at the input end with no revenues at the output end.

Technology is the application of knowledge to the production process. It can improve the process to make it more efficient or it can improve the resource input to make the tools and equipment more effective and productive.

What Do We Know about Scarcity?

Why must we study economics? If there were always an unlimited number of resources available to fully satisfy everyone's wants and needs, then there would be no need to study economics. However, everyone will always have more wants and needs than can be satisfied.

Resources are limited and our wants and needs are unlimited. The difference between our unlimited wants and the limited resources defines **scarcity.** We are constrained by the resources we have available at any one time. Meanwhile, many of our wants and needs are recurring, like hunger and thirst and other biological needs. We must satisfy them repeatedly. Other wants and needs are new, and we want to fill them.

The condition that comes out of this situation is **scarcity. Anything is scarce if it is useful and there is a limited amount of it.** Scarcity has always existed and always will exist in the future.

Since not all wants and needs can be satisfied at any one time, decisions must be made to determine which wants and needs will be satisfied now, and which ones will be put off until a later time or may never be satisfied. How we as individuals and as a society figure this out is what we study in economics.

You are already skilled in making these decisions. Consider time management. You must figure out how to use the 24 hours in any one day to the best of your advantage. Your goal is to make yourself as better off as possible by combining work, sleep, grooming, study, school attendance, commuting, play, using your cell phone, and all the other things you do in those 24 hours. Being rational, you usually select those activities that have the highest priority (according to you) and include them, while postponing other, lower priority activities to another day.

What is a Good Definition of Economics?

Based on scarcity, **economics is a study of how individuals and society try to make the best use of the scarce resources** available to them. How do people allocate their scarce resources to fulfill their most-valued unmet wants and needs? Whose wants and needs get satisfied? Who must go without? As individuals and as a society, we should try to maximize efficiency to get the most satisfaction out of the resources we use up. Maximizing the efficient use of resources will lead to maximizing the overall economic well-being of society.

How Do We Make Decisions?

No matter who does the deciding, we will assume they are rational in doing so. That means the decision-maker will think things through, gather information, recall past experiences, weigh the value of what will be obtained (**the benefit**) and the value of what must be given up (**the cost**), and decide whether or not to take the next step. The decision-maker does this by using a technique called **cost-benefit analysis.**

Good decision-makers will also work on the margin, where the **margin is the next step taken.** It is best to keep the size of this next step to be small, especially in uncertain situations.

The key tool you, the decision-maker, will use is your **valuation system.** You create your own valuation system by evaluating all the experiences, likes and dislikes, and other available information and formulating an opinion of the worth of a particular thing. Each person's valuation system is unique. It is highly unlikely that two people would have the same valuation system. A consequence of this is that you are better at making decisions about satisfying your wants and needs than somebody else doing it for you.

A **cost** is your valuation of what you must give up when you make a decision. When working on the margin it is called **marginal cost (MC).** This is the cost of taking the next step (or making the next item).

A **benefit** is your valuation of what you expect to get when you make a decision. When working on the margin it is called **marginal benefit (MB).** This is the benefit you get from taking the next step (or making the next item).

If the marginal benefit exceeds the marginal cost (MB > MC), then taking the next step is worthwhile. You will end up with more if you do so, since you get back more than you give up. Your net worth increases, and you will be better off.

If MB > MC, do it! Because if you do, your net worth increases.

If the marginal benefit is less than the marginal cost (MB < MC), then taking the next step is not worthwhile. You will end up with less if you do so, since you give up more than you get. If you go ahead and take this step, your net worth would decrease, and you would be worse off.

If MB < MC, don't do it! Because if you do, your net worth decreases.

Scarcity forces decisions to be made, since not everyone can have everything that they want. Rational people use cost-benefit analysis to make these decisions. This is so natural to people that often they are not even aware they are doing it.

What Is an Opportunity Cost?

Every decision has at least one cost. It is the **opportunity cost**. A resource used to make one product is no longer available to make another product. In other words, you lose the opportunity to use it to make another product.

Rational decision-making implies you will elect to use the resource to make the product that is most valuable to you. You get the most valuable (to you) product and must give up getting the lesser-valued product. Therefore, **the opportunity cost of any decision you make is the value you place on the next best alternative that you could have chosen but did not.**

Here are some examples of opportunity cost:

- Come to your 8 AM class and you lose the value of an extra hour of sleep.

- Sleep an extra hour and you lose the value of your 8 a.m. class.

- Buy a $20 shirt and you can't use the money to buy $20 worth of gasoline.

- Use all your study time on English and see your Economics grade drop.

Most decisions involve giving up one thing of value to get another thing of value. Deciding whether to do so is called making a **trade-off**. You will take the next step in a sequence of trade-offs if you perceive the marginal benefit (MB) you would get in the next step exceeds the marginal cost (MC) of taking that next step. You would keep taking the next step as long as you continue to perceive that MB > MC for that step. Ultimately, you will perceive that you have reached the step where MB = MC and that the next step would have MB < MC. This is the decision point where you would reject taking the next step and you will stop.

How Does a Society Answer the Three Basic Economic Questions?

All economic societies must answer these questions:

- **What to produce**
- **How to produce?**
- **For whom to produce?**

There are three basic ways society can organize to answer these questions:

- In a **traditional** economy, people will do everything the way it has always been done.

- In a **market capitalist** economy, individuals decide for themselves.

- In a **command dictatorship** economy, the rulers make all the decisions.

How Does a Society Answer "What to Produce?"

In a traditional society, this generation will produce exactly the products that were produced by the previous generations. There are no new decisions to make.

In a market capitalist society, each buyer decides what he or she wants to buy, or not. Buyers send a message to producers each time they buy or do not buy a good or service. If you decide to buy a good, the inventory stock decreases by one. If you decide not to buy, the item remains on the shelf. Millions of these messages are sent each day. Producers adjust their production process in response to those messages. They produce more of the goods that are selling. They produce less of the goods that do not sell. This insures they are producing what customers want to buy, thereby maximizing sales revenues.

In a command dictatorship society, the rulers decide what people should have. Producers only make those things the rulers allow them to make. Individual preferences have extraordinarily little influence in this type of society.

How Does a Society Answer "How to Produce?"

In a traditional society, sons will train to do the work their fathers did, and daughters will do the work their mothers did. Everything will be done in the time-honored and old-fashioned way.

In a market capitalist society, entrepreneurs will choose the most profitable way to produce a satisfying, salable product, keeping the use of resources as low as possible. An employer will hire those workers who will be most productive. Employees will accept jobs that are most satisfying, both in pay and in other ways. Entrepreneurs will establish new markets or enter existing markets if they see the prospect of a greater return on their time, talent, and investment in relationship to the risk.

In a command dictatorship society, producers will operate production facilities by following the orders of the rulers. The only new ideas that will be implemented are those approved by the dictator.

How Does a Society Answer "For Whom to Produce?"

Since resources are scarce and wants and needs are unlimited, some form of **rationing**, that is, a distribution method, is necessary in every society.

In a traditional society, products will be distributed to users in the way that they always have been distributed. There is no incentive for anyone to try to break out of this preconceived mold, for that would render them to be an outcast of their society.

In a market capitalist society, available products will be placed in a market where prospective buyers can look them over. Only those who want to buy and can afford to pay for a product will get the product. Those who do not want the product, or who will not be willing to pay for it, do not have to buy. Those who cannot afford to pay for the product will not get one. Those who choose to spend their limited income on other, higher priority goods also will not get one.

Purchasing power is the rationing mechanism in a market capitalist society. Those employees more valued by employers will earn more income and have more purchasing power. Thus, there is an incentive for each individual to become more valuable in the eyes of a current or prospective employer. Highly valued, productive employees receive high income. Low valued, unproductive employees receive low income.

In a command dictatorship society, only those who are in favor of the ruler will get the product. Those out of favor will not get any. **Favoritism** is the rationing mechanism in a command dictatorship. Those who have the most pull with the ruler get the most products. People with no pull get very little or must wait in line for leftovers. Thus, the principal incentive for each individual is to become more liked by the ruler.

There is no pure society adhering only to one of these systems. There is a mixture of all three in each country. Some are heavily oriented toward market capitalist, and some are heavily oriented toward command dictatorship. The United States is mainly market capitalist, but has a large element of command dictatorship, where the government tells us what to do and how to do it, also, Americans adhere to many traditional practices.

What Were Adam Smith's Great Ideas?

In a market capitalist society, individuals make decisions. Resources and property are privately owned. Privately owned firms produce goods and services.

Competition is the key. Firms compete for customers. Customers compete for goods and services. Employers compete for the most valued employees. All are trying to maximize their own betterment. All must satisfy others to be successful.

In 1776, Adam Smith wrote of this in "The Wealth of Nations." He said that the wealth of a nation is not the gold in the king's treasury but in the capability of its people to create and produce.

He further said that it is as if an "invisible hand" is guiding all the participants in an economic society to operate for the betterment of all society as they go about their daily business. Each act in his own self-interest to improve his net worth. To succeed, he must cooperate with others to cause them to improve their net worth. As a result, all of society's economic betterment is improved. Smith stated that this form of society would be far wealthier than the existing command dictatorship that existed in Great Britain at the time.

A decision-maker selects the option that will be the best in his own self-interest. To maximize one's own betterment, there is a need to contribute to others' betterment. The seller, to increase sales revenue, must satisfy the desires of the buyer, or there will be no sale. The buyer, to acquire the goods he desires, must be willing to pay the seller enough to make the transaction profitable, or there will be no sale. A successful transaction raises the net worth of both parties. Acting in one's own self-interest does not mean being selfish. A selfish person acts with no concern for the betterment of others.

In a market capitalist society, everyone makes decisions for himself. Individuals own and control the use of resources and property. In a command dictatorship society, the rulers make decisions. The rulers control the use of resources and property, no matter who owns them. This is true no matter what form of command dictatorship: slavery, communism, socialism, fascism, autocracy, and to a lesser extent, burdensome government bureaucracy.

What Are Private Property Rights?

Private property is the right of private persons and firms to obtain, own, control, employ, dispose of, and bequeath land, capital, and other property. One role of an enlightened government is to provide for the protection of individual property rights. People work to obtain an income. People use their income to buy satisfying goods.

One incentive to work is to better yourself by purchasing products that make your life more comfortable and enjoyable. Once you buy a good, it becomes your property. You have the right to use that property as you wish (if you do not use it to harm or hinder others).

It was the usual case in the past in most countries, and continuing in the present in some countries, that the government may confiscate anyone's property without recourse. If you had no right to keep your property, you lose the incentive to work hard.

You would not want to spend your income on things that could be taken away from you. Thus, in societies like these, individuals have no incentive to accumulate goods or to take risks to improve their lot. Consequently, this dooms the people at the bottom of the wealth ladder to stay there, while those in power control most of the wealth.

On the other hand, if an individual's right to own and keep private property is protected from confiscation by the government; individuals have an incentive to accumulate goods and to take risks to improve their lot. Depending upon their ingenuity, talents, hard work, and even luck, many people succeed and begin to accumulate wealth. They move up the wealth ladder and, in the process, create a prosperous middle class.

The rulers are still located high on the wealth ladder, but now many people who would have been doomed to stay at the bottom of that ladder move up. Thus, in a society that protects private property, the number located in poverty at the bottom of the wealth ladder is significantly reduced.

What about publicly owned property? The government controls publicly owned property. It includes national parks and forests, city property, public spaces, and the like. You take good care of your privately owned property and put it to its best use. You do not necessarily do this as well for the property you do not own, including publicly owned property.

Resources owned by the public are not owned by anyone. People tend to use them harshly and expect the government to take care of them. Thus, publicly owned resources suffer more abuse and do not get used as efficiently as privately owned resources. For example, the major pollution problems involve the atmosphere, lakes and rivers, and the oceans. None of these are private property; all are publicly owned.

What Can We Learn from a PPC?

A PPC is a graph showing all possible combinations of two goods that are possible to be produced with an available set of resources and with the existing technology in a given time period.

Any two goods will do—cookies and cake, cars and trucks, shirts and slacks, yogurt, and ice cream—as long as the production facility can be adjusted to switch to making more of one and less of the other.

The PPC represents the capacity to produce goods and services, assuming a fixed number of limited resources, time, and technology. The PPC bows outward because resources are not equally suited to produce both goods. In the example, where we describe the trade-off between cookies and cake, there is a trade-off that gets worse each time a decision is made. To get each additional unit of cookies, increased amounts of cake must be given up.

This example uses a basic production facility, the family kitchen. Mom provides the labor, the available ingredients are the land resource, and all the appliances and equipment in the kitchen are the capital resource. Mom has recipes, thought up long ago by some entrepreneur, for cake and cookies. The recipes outline the process, a series of steps to convert the inputs into the desired outputs, in this case, cake or cookies. All production processes operate in this way. **Figure 1-2** shows a PPC for morn's choice between making cake and baking cookies.

In another example, a society must choose what combination of consumer goods and capital goods it wants to produce with its available resources and the state of its current technology. Just like mom, it can choose to be efficient and produce a combination shown on the PPC.

Exactly where on the PPC mom chooses to be depends on the relative value the family places on how many cookies and how much cake they want at the decision-making time. This is true in any society. Society must choose whether it wants more consumer goods and fewer capital goods, or vice versa. **Figure 1-3** shows the trade-off morn faces when she decides whether or not to increase the number of cookies she might make at the cost of decreasing the amount of cake.

Any of the points on the curve is the result of an efficient use of resources and existing technology. Any point under (inside) the curve is inefficient because the available resources are not being used efficiently. Any point outside the curve is not possible to attain until society adds more resources or uses better technology (or when mom buys more resource inputs or gets new equipment in the kitchen). **Figure 1-4** locates points of efficiency, inefficiency, and unattainable points on a PPC graph.

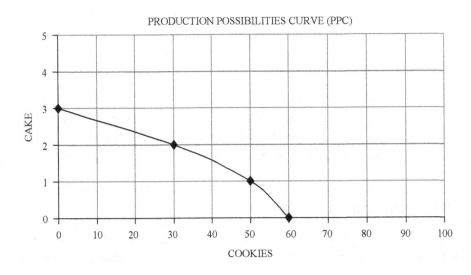

FIGURE 1-2. PPC: data and graph

Mom is limited by the number of resources she has available, including her time, and the current state of technology in her kitchen. Thus, she must choose one of the combinations of cake and cookies to bake that are shown in the data above.

Source: Mikel Cohick.

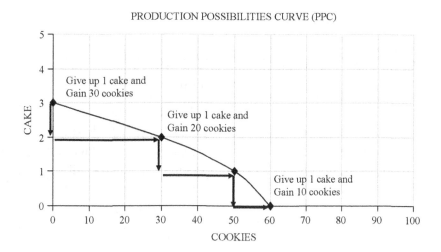

FIGURE 1-3. PPC: Trade-Off

Because most resources and technology are specialized to do one job well, they do that job better than the other. This means that the trade-off gets worse as resources are shifted from one job to the other. Notice that mom gets fewer additional cookies each time she shifts resources equivalent to producing one cake.

Source: Mikel Cohick.

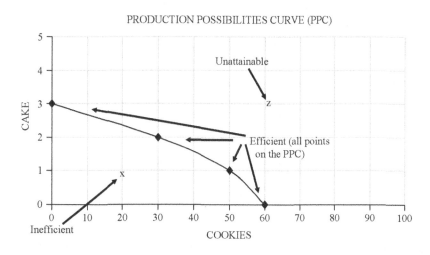

FIGURE 1-4. PPC: efficient, inefficient, and unattainable points

Combinations inside the PPC (*x*) can be produced without using all available resources and technology, leaving many of them idle. Fewer satisfying goods will be produced. This is inefficient. All available resources and technology put to use will produce the combinations on the PPC. This is efficient. Not enough resources or technology exist to produce combinations outside the PPC (*z*). Point *z* is unattainable.

Source: Mikel Cohick.

Why Should We Want Economic Growth?

Economic growth can occur if the curve shifts outward, enabling society to produce more of both kinds of goods and provide for more satisfaction of wants and needs. Adding resources, improving technology, or reducing the burden of government can accomplish this.

In the example of mom producing cake and cookies in the kitchen, mom could run to the grocery store to get more ingredients. She could enlist the aid of the children to help do the work. She could upgrade to more efficient appliances and tools. She could find a better, more productive recipe. In each instance, she would be increasing her available resources or improving the process. All would push the PPC outward, and she could produce larger combinations of cake and cookies. A manufacturer of vehicles or clothing could do the same thing to reach previously unattainable combinations of production.

Figure 1-5 demonstrates the outward shift of the PPC (into previously unattainable possibilities) when either resources are increased or when new technology is implemented, or both. We will examine economic growth in greater depth in Chapter 13.

This example used the trade-off between cookies and cake. There is the same phenomenon when Ford must choose between producing cars or trucks and when the United States government must choose between military expenditures and social welfare expenditures.

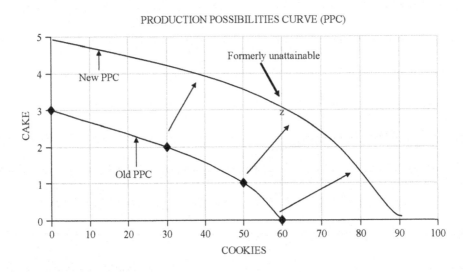

FIGURE 1-5. PPC: economic growth

Increase resources and/or technology and the PPC moves outward into the previously unattainable region. Now combination *z* is possible to produce. Thus, more wants and needs can be fulfilled. This is the essential good of economic growth.

Source: Mikel Cohick.

SUMMARY

1. **Tell how individuals, consumers, producers, and governments make decisions.**

   Economists assume that each of us acts rationally by gathering information and thinking the problem through before we make any decision. This does not mean that we wait for all available information. That is rarely possible. We strive to better ourselves. In small steps, we do this by valuing the benefit to be received (marginal benefit. MB) and what must be given up (marginal cost. MC). If MB > MC, do it and you are better off. If MB < MC, don't do it, and you will be no better or no worse off. If you do it in this situation, you will be worse off.

2. **Tell why the existence of scarcity forces us to make decisions.**

   Scarcity is the condition where we have unlimited wants and needs to be fulfilled but have a limited number of resources available for use in making satisfying goods and services. Therefore, not all wants and needs will be fulfilled. Someone must decide which wants and needs will be fulfilled, and which ones will be put off until another time. Either you will decide for yourself, or someone will decide for you.

3. **Describe how goods and services are produced.**

   Entrepreneurs create a production process, essentially a recipe, which will transform inputs—land, labor, and capital—into satisfying outputs—goods and services. Entrepreneurs will strive for efficiency and will improve the process by implementing new technology.

4. **Tell why there is always a cost in making decisions, even if no money changes hands.**

   Each resource has alternative uses. If we use a resource to satisfy one want or need, we no longer can use it to satisfy some other want or need. Therefore, we suffer a lost opportunity. The value we place on the next best alternative that could have selected (instead of the one we chose) is the opportunity cost of making that decision.

5. **Describe what alternative organizing mechanisms exist for a society.**

   Society can be organized in one of three ways (or, in some combination of the three ways): a traditional society, a command dictatorship, or market capitalism.

6. **Describe how these alternative organizing mechanisms differ in answering vital economic questions.**

   The three vital economic questions are: What to produce? How to produce? For whom to produce?

   A traditional society answers each of these questions by requiring people to do everything the way it always has been done.

   A command dictatorship answers each of these questions by commanding people to do what the dictator says. Deviations from what the dictator says are met with punishment. To get ahead in this system, the principal incentive is to gain favor with the dictator.

Market capitalism is heavily driven by individual decision-making. Each person strives to become better off. Producers produce what customers are willing to buy. Producers seek to be profitable, so they choose how to produce by developing a process to produce a satisfying, salable product, while at the same time, they keep the cost of inputs low. Products are then made available to consumers in a market where those willing and able to pay the price to choose what they want to buy. The incentive in a market system is betterment. To achieve this, each participant must strive to make others better off, so that they might become better off.

7. Describe what payoff exists when there is state protection of private property rights.

If one is assured that he can own private property, and it will not be confiscated by the government or stolen by someone, he has an incentive to work hard to accumulate property, which improves his standard of living. This is the basic step in the accumulation of wealth and the progress upward on the wealth ladder. The result of wealth accumulation is the creation of a prosperous middle class. If the government or a thief can confiscate private property at will, there will be no incentive to work hard and accumulate wealth. Society will remain divided into the ruling elite, the haves and everyone else, the have nots.

8. Outline what the PPC shows ns.

The PPC shows us the various combinations of two goods that can be produced given a fixed number of resources and a fixed technology. The fact that the PPC bows outward indicates that resources and technology are better used to produce one good than the other. As we shift resources and technology, step by step, from producing one good to producing the other, the trade-off gets worse and worse for each additional step. The PPC also shows us what happens when our resources and technology are inefficiently used or not used at all. To achieve economic growth, the PPC must be pushed outward into previously unattainable combinations. This is done by adding resources or improving the technology.

9. Tell why we want economic growth.

If the economy grows, more goods and services can be produced. Therefore, more wants and needs can be fulfilled, and fewer people will have to do without. Economic growth leads to a rising standard of living.

Homework Chapter 1

Name_____

DESCRIPTIONS

Match the key terms with the descriptions.

_____ The process of thinking things through before making a decision.

_____ What can be fulfilled by acquiring goods and services.

_____ People working.

_____ Tools and equipment used for production.

_____ Funds to acquire capital goods.

_____ Risk taking.

_____ Goal of a business.

_____ The transformation process.

_____ Maximum output at lowest cost.

_____ Application of knowledge.

_____ Limited resources unlimited wants and needs.

_____ Evaluation of whether to take the next step.

_____ Cost of taking the next step.

_____ Benefit of taking the next step.

_____ Alternative foregone when you make a decision.

_____ Consumer decides what gets produced.

_____ The ruling elite makes decisions.

_____ Individual ownership of farms, factories and homes.

_____ Description of how self-interested activity benefits society by Adam Smith.

_____ What a society can produce.

_____ More production to satisfy wants and needs.

_____ Things people buy.

KEY TERMS

1. Capital (capital goods)
2. Command dictatorship economy
3. Cost-benefit analysis
4. Economic growth
5. Efficiency
6. Entrepreneurship
7. Financial capital
8. Goods and services
9. Labor
10. Marginal benefit (MB)
11. Marginal cost (MC)
12. Market capitalist economy
13. Opportunity cost
14. Private property
15. Production
16. Production possibilities
17. Making profit
18. Rational action
19. Scarcity
20. Technology
21. The "Invisible Hand"
22. Wants and needs.

EXERCISES

1. Joe decides to go to a hockey game and buys a ticket for $40. He must drive one hour each way to get to the arena. The game will take three hours. He decides to eat his dinner at the arena. It will cost him $8. List all of Joe's opportunity costs of going to the hockey game.

2. Look at a typical pencil. Make a list of some of the resources (land, labor, capital) that are consumed in producing a pencil.

3. Describe how a potential buyer might use cost-benefit analysis to determine whether to buy a particular pair of shoes.

4. Describe how a shoe producer might use cost-benefit analysis to determine whether to produce the shoes.

5. If the rulers could confiscate your private property any time they wished, how would that affect your incentive to work harder or to get an education?

6. How is morn going to know where to position herself on the cookies-cake production possibilities curve?

2 How the Market System Works

Of the three major ways a society can organize—**traditional, command dictatorship, and market capitalist**—the operation of the first two are easy to describe.

In a traditional system, everyone does exactly as has been done in the past. Those who want to defy the system are usually banished from the society or willingly leave.

In a command dictatorship system, everyone does exactly what the ruler tells them to do, under the risk of punishment if they do not.

In a market capitalist system, everyone acts individually to better themselves in their own self-interest, without needing direction from anyone. In such a system, how do things get done? Why are the right things done? If nobody is in charge, how does it all work out right? Why is it the best method of organizing a society? In this chapter, we explore these and other questions.

After studying this chapter, you should be able to:

1. Describe the law of demand.
2. Describe the law of supply.
3. Tell how market equilibrium is achieved.
4. Describe what causes buyers to change their demand behavior.
5. Describe what causes sellers (producers) to change their supply behavior.
6. Tell what causes the price of a good to change.
7. Describe what happens when government imposes a price on the market.

What Is Trade?

We are all specialists. In the modern world, it is not practicable to be self-sufficient. Each of us specializes in doing one task; usually what we are good at doing. Each of us produces more of that one item than is needed to satisfy our own wants and needs. Thus, we have an excess amount that we make available for sale to others who are not as good at producing this item, but who specialize in producing some other item.

We rely on others to make those things we want but cannot make for ourselves or have no time available to make them ourselves. Therefore, we engage in trade with others. We offer to others our excess goods that are our specialty in exchange for their excess goods they specialize in.

Simple Trade. Able trades one of his good X to Baker who wants it. Baker trades one of his good Y to Able who wants it. Able values a unit of good Y he is getting more than he values the unit of good X he is offering. Baker values a unit of good X he is getting more than he values the unit of good Y he is offering. Both will become better off because of the trade because what they each get (marginal benefit, MB) is more valuable to them than what they must give up (marginal cost, MC). **This process of direct trade of one item for another is called barter.**

Barter is inconvenient in that Able must find someone (in the case, Baker) who has what Able wants and wants what Able has. This is called a **double coincidence of wants**. This is time-consuming and might be impossible to accomplish. Modern trade removes the inconvenience of barter from trade.

Modern Trade. Able sells good X to Baker in exchange for money. Able values the money received more than he values keeping good X for himself. Baker values good X more than the money he must spend to acquire it. Using the same logic, Able uses the money he received from Baker to buy good Y from Charlie. Charlie uses the money to buy good Z from Delta, and so forth. This trading activity uses money as a tool that enables us to make trades without the necessity of matching wants and needs. It eliminates the double coincidence of wants. Money is called a **medium of exchange** because it is the middle step in the exchange process. Money's value is in its **purchasing power**, the ability to let you buy things you want to buy.

What Are the Basic Ideas of Trade?

Buyers are a group of people who are willing and able to exchange money to acquire a particular amount of a good or service made available by sellers.

Sellers are a group of people who can produce and make available to buyers a particular amount of a good and service and are willing to offer it up in exchange for money.

Trade occurs in markets where potential buyers and sellers interact. Buyers and sellers need not physically meet one another in a market, although they may.

Trade occurs only when both the buyer and seller perceive that he or she will become better off after the trade is made than before the trade. If either side perceives they will not be better off after the trade, the trade will not occur.

Price. This is the **rate of exchange for a trade**. In modern trade, it is expressed in terms of money.

The buyer does a **benefit-cost analysis** when deciding whether to buy a particular good. **The buyer pays the price** (the buyer's marginal cost, MC). The buyer will do so only if he or she perceives the value of the good or service received (the buyer's marginal benefit, MB) is greater than the money to be spent. Also, the buyer will consider alternative uses of the money (that is, his or her opportunity cost) and decide if using the money to purchase this good or service is the best alternative.

The seller also does a **benefit-cost analysis** when deciding to sell a particular good. **The seller receives the price** (the seller's marginal benefit, MB). The seller will partake in the transaction only if he or she perceives the price received by selling the good or service is of greater value to him or her than the cost the seller incurred producing the good and bringing it to market (the seller's marginal cost, MC). If it is not, the seller will keep the goods for his or her own use.

Because of this, the price of a good or service can never be more than the value the actual buyer places on the good or service and can never be less than the value the actual seller has invested in bringing that good or service to market. Otherwise, there is no trade.

Buyer's value > Price > Seller's cost? Trade!

Buyer's value < Price? No trade!

Price < Seller's cost? No trade!

The price will be determined by the free market interaction of the behavior of the buyers, called **demand**, and the behavior of the sellers, called **supply**. This interaction will create the price.

In the real world, we buyers sometimes ask, "What does it cost?" when we actually mean, "What is the price?" Price and cost have separate meanings in economics. You see the concepts of marginal benefit, MB, marginal cost, MC, and opportunity cost in operation. You see what you must give up to get something. You, as a buyer, must give up the price so it is your marginal cost, MC, but the seller does not give up the price. The seller gets the price, so the price is his or her marginal benefit, MB. The seller's expense to bring the good to market is the seller's marginal cost, MC.

Buyer's MC = Price = Seller's MB

What Is Demand Behavior?

Buyers compare their perceived value of a product with the price and decide whether it is in their best interest to buy the product. Thus, buyers are sensitive to changes in the price. They react to price changes in a very predictable way. This behavior pattern of buyers is called the **law of demand: Assuming nothing else is changing, if the price rises, buyers will buy less and if the price falls, buyers will buy more.**

The law of demand says that the quantity of a product that buyers want to buy (quantity demanded, Q_d) increases when price (P) decreases, and vice versa. For an individual buyer or for an entire market of buyers we represent their demand behavior on a graph as a downward-sloping line, called the **demand curve**. The demand curve shows how much of a goodwill be bought at each price. More will be bought at lower prices; less will be bought at higher prices. **Figure 2-1** describes the demand curve and the buyers' demand behavior.

Why do buyers behave this way? There are two ways to explain why buyers follow the law of demand.

The income effect. If the price of good X goes up, but your income doesn't, you can't buy as much of good X as you could before. The opposite is true—if the price of good X goes down, you can buy more with the same income. This makes sense when you consider your income to be so much purchasing power. Your income doesn't go as far after the price increases as it did before the prices rose.

The substitution effect. If the price of good X goes up, you no longer have the income to buy as much of good X as before, so you switch to a substitute good Y that will satisfy the want or need but has a lower price.

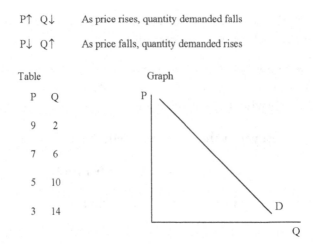

P↑ Q↓   As price rises, quantity demanded falls

P↓ Q↑   As price falls, quantity demanded rises

Table

P	Q
9	2
7	6
5	10
3	14

Graph

FIGURE 2-1. Law of Demand

The law of demand tells how buyers will behave when the price of a good changes. It is a stimulus-reaction behavior: When the price goes up (stimulus), buyers buy less (reaction). When the price goes down (stimulus), buyers buy more (reaction).

Source: Mikel Cohick

Later, we shall look at what happens when buyers—individually and collectively—change their behavior and how that behavior change upsets the market. But first, let us look at the supply side of the market.

What Is Supply Behavior?

Sellers (and also producers) compare the costs they incur to produce and market their product to the price and decide whether or not it is in their best interest to bring the product to market. Thus, sellers are sensitive to changes in the price. They react to price changes in a very predictable way. This behavior pattern of sellers is called the **law of supply: Assuming nothing else is changing, if the price rises, sellers will bring more to market and if the price falls, sellers will bring less to market.**

The law of supply says, then, that the quantity of a product that sellers are willing to sell (quantity supplied, Q_s) increases when price (P) increases, and vice versa. For an individual seller or for an entire market of sellers, we can represent their supply behavior on a graph as an upward-sloping line. This line is called the **supply curve.** The supply curve shows how much of a good will be brought to market at each particular price. More will be brought to market at higher prices; less will be brought to market at lower prices. **Figure 2-2** describes the supply curve and the sellers' (and producers') supply behavior.

Why do sellers behave this way? The principal reason explaining why sellers follow the law of supply is their desire to be profitable; to become better off having engaged in their business activity than they were before. This is the **profit motive.** Profit is essentially the difference between the price the seller receives when he or she sells the product and the costs of producing and marketing that product. If the price exceeds costs, the transaction will be profitable; if not, a loss will be made. Sellers like profits and dislike losses.

If the price of good X rises, but the costs to make good X do not change, then the profit the seller makes on each unit sold increases. This is a strong incentive for the seller to produce more of good X and bring more to the market.

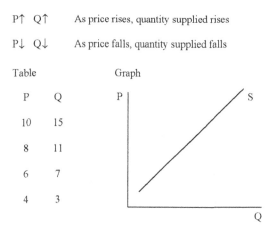

FIGURE 2-2. Law of Supply

The law of supply tells how sellers (and producers) will behave when the price of a good changes. It is also a stimulus–reaction behavior: When the price goes up (stimulus), sellers provide more (reaction). When the price goes down (stimulus), sellers provide less (reaction).

Source: Mikel Cohick

If the price of good X falls, but the costs to make good X do not change, then the profit the seller makes on each unit sold decreases. This is a strong incentive for the seller to produce less of good X and bring less to the market. If the price falls below the costs, the seller will cease bringing any of good X to the market. It is likely the seller will use his or her resources to produce something else.

There is another reason underlying the law of supply. At all times, the producer and seller are operating out of a fixed-sized facility that limits the capability to expand production. Because of this limitation, costs of producing more of good X will increase as the producer increases production. Therefore, the producer will only want to produce more if the price increases enough to cover these higher costs.

How Is A Market Created?

A market for any good occurs when the buyers and the sellers interact. The demand curve represents the buyers' behavior, and the supply curve represents the sellers' behavior. Putting them together creates a market. Since the demand curve slopes downward and the supply curve slopes upward, the two curves can intersect in only one place. See **Figure 2-3**. What this means is that the buyers and the sellers will come to an agreement only at one point on a market graph, at the price and the quantity where the two curves intersect.

In the beginning, the offering price could be above, at, or below the price where the two curves intersect. Left on its own, any market will, by trial and error, reach the price at the intersection, this specific point where buyers and sellers agree. Once it reaches this point, the market settles down and all buyers who are willing and able to buy are happy. Also, all sellers who are willing and able to sell are happy. All others—those unwilling or unable to buy or sell at this price—go away and do not participate. The price stabilizes and so does the quantity bought and sold. This happy situation is called **market equilibrium**.

How does a market reach equilibrium? That story is best told by examining the two other starting point possibilities: when the price starts out higher than the equilibrium price (a **surplus** situation) and when the price starts out lower than the equilibrium price (a **shortage** situation).

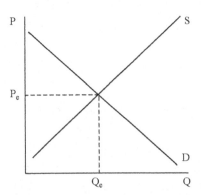

• Buyer behavior (demand) and seller behavior (supply) intersect.

FIGURE 2-3. Making a Market

Notice that the buyer behavior pattern, called demand, intersects with the seller behavior pattern, called supply, at one point only. Since the offering price could be any number, the market could start at a price above P_e, at P_e, or below P_e.

Source: Mikel Cohick

Surplus—The price is too high. At a high price, many sellers wish to sell because of the expectation of high profits. However, not many buyers are willing to buy because their valuation of the good is less than the price they must pay. Buyers think the good is too expensive. Many buyers do not come to market. Eager sellers find out that they have a lot of unsold goods left over at the end of the day. **The quantity demanded (Q_d) is less than the quantity supplied (Q_s).** The difference between Q_s and Q_d is called a **surplus**. **Figure 2-4** shows the surplus situation.

The buyers, who bought, even at this high price, are happy. The sellers who made sales are happy. However, many sellers were stuck with unsold goods. They are unhappy. Unhappy people take action to remove the unhappiness. Sellers with unsold goods mark down the price of the goods. They have a clearance sale. As the price falls, the law of demand kicks in, and buyers will want to buy more. Also, the law of supply kicks in, and some sellers cut back on orders from the factory or decide to quit selling this **good** at all. This dynamic process continues—price dropping, buyers increasing in number, sellers decreasing in number—until the price drops to the **equilibrium price** where the behavior of the buyers and the behavior of the sellers intersect. At that point, the quantity demanded by the buyers exactly equals the quantity supplied by the sellers ($Q_d = Q_s$), and the price stops falling. The market has reached equilibrium.

Shortage – The price is too low. At a low price, many buyers wish to buy because the good is a great bargain! The buyers value it much higher than the small price and want to acquire it. However, not many sellers are willing to produce and sell the goods at this low price, because there is no profit in doing so. Eager buyers storm the market, and the early arrivers clean off the shelves. Sellers run out of goods for sale. Those buyers who got there too late are told that the store is sold out. They are unhappy. **The quantity demanded (Q_d) is greater than the quantity supplied (Q_s).** The difference between Q_d and Q_s is called a **shortage**. **Figure 2-5** shows the shortage situation.

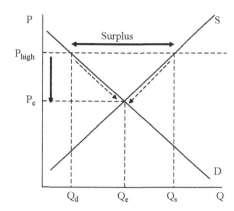

FIGURE 2-4. Surplus

At the price P_{high}, sellers will bring too much to the market and buyers will not want to buy that much. What is left over is called a surplus. This spurs the sellers to mark down the price to move out the goods. As price falls, some sellers leave the market and Q_s decreases. Also, more buyers show up and Q_d increases. This continues until price drops to P_e.

Source: Mikel Cohick

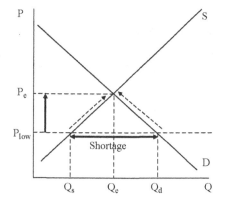

FIGURE 2-5. Shortage

At the price P_{low}, sellers will not bring much to the market and buyers will want to buy a large amount. Sellers run out and buyers face a shortage. This spurs the buyers to bid up the price in an attempt to acquire the good. As price rises, more sellers enter the market and Q_s increases. Also, some buyers drop out of the bidding and Q_d decreases. This continues until price rises to P_e.

Source: Mikel Cohick

The buyers who bought are happy with their bargains. The sellers who sold are happy. However, many buyers went home empty-handed. They are unhappy. Unhappy people take action to remove the unhappiness. Some of these unhappy buyers begin to bid up the price, telling the sellers that if a product is reserved for them, they will pay more for it. Word gets out and other buyers begin to participate in the bidding. An auction begins. As the price rises, the law of demand kicks in and some buyers will opt-out and no longer take part in the bidding. Also, the law of supply kicks in, and more sellers are willing to produce this product and bring it to market since a higher price means a better profit.

This dynamic process continues—price rising, buyers decreasing in number, sellers increasing in number—until the price rises to the equilibrium price where the behavior of the buyers and the behavior of the sellers intersect. At that point, the quantity demanded by the buyers exactly equals the quantity supplied by the sellers ($Q_d = Q_s$), and the price stops rising. The market has reached equilibrium.

When Is a Market in Equilibrium?

No matter at what price a market starts, if the participants—the buyers and the sellers—are in control, the dynamic processes described above will drive the market to the equilibrium price. **At the equilibrium price, quantity demanded (Q_d) equals quantity supplied (Q_s).** All buyers who are willing and able to pay the equilibrium price are happy. All sellers who are willing and able to bring the product to market at the equilibrium price are happy. All others go away and no longer participate in this market. There is no surplus and no shortage. This is shown in **Figure 2-6.**

If the behavior of the buyers (demand) and the behavior of the sellers (supply) do not change the market will stay in equilibrium with unchanging price and unchanging quantity.

How Does a Price Change?

In any market that is in equilibrium, the price will remain unchanged until either the buyers' behavior changes or the sellers' behavior changes. If buyer behavior changes, the demand curve will shift to a new location. If seller behavior changes, the supply curve will shift to a new location. Either of these behavioral changes upsets equilibrium and puts this market back into either a surplus or shortage situation. Once either of those events occurs, the market must seek out a new equilibrium point in the same way as described above.

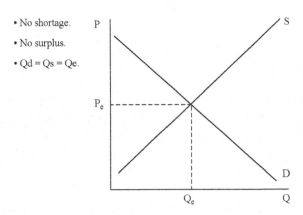

FIGURE 2-6. Equilibrium

As the shortage or the surplus disappears, the market reaches equilibrium, where all buyers who wish to buy at price P_e can do so and all sellers who wish to sell at price P_e can do so. The market will remain in equilibrium until either the buyers or the sellers, or both, change their behavior pattern, thereby upsetting the equilibrium.

Source: Mikel Cohick

If you notice the price of a good changing, therefore, you know automatically that its market is not in equilibrium and the buyers and sellers are seeking the new equilibrium point. When it is found, the price will stop changing and settle down.

Now it is time to investigate what causes buyers' demand behavior to change and what causes sellers' supply behavior to change. Then we will apply these changes to an equilibrium market and see what happens to the price and the quantity.

What Can Cause Demand Behavior to Change?

Our demand behavior changes every time there is a change in one of these determinants: **income, tastes and preferences, the number of buyers, expectations of future prices, or the price of an interrelated product**. We will look at these reasons one by one. But first, let us see what the change looks like on a graph.

If buyers increase their demand, they want to buy more than they did before at the old equilibrium price and at any other price this product might sell for. On a graph, the demand curve will jump to a position to the right of the old demand curve. For each price (P), the quantity demanded (Q_d) will be higher. This new demand curve represents the new demand behavior. The old demand curve is no longer a reality. **Figure 2-7** shows an increase in demand.

If buyers decrease their demand, they want to buy less than they did at the old equilibrium price and at any other price this product might sell for. On a graph, the demand curve will jump to a position to the left of the old demand curve. For each price (P), the quantity demanded (Q_d) will be lower. This new demand curve represents the new demand behavior. The old demand curve is no longer a reality. **Figure 2-8** shows a decrease in demand.

- Demand shifts right.
- Old equilibrium is upset Shortage.
- A new equilibrium is established.
- Price rises from P_1 to P_2.
- Quantity rises from Q_1 to Q_2.

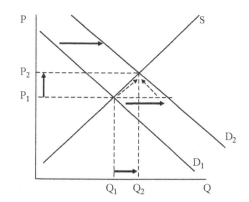

FIGURE 2-7. Demand increases

One or more of the determinants of the buyers' demand behavior has changed. Buyers now want to buy more at all prices, and particularly at the old equilibrium price, P_1. This generates a shortage as equilibrium is upset. Review what happens in a shortage situation. A new equilibrium will be established at price P_2 and quantity Q_2.

Source: Mikel Cohick

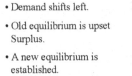

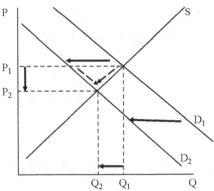

- Demand shifts left.
- Old equilibrium is upset Surplus.
- A new equilibrium is established.
- Price falls from P_1 to P_2.
- Quantity falls from Q_1 to Q_2.

FIGURE 2-8. Demand decreases

One or more of the determinants of the buyers' demand behavior has changed. Buyers now want to buy less at all prices, and particularly at the old equilibrium price, P_1. This generates a surplus as equilibrium is upset. Review what happens in a surplus situation. A new equilibrium will be established at price P_2 and quantity Q_2.

Source: Mikel Cohick

How Can Determinants of Demand Change?

Consumer demand is set by several things: income, tastes and preferences, the number of buyers, buyers' expectations of future price changes, and the prices of interrelated goods.

Income. If our income increases, we can afford to buy more of any products at the existing price. Thus, the demand curve shifts right. Vice versa applies. If our income decreases, we must cut back on the amount of a product we buy. Thus, the demand curve shifts left.

Tastes and preferences. If our tastes and preferences for a product increase, we will want to buy more of that product than we used to buy. Thus, the demand curve shifts right. Vice versa applies. If our tastes and preferences for a product decrease, we will want to cut back on the number of that products we buy. Thus, the demand curve shifts left.

Number of buyers. If the number of buyers increases, they will want to buy more of a product. Thus, the demand curve shifts right. If the number of buyers decreases, they will want to buy fewer of a product. Thus, the demand curve shifts left.

Expectations. If we expect the price of a product to go up tomorrow or in the very near future, we will increase the number of items we buy now and stock up before the price rises. Thus, the demand curve will shift right today. If we expect the price of a product to go down tomorrow or in the very near future, we will decrease the number of items we buy now and wait until the price falls. Thus, the demand curve will shift left today.

Price changes for interrelated goods. Some products interrelate. There are several products in competition with each other because each one could be a **substitute** for the other. Examples are Coke and Pepsi or Ford and Chevrolet. Because of this, if the price of one product changes, we might modify our behavior toward its substitute.

If the price of Coke rises and the price of Pepsi does not change, we might switch from the now higher-priced Coke to Pepsi, shifting our demand curve for Pepsi to the right. If the price of Coke falls and the price of Pepsi does not change, we might switch from the now higher-priced Pepsi to Coke, shifting our demand curve for Pepsi to the left. In both cases, while the demand curve for Pepsi shifts, the demand curve for Coke did not shift, because we simply reacted to the price change for Coke along our existing behavior pattern.

Another interrelationship exists when we buy two products together. These are called **complements**. An example is a hamburger and French fries. If the price of one product changes, we might modify our behavior toward the other one.

If the price of a hamburger rises and the price of French fries does not change, we will decrease the number of hamburgers we buy and we also buy fewer orders of French fries, even though the price of French fries did not change. The demand curve for French fries shifts left. If the price of a hamburger falls and the price of French fries does not change, we will increase the number of hamburgers we buy and we also buy more orders of French fries, even though the price of French fries did not change. The demand curve for French fries shifts right.

What Can Cause an Increase in Demand?

The demand curve for good X will shift to the right if:

- **Income rises.**
- **Our tastes and preference for good X rise.**
- **The number of buyers rises.**
- **The price of a substitute good Y rises.**
- **The price of a complement good Z falls.**
- **We expect a higher price for good X soon.**

What Can Cause a Decrease in Demand?

The demand curve for good X will shift to the left if:

- **Income falls.**
- **Our tastes and preferences for good X decrease.**
- **The number of buyers decreases.**
- **The price of a substitute good Y falls.**
- **The price of a complement good Z rises.**
- **We expect a lower price for good X soon.**

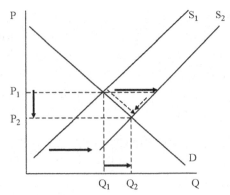

- Supply shifts right.
- Old equilibrium is upset Surplus.
- A new equilibrium is established.
- Price falls from P_1 to P_2.
- Quantity rises from Q_1 to Q_2.

FIGURE 2-9. Supply increases

One or more of the determinants of the sellers' supply behavior has changed. Sellers now want to provide more at all prices, and particularly at the old equilibrium price, P_1. This generates a surplus as equilibrium is upset. Review what happens in a surplus situation. A new equilibrium will be established at price P_2 and quantity Q_2.

Source: Mikel Cohick

What Can Cause Our Supply Behavior to Change?

Our supply behavior changes when the costs of producing a product and bringing it to market change, or the costs of running a business change, or the number of sellers changes, or the technology used to make the product changes. We will look at these reasons one by one. First, let's see what the change looks like on a graph.

If costs fall and sellers increase their supply, they want to sell more at the old equilibrium price and at any other price this product might sell for. On a graph, the supply curve will jump to a position to the right of the old supply curve. For each price (P), the quantity supplied (Q_s) will be higher. This new supply curve represents the new supply behavior. The old supply curve is no longer a reality. **Figure 2-9** shows an increase in supply behavior.

If costs rise and sellers decrease their supply, they want to sell less at the equilibrium price and at any other price this product might sell for. On a graph, the supply curve will jump to a position to the left of the old supply curve. For each price (P), the quantity supplied (Q_s) will be lower. This new supply curve represents the new supply behavior. The old supply curve is no longer a reality. **Figure 2-10** shows a decrease in supply behavior.

How Can the Determinants of Supply Change?

Producers' and sellers' supply is set by several things: business costs, the number of sellers, and changes in technology.

Business costs. If the cost of operating a business rises and the price of the product does not, then profits shrink. This is a disincentive to produce. The seller will be less willing to provide the same amount of this product than before. The supply curve shifts to the left. Vice versa applies. If the costs of operating a business fall and the price of the product does not, then profits grow. This is an incentive to produce

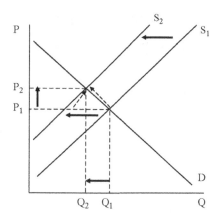

- Supply shifts left.
- Old equilibrium is upset. Shortage.
- A new equilibrium is established.
- Price rises from P_1 to P_2.
- Quantity falls from Q_1 to Q_2.

FIGURE 2-10. Supply decreases

One or more of the determinants of the sellers' supply behavior has changed. Sellers now want to provide less at all prices, and particularly at the old equilibrium price, P_1. This generates a shortage as equilibrium is upset. Review what happens in a shortage situation. A new equilibrium will be established at price P_2 and quantity Q_2.

Source: Mikel Cohick

more. The seller will be willing to provide the more of this product than before. The supply curve shifts to the right. The costs we're talking about here are of many kinds. Some of the more obvious ones are costs to comply with regulations, labor and raw materials costs, energy costs, administrative expenses, and taxes on business.

Number of sellers. If the number of sellers increases, they will provide more products to the market. Thus, the supply curve shifts right. If the number of sellers decreases, they will provide fewer products. Thus, the supply curve shifts left.

Changes in technology. Scientists and engineers are coming up with new ways of doing things all the time. Those techniques that can be applied to production and distribution of goods and services while, at the same time lowering the cost per unit of the product, will be adopted by business. Therefore, making products with the newly adopted technology lowers costs and improves profits. The supply curve will shift to the right. Technologies that do not lead to lower production costs, will not be adopted.

On the other hand, old technologies, represented by continued use of obsolete equipment and techniques, contribute to rising costs and squeezed profits as the equipment breaks down and repairs become more costly. In this situation, supply curve shifts to the left.

What Can Cause an Increase in Supply?

The supply curve for good X will shift to the right if:

- **Costs of production and distribution fall.**
- **The number of sellers rises.**
- **New technology is implemented.**

What Can Cause a Decrease in Supply?

The supply curve for good X will shift to the left if:

- Costs of production and distribution rise.

- The number of sellers falls.

- Old technology becomes obsolete.

When Do Prices Change?

When demand shifts right, equilibrium is upset. Buyers now want to buy more than they did before. Sellers have not changed; they want to sell the same amount as they did before. Therefore, quantity demanded (Q_d) is greater than quantity supplied (Q_s) and there is a shortage situation. Read about the shortage process again. When the market sorts itself out and gets back to a new equilibrium, it will settle at a new, higher equilibrium price and at a new, higher equilibrium quantity. Review **Figure 2-7**.

When demand shifts left, equilibrium is upset. Buyers no longer want to buy the amount they did before. Sellers have not changed; they want to sell the same amount as they did before. Therefore, quantity demanded (Q_d) is less than quantity supplied (Q_s), and there is a surplus situation. Read about the surplus process again. When the market sorts itself out and gets back to a new equilibrium, it will settle at a new, lower equilibrium price and at a new, smaller equilibrium quantity. Review **Figure 2-8**.

When supply shifts right, equilibrium is upset. Sellers now want to sell more than they did before. Buyers have not changed; they want to buy the same amount as they did before. Therefore, quantity demanded (Q_d) is less than quantity supplied (Q_s), and there is a surplus situation. Read about the surplus process again. When the market sorts itself out and gets back to a new equilibrium, it will settle at a new, lower equilibrium price and at a new, higher equilibrium quantity. Review **Figure 2-9**.

When supply shifts left, equilibrium is upset. Sellers no longer want to sell the amount they did before. Buyers have not changed; they want to buy the same amount as they did before. Therefore, quantity demanded (Q_d) is greater than quantity supplied (Q_s), and there is a shortage situation. Read about the shortage process again. When the market sorts itself out and gets back to a new equilibrium, it will settle at a new, higher equilibrium price and at a new, smaller equilibrium quantity. Review **Figure 2-10**.

Can Both Demand and Supply Shift at the Same Time?

Yes. Notice that those behavior changes that cause the demand and the supply curves to shift are totally independent of each other. Several behavior changes could occur at the same time. How can we handle this? Do it the same way you tie your shoes. You never tie them both at the same time. First, you tie one; then you tie the other. It doesn't matter which one you tie first. The result will be the same.

Let's apply this to our double shift. First, deal with the shift in the demand curve and get to a new, but temporary, equilibrium point. Then, deal with the shift in the supply curve from the temporary equilibrium point and get to the new, final equilibrium point. You can start with the supply curve first, followed by the demand curve, but the final equilibrium point will be the same. See **Figure 2-11**.

- Demand shifts right.
- Supply shifts left.
- A new equilibrium is established.
- Price rises from P_1 to P_2.
- Quantity moves to Q_2.

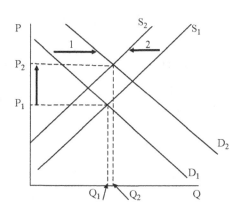

FIGURE 2-11. Demand Increases and Supply Decreases

It does not matter which curve is shifted first. The ending point will be the same. When demand increases and supply decreases, prices rise but quantity could change either way. When demand decreases and supply increases, prices fall but quantity could change either way. When both demand and supply increase, quantity increases but price could change either way. When both demand and supply decrease, quantity decreases but price could change either way. The reader should graph these possibilities.

Source: Mikel Cohick

Does a Price Change Cause a Shift in Demand or Supply?

For any good or service, its market price will change only if the demand curve or the supply curve shifts. Therefore, only the events that shift the demand or supply curves can generate a price change. Remember, price changes only if the market is out of equilibrium and is searching for its new equilibrium.

The reverse does not happen. **A changing price does not alter either buyer or seller behavior.** Thus, a changing price cannot shift either the demand curve or the supply curve. Remember that the demand curve indicates that buyers buy more when the price falls and less when the price rises. Also, remember that the supply curve indicates that the sellers will provide more when the price rises and less when the price falls. A change in price can change only quantity demanded and quantity supplied.

What If?...

...One seller sets his or her price higher than the equilibrium price? If the buyers have the freedom to do so, they will buy the product at the lower, equilibrium price from competing sellers. This seller will not see any customers until all the goods selling at the lower price have been sold. By then, there may not be any more buyers. Greed is not necessarily a good thing.

...One seller sets his or her price lower than the equilibrium price? This seller will sell out first. Customers will want to buy from this seller at the lower price than from the competitors who are asking the equilibrium price. However, this seller could have sold his or her goods at the equilibrium price and made a larger profit. Perhaps the seller wanted the afternoon off.

...Government sets the price? If this is the situation, we are no longer talking about a free market system. Now the command dictatorship system intrudes into the marketplace. Typically, the government interferes in a market to help a special interest group (a favored group). A government legislative body will do this by enacting legislation that restricts price movements. This is called a **price control**. There are two kinds of price control: a **price ceiling** and a **price floor**.

Price ceiling. A law fixes the maximum price for a product or service. The maximum price is set below the market equilibrium price. Thus, it is a price ceiling; the law allows no higher price. This is done to favor the buyers, particularly low-income buyers. It is impossible to favor one side without hurting the other side, so a price ceiling hurts the sellers.

A typical example of a price ceiling is the imposition of rent controls on apartments by a city council. The intent is to keep rents low enough so low-income families can afford apartments. It fails to accomplish this task.

Remember the shortage situation. If the price is below the equilibrium price, buyers think it is a big bargain and quantity demanded (Qd) is high. However, sellers see there is much reduced profit in providing the product at this low price, so quantity supplied (Qs) is low. Many landlords may take their apartment complexes off the market and turn them into condominiums or storage facilities, where profits might be higher. A shortage (Qd > Qs) is created by the legislation. **Figure 2-12** describes the price ceiling.

This shortage, however, cannot be eliminated. It is illegal to charge a higher price. Because of this, the remaining sellers must cope with large numbers of applicants. They must use some artificial means to decide which of the applicants to accept. They may use one or more of several techniques, including first come, first served, or drawing names out of a hat, but the most likely method will be by preferential treatment or discrimination.

It is possible that some sellers will break the law and demand an extra payment under the table. Other shady techniques may be used. Suddenly, a perfectly legitimate market has become a **black market** where illegal business practices become the typical practice.

Even though the legislative body's intention may have been honorable, the consequences are severe. Perfectly good apartments are taken off the market. No builder of apartments will come into this city, for there is no profit to build there. Fewer families will end up with an

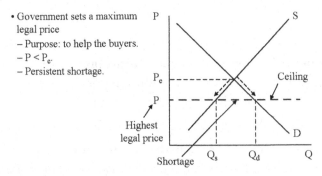

FIGURE 2-12. Price Ceiling

The intention is to keep the price low for the buyers. The result is that is chases sellers from the market and creates a persistent shortage

Source: Mikel Cohick

apartment. Low-income families will most likely be discriminated against in the application process. Landlords who remain in the city will have much smaller profits and may try to cut costs by skimping on maintenance. As the apartments deteriorate from reduced maintenance, slums are created.

Price floor. A law fixes the minimum price for a product or service. The minimum price is set above the equilibrium price. Thus, it is a price floor; the law allows no lower price. This is done to favor the sellers, particularly sellers who have political influence. It is impossible to favor one side without hurting the other side, so a price floor hurts the buyers. **Figure 2-13** describes the price floor.

An agricultural subsidy is a good example of a price floor. Congress might be concerned about the income of wheat farmers, so they pass legislation that fixes the minimum price of a bushel of wheat above the market equilibrium price of wheat. Each bushel sold at the price floor would then bring in more income to the farmer than if he had sold it at the equilibrium price. Wheat farmers would like this situation and will increase their quantity supplied (Qs). On the other hand, wheat buyers note these higher prices and cut back on the quantity demanded (Qd). For example, cereal makers will switch to cheaper corn or oats to make cereal instead of using higher priced wheat. A surplus (Qs > Qd) is created by this legislation.

This surplus, however, cannot be eliminated. It is illegal to sell wheat at a lower price than the price floor. Farmers produced more wheat in anticipation of getting a larger income; not only on each bushel sold but also on all the added bushels they produced. Sadly, in the worldwide wheat market all buyers who still wish to buy wheat at this artificially imposed higher price do so and go home. There are no more buyers for the surplus of wheat. So, the farmers get no income from this surplus production, although they have to pay the added costs of production.

The wheat farmers complain to Congress about the situation. Congress comes to their rescue by having the government buy up the surplus wheat and getting the income to the farmers. Unfortunately, the government has no use for the wheat. They cannot sell it and they cannot legally give it away. (When something is given away, it has a price of $0, which is lower than

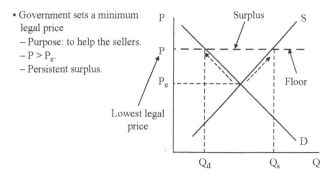

FIGURE 2-13. Price Floor

The intention is to keep the price high for the sellers. The result is that is chases buyers from the market and creates a persistent surplus.

Source: Mikel Cohick.

the price floor.) Taxpayer dollars were used to buy it and taxpayer dollars will be used to store it in silos, where it most likely will rot.

Even though the intention of Congress may have been honorable, the consequences are severe. Perfectly good resources are shifted from making other products to making more wheat that nobody wants. Taxpayer dollars are diverted to increase farmer's income instead of being used for other needed projects or simply returned to the taxpayer who earned them. Less wheat is bought and used. Fewer wants and needs get satisfied from using up more resources.

Another example of a price floor imposed by Congress is the minimum wage. Go back over this story about wheat and apply it to unskilled workers who would receive minimum wage. Remember that the "wheat buyers" become employers and the "farmers" become the job applicants. As the minimum wage rises, are there surplus workers? Why? For low skill, low-income jobs, fewer jobs are still available at the higher minimum wage and there are more applicants looking for them. The surplus of workers—unemployment— grows.

...Government controls the quantity instead of the price? The government can forbid the production, purchase, and sale of a product. If there is a demand for the product and there are suppliers willing to supply it, it is most likely that a **black market**, an illegal market, for this product will appear.

If being caught participating in this illegal market carries a penalty, for example, a fine or jail time, then both the buyers' and sellers' benefit-cost analysis will be affected. The buyer will consider the risk of being caught in determining his tastes and preferences for the product and, because of that, will shift his demand curve to the left. Alternatively, the buyer may be intrigued by the fact that this product is now "forbidden goods" and, therefore, more desirable, which will shift his demand curve to the right

The seller will include the risk of being caught in the cost of bringing the product to market and, because of that, will shift his supply curve to the left. Alternatively, the seller may no longer adhere to quality control standards and lower the quality of the product as well as its costs of production and, because of that, will shift his supply curve to the right.

Which incentives will dominate? Nobody knows when the legislation is passed. All of these happened when the United States passed Prohibition Laws forbidding the production, sale, purchase, and use of alcoholic beverages during the 1920s. More people wanted to drink alcoholic products. A lot of the product made available was bad booze that blinded and killed. A huge amount of police time was committed to handling all the illegal market activities for these products. Legitimate producers quit the business and criminal elements took over.

Is there such a situation today in the United States? Go over this story again and apply it to the street drug trade.

Which System is Best—Market or Command?

The market system will accomplish the following better than either the traditional or the command system:

> Individual wants and needs will be more closely and more fully satisfied.

> Preferential treatment will give way to the ability to pay as a method of determining who receives produced goods and services.

Scarce resources will be directed to producing goods and services that satisfy the more valued wants and needs.

Since individuals' behaviors determine the market outcome, changes in those behaviors immediately will be accommodated in the market system. Remember, in a traditional system, change is unwelcomed and in a command dictator system, the only changes that will be accommodated are changes the dictatorship wants to be considered.

None of the systems can guarantee that everyone's wants and needs will be satisfied. This is because scarcity exists in all systems, now and in the past and in the future, too. Some will have to forego satisfactions in each system, but, in the market system, the incentive to succeed in acquiring access to purchasing power is great. This incentive is stifled by tradition or command dictatorship. For each individual participant in the market system, talent, skill, drive, and sheer hard work will impel one to success.

SUMMARY

1. **Describe the law of demand.**

   The law of demand states that buyers will behave in the following way when the price changes: If the price of a good rises, the buyer will buy a smaller amount of the good, and vice versa. That is, if price increases, quantity demanded decreases, and if price decreases, quantity demanded increases.

2. **Describe the law of supply.**

   The law of supply states that sellers (and producers) will behave in the following way when the price changes: If the price of a good rises, the seller will want to bring a larger amount of the good to the market, and vice versa. That is, if price increases, quantity supplied increases, and if price decreases, quantity supplied decreases.

3. **Tell how market equilibrium is achieved.**

   Buyers and sellers interact in a market. At any particular point in time, the asking price of a good could be too high, too low, or just right.

   If the price is too high, sellers will want to supply a large amount to the market, but buyers will not want to buy the larger amount. Therefore, quantity supplied exceeds quantity demanded, and a surplus exists. Unhappy sellers will begin to mark down the price to get rid of unsold goods. As the price falls, buyers increase the quantity demanded while sellers decrease the quantity supplied. The price will continue to fall until quantity demanded equals quantity supplied, and equilibrium is achieved.

   If the price is too low, buyers will want to buy a large amount of the good, but sellers will not want to provide the larger amount to the market. Therefore, quantity demanded exceeds quantity supplied, and a shortage exists. Unhappy buyers will begin to bid up the price to make sure they get one of the goods. As the price rises, buyers decrease the quantity demanded (drop out of the bidding) while sellers increase the quantity supplied. The price will continue to rise until quantity demanded equals quantity supplied, and equilibrium is achieved.

   If the price is the equilibrium price, it is just right. All buyers who wish to buy at that price can do so and all the sellers who wish to sell at that price can do so.

4. **Describe what causes buyers to change their demand behavior.**

   Several factors determine buyer behavior. If any one of them changes, buyer behavior changes and the demand curve shifts away from its previous location. The determining factors are: income, tastes and preferences, number of buyers, prices of interrelated goods, and expectations of future prices. If demand increases (shifts to the right), a shortage situation replaces equilibrium. If demand decreases (shifts to the left), a surplus situation replaces equilibrium.

5. **Describe what causes sellers (producers) to change their supply behavior.**

   Several factors determine seller behavior. If any one of them changes, seller behavior changes and the supply curve shifts away from its previous location. The determining factors are business costs, number of sellers, and technology. If supply increases (shifts to the right), a surplus situation replaces equilibrium. If supply decreases (shifts to the left), a shortage situation replaces equilibrium.

6. Tell what causes the price of a good to change.

The price will change only when the market is not in equilibrium, that is, when a surplus or a shortage exists. If neither demand nor supply behavior change, the price will not change. If either demand behavior changes or supply behavior changes, or both behaviors change, the market is no longer in equilibrium and the price will change as the market moves toward a new equilibrium. Also, note that a change in a good's price does not cause either the buyer or the seller to modify his behavior pattern. A change in price is the result of either demand or supply shifting, not the cause of the shift.

7. Describe what happens when government imposes a price on the market.

Government can impose a price ceiling, which is a price that is lower than the equilibrium price, causing a persistent shortage. The intention is to enable low-income earners greater access to the goods. This fails. The result is that fewer people will get their wants and needs satisfied and previously available goods are removed from the market.

Government can impose a price floor, which is a price that is higher than the equilibrium price, causing a persistent surplus. The intention is to enable the sellers to gain greater income when they bring this good to market. This fails. The result is that fewer people get their wants and needs satisfied and a lot of resources are wasted.

Homework Chapter 2

Name_____

DESCRIPTIONS

Match the key terms with the descriptions.

_____ Government imposed minimum price.

_____ Goods used together.

_____ Excess of demand oversupply.

_____ Price increases, quantity demanded decreases.

_____ Direct trade of one item for another without money.

_____ Quantity demanded equals quantity supplied. No surplus or shortage.

_____ Excess of supply over demand.

_____ Government imposed maximum price.

_____ Rate of exchange for a trade.

_____ Behavior of buyers.

_____ As prices change, buyers' incomes change.

_____ Switching from one good to another similar good with a lower price.

_____ Price increases, quantity supplied increases.

_____ A curve showing the quantities that sellers are willing and able to sell at each particular price.

_____ People are willing and able to exchange money to acquire a particular amount of a good or service.

_____ Behavior of sellers.

_____ People are willing to exchange a particular amount of good or service for money.

_____ What occurs when buyers and sellers interact.

_____ A good with similar qualities to another good that can take its place.

_____ A curve showing the quantity that buyers are willing and able to buy at each price.

KEY TERMS

1. Barter
2. Buyers (Consumers)
3. Complementary Goods
4. Demand
5. Demand Curve
6. Income Effect
7. Law of Demand
8. Law of Supply
9. Market
10. Market Equilibrium
11. Price
12. Price Ceiling
13. Price Floor
14. Sellers (Producers)
15. Shortage
16. Substitute Good
17. Substitution
18. Supply
19. Supply Curve
20. Surplus

EXERCISES

1. What are the difficulties of barter, or trading goods for goods?

2. Describe how the market price system eliminates a shortage.

3. List five sets of complementary goods. A set should include both the primary good and its complement.

4. List all the determinants that affect demand behavior. **Hint: price is not one of them.**

5. Describe a real-world event might cause demand behavior to change so that demand decreases (the demand curve moves to the left)?

6. Draw a demand and supply graph to demonstrate how the market will change the price of a good if consumers lose their taste for it. Make sure you label each axis and each curve.

7. Suppose the government sets a price ceiling on apartment rents. How would the resulting shortage be rationed if the price cannot be raised above the ceiling?

3 The Economics of Consumers

The United States is a nation of consumers. Each year American consumers spend over $13.8 trillion for the purchase of goods and services. This is called consumption spending. About two-thirds of the nation's output, its gross domestic product (GDP), is consumption spending. Consumers spend most of (and sometimes more than) their after-tax income to acquire the goods and services they individually believe will best satisfy their wants and needs.

Consumers are intensely individual, because each has developed a unique system of evaluating his or her tastes and preferences. This value system identifies how much utility, benefit, or satisfaction would be obtained when one more unit of a good is consumed.

Some other characteristics are common to us all. One is the concept of diminishing marginal utility. If you consume successive amounts of the same good, each time the next unit is less useful to you, that is, it has less utility, than the previous one.

Another is the concept of elasticity, which measures how intensely consumers will react to a price change. Consumers react to a good's price change with different intensity depending on the characteristics of the good.

In this chapter, we will explore these and other concepts.

After studying this chapter, you should be able to:

1. Determine what kinds of goods do consumers spend their income on.
2. Describe diminishing marginal utility.
3. Describe how consumers maximize utility over a range of products.
4. Identify the difference between inelastic demand and elastic demand.
5. Determine the main factor affecting elasticity of supply.
6. Determine why both retailers and government policymakers prefer taxes to be levied on inelastic goods rather than elastic goods.

How Is Income Earned?

To be a consumer, one must have purchasing power. People obtain purchasing power by selling the resources in their possession, preferably to the highest bidder. Recall from Chapter 1 that the resource categories are land, labor, capital, and entrepreneurship. We will discuss these resources and their generation of income more fully in Chapter 8, but for now, here is a thumbnail sketch of each:

Owners of the land resources earn an income by selling their natural resources to businesses that need them as raw material inputs to their production process.

Everyone possesses a labor resource. Most people earn an income by taking a job with a firm and get paid wages or a salary.

Those with savings can earn some income from interest payments when they deposit their savings in a bank. The bank then finances the acquisition of capital goods by businesses using the deposits of savers to make those loans.

The entrepreneur will earn an income only if he or she is successful. A successful venture will generate a profit for the entrepreneur. An unsuccessful entrepreneur will suffer a loss.

What Do We Do with Our Income?

Once he or she earns income, the income-earner will apportion the income in three ways: pay taxes, save some, and spend the rest. How much goes to taxes depends on the current tax laws. Usually, the consumer has no control over that. **After the consumer pays taxes, the remainder of the consumer's income, the after-tax income, or take-home pay, is disposable income.**

The income earner now chooses how he or she will dispose of this income. It will be spent on the purchase of goods and services designed to best satisfy the buyer's most pressing wants and needs. **Whatever remains after spending is saving.** A smart person will place these savings into a bank and earn some interest on the deposit.

On What Do Consumers Spend?

There are three categories of consumer spending: durable goods, nondurable goods, and services.

Durable goods are items that are expected to provide satisfaction to the user over an extended period of time, say three years or more. Examples are furniture, appliances, electronic gear, and automobiles. About 12 percent of consumer spending is for durable goods.

The durable goods category is the **most volatile** segment of consumption spending. When the economy takes a downturn people begin to put off buying new durable goods and make do with the old model, so sales plummet. When good economic times return, the same people rapidly increase their purchases of durable goods, especially those that are wearing out, and their sales increase rapidly.

Nondurable goods are items that consumers expect to use up in a short period of time. Examples include food items, cosmetics, cleaning supplies, gasoline, newspapers, and magazines. About 28 percent of consumer spending is for nondurable goods.

The nondurable goods category is the **most stable** category. Regardless of the state of the economy, people typically continue to buy non-durable goods to replace the ones used up. Therefore, sales of non-durable goods are much steadier than those of durable goods.

Services are activities that consumers pay somebody else to do for them, because they are not capable of doing them for themselves or, more likely, they just do not want to take the time to do for themselves. Examples include haircuts, medical procedures, nail salons, oil changes, yard maintenance, and house cleaning. About 60 percent of consumer spending is for services. The service category is the **fastest-growing segment** of our economy.

How Do Consumers Decide What to Buy?

In Chapter 2 we identified an inverse relationship between price and quantity demanded (when the price goes up, we tend to buy less of a product and when the price goes down, we tend to buy more). The income effect means that as the price of something goes up, our real incomes are reduced because when we are paying more for each item, we can afford to buy less of it. If the price falls, our real incomes are increased because we do not have to pay as much for each item so we can afford more of it. The substitution effect means if the price of one item rises, we go looking for a close substitute that is less expensive.

Another explanation has to do with the amount of pleasure or satisfaction we get from consuming a specific item at one time. We will use the word **utility to describe the pleasure, satisfaction, or usefulness we get when we consume a good or a service.**

Utility is a subjective measure. It is said that beauty is in the eyes of the beholder and utility is much like that. We are all individually unique in our tastes. One person may get much pleasure from watching a romantic, emotion-packed, tear-jerking movie, while someone else may prefer a good hard-hitting football game. Also, while consumers may have unlimited wants for goods and services in general, specific wants will be satisfied during a particular time.

For instance, there are limits to the amount of pizza a person can eat in one hour. While different people have different limits, everyone eventually reaches a limit. All of this is just another way of saying that people are different, and their value systems have developed in separate ways. We use our value system to subconsciously assign values to the goods and services we are thinking of purchasing and using.

Total utility is the sum of all the utility we obtain when we consume a series of goods or services. However, we do not start off deciding the total number we shall consume. Rather, we decide one step at a time, that is, on the margin. We apply marginal cost-benefit analysis. We make decisions on margin every day. The benefit in this case is called utility. The marginal benefit we get is the added utility we predict we will get from consuming one more of the items. This is called **marginal utility (MU)**. The added cost of that one more item is called **marginal cost (MC)**.

What Is Diminishing Marginal Utility?

Imagine sitting down to eat pizza in a place where you buy pizza by the slice. If you want to maximize your utility from eating pizza, you will subconsciously compare the cost of one more slice of pizza, the marginal cost (MC), to your predicted benefit of eating one more slice of pizza, marginal utility (MU).

If you are very, very hungry when you sit down to eat pizza by the slice, you will assign a high marginal utility to that first slice of pizza. The cost of the first slice is modest, so you decide to buy and eat the first slice.

Now you must decide whether to buy and eat another slice. Since you just ate a slice of pizza, you are not as hungry as you were when you started, but you still have hunger pangs. You will assign a lower marginal utility to the second slice. But, if you are still hungry, the marginal utility still exceeds the marginal cost, and you buy another slice and eat it.

As you continue to eat additional slices of pizza, you quickly notice that the utility you get from eating each additional slice seems to be less than the previous slice.

If the marginal cost of buying a slice of pizza stays the same, and the marginal utility of successive slices is decreasing, you will soon find that one of the slices you consider buying and eating has a marginal utility that you will predict will be less than the cost of buying the slice. At that point, you will rightly decide that you have had enough pizza.

The quitting point will come at a different number of slices for different people, depending upon their size, appetite, and taste for pizza, but it will come. Any additional slice would be worthless to you than its cost. In economic terms, the marginal utility of the next slice is less than the marginal cost, and you will be worse off if you buy and eat it. **Figure 3-1** shows how marginal utility diminishes as more and more slices of pizza are eaten. Marginal utility can fall below zero. If eating the next slice will make you sick, you receive negative marginal utility.

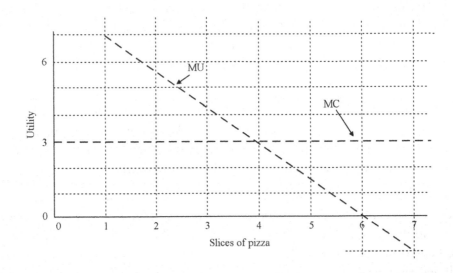

FIGURE 3-1. Diminishing Marginal Utility

As you eat more and more slices of pizza, marginal utility diminishes. When marginal utility exceeds marginal cost (MU > MC) as it does for slices 1 through 3, you will predict that the next one will be worth buying. However, after eating slice 4, where you just broke even, you can no longer predict that the next slice is worth buying, and you will stop. If the pizza slices were free (MC = 0), you would then eat the sixth slice, whose MU = 0. If you eat more than six slices in this example, you will feel ill (negative marginal utility).

Source: Mikel Cohick

What if the price of the next slice were zero? Since you can have it for free; you would accept it as long as your predicted marginal utility is greater than zero. This is the reason people tend to eat more than they really should at an all-you-can-eat buffet table.

The concept of diminishing marginal utility outlined above explains our individual demand behavior. Imagine that the salesperson wants you to buy two instead of one. Your marginal utility of the second one is less than the first one, so to induce you to buy the second one, the salesperson lowers the price of the second one, by saying, "Buy the first one at the regular price and you can buy the second one at half price." Diminishing marginal utility is inherent in the demand curve. You will buy more if the price is lower.

Diminishing marginal utility is one reason that a case of soda costs less per ounce than an individual bottle of soda and a 32-ounce bottle of soda costs less per ounce than a 12-ounce bottle of soda.

How Can We Maximize Utility Over Different Products?

At some point during our pizza consumption spree, we may desire to consume a different product. Most people get thirsty during the first slice, especially if it contains red pepper. Something to drink, say, a soft drink or (if it is legal to do so) a beer, is our next acquisition.

If pizza is $3.00 a slice and beer is $3.50 a bottle, after a couple of slices of pizza the bottle of beer at $3.50 looks like a bargain compared to another slice of pizza at $3.00. This is because of diminishing marginal utility of the pizza. The third slice does not give us as much marginal utility so it might not be worth as much to us as a beer, especially if we are thirsty. We get more usefulness out of the beer compared to its price of $3.50 than the usefulness we would get from eating yet another slice of pizza compared to its price of $3.00. At some point, the usefulness we get out of both the beer and the pizza has diminished but renting a movie at $3.00 seems like the real bargain.

To summarize, consumers maximize their utility by comparing the marginal utility they get from each additional product to its price. We call these comparisons **value-to-money ratios**. They indicate how much "bang for the buck" you will receive. They will reach a utility maximizing state where, for the next purchase of all options, all the ratios of marginal utility to price are the same:

$$\frac{\text{Marginal Utility of Pizza}}{\text{Price of Pizza}} = \frac{\text{Marginal Utility of Beer}}{\text{Price of Beer}} = \frac{\text{Marginal Utility of Movie}}{\text{Price of Movie}}$$

Do we go through a conscious calculation of the ratio every time we buy and consume a product? Probably not, but you may ask yourself: "Which should I buy next? One more slice of pizza, another beer, or a movie?" Your response is to buy the one that delivers the most value for the money spent. If the equality above does not exist, one of the items will have a higher value to money ratio than the others and it will be the preferred item. You continue to choose the one with a higher value for money ratio until all have the same ratio as indicated in the equation above.

What Is Consumer Equilibrium?

When you reach the point when all your next choices have the same "value received for money spent" ratio, you have reached **consumer equilibrium**, and you will quit buying. You have maximized your total utility.

Consumer equilibrium can be upset easily. All it takes is for one price to change or for you to modify your opinion of one of the products. If either of these occurs, one of the products will have a higher value-to-money ratio than the others and you will buy more of that one.

Advertising attempts to get you to do just that. The advertiser either tries to convince you that his product is a better buy, that is, you raise your value of it, or the advertiser announces a big sale where the product's price is lower. Both techniques will increase the ratio of that product compared to the others and induce you to buy more of that product.

What Is The Diamond-Water Paradox?

Economists wondered for years why diamonds, which are clearly a luxury item, had so much more value than water, which is clearly necessary to sustain life. We can explain this paradox by the abundance of water compared to diamonds, which are much scarcer. The answer lies in a comparison of marginal utility to total utility. While a cup of diamonds has much more marginal utility than a cup of water (unless you are lost in the Sahara), water has much more total utility than diamonds. We can easily do without all the diamonds in the world but cannot survive without water.

Typically, we are buying our first diamond, which has high marginal utility to us and we are willing to pay a high price for it. However, the next glass of water is not our first glass, and our marginal utility of that glassful is low (unless you are stranded in the Sahara). Thus, we would be willing to pay only a low price for it. Economic decision-making is based on marginal utility and not on total utility. We decide based on what valuation we make on the next cup of water and the next diamond.

What Is the Elasticity of Demand?

Are there products you continue to buy in the same amount, even if its price goes up? Tobacco, if you use it, maybe one. Did you ever hear someone say, "there is just no substitute for my cigarette after lunch"? Necessities like food, gasoline, and medicine could also fit in that category. For other goods, for example, specific foods like tacos, or expensive items like a new car, we immediately look for substitutes when their prices go up.

Demand behavior tells us that we buy more when the price falls and less when the price rises. We introduce the concept of elasticity to expand on those answers. When the price goes up, how much less will we buy? When the price falls, how much more will we buy? A little, or a lot? **Elasticity of demand is a measure of the intensity of our response when a product's price changes.**

When demand is **elastic**, if the price goes down even a little, we tend to buy much more of the item. Or, if the price goes up even a little, we tend to buy much less of the item. **Consumers respond greatly to even a small price change.**

Typical characteristics of goods having an elastic response are:

- **Substitutes are readily available.**

- **Big price tag compared to our income.**

- **We don't need to buy it right now.**

When demand is **inelastic**, if the price goes up a lot, we cut back only a little bit on our purchases of the item. If the price goes down a lot, we usually do not increase our purchases of the item very much. **Consumers do not respond very much even to large price changes.**

Typical characteristics of goods having an inelastic response are:

- **No substitutes are available.**

- **Small price tag compared to our income.**

- **We need to buy it right now.**

How Is Elasticity Measured?

We measure elasticity by the "percent change" method. Percent change is calculated by dividing the change (the new number minus the original number) by the original number, then multiplying by 100 to make it a percent. For example, if a price rises from $10 to $15, the percent change is:

$$\% \text{ Change} = 100 \times (\$15 - \$10) / \$10 = 100 \times (+\$5 / \$10) = 50 \text{ percent.}$$

Calculate the percent change in quantity and the percent change in price. Then, to calculate demand elasticity, divide the percentage change in quantity by the percentage change in price (ignore the minus sign), or:

$$\text{Elasticity} = \frac{\% \text{ Change in Quantity}}{\% \text{ Change in Price}}$$

If the result is greater than one, demand is elastic. The percent change in quantity is greater than the percent change in price. We had a big response to a small price change. An elastic demand curve will appear to be shallow, or flat.

If the result is less than one, demand is inelastic. The percent change in quantity is less than the percent change in price. We had a small response to a big price change. An inelastic demand curve will appear to be steep.

Figure 3-2 shows how the demand curve looks for both elastic goods and inelastic goods. If demand is equal to one, demand is unitary. The percent change in quantity is just equal to the percent change in price. A ten percent price cut generated a ten percent increase in sales.

What Are Some Business Uses of Elasticity?

Knowledge about the elasticity of demand for its products can be a valuable bit of information for a producer and a retailer.

If demand is elastic, the producer can offer lower prices and create a whole new customer base. Southwest Airlines does that. They found very efficient ways to use their capital and labor resources (their planes

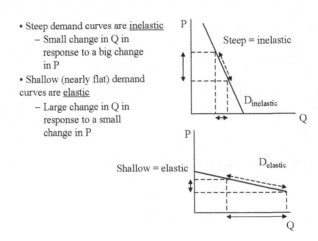

FIGURE 3-2. Demand Curve Elasticity

Inelastic demand results in a small percent change in Q in response to a large percent change in P. Thus, the demand curve is steep. Elastic demand results in a large percent change in Q in response to a small percent change in P Thus, the demand curve is shallow.

Source: Mikel Cohick

and crews), which allowed them then to offer lower prices for fares. The lower fares resulted in a large increase in the passengers and became their new customer base.

If a business firm sells elastic goods, it should always maintain the appearance of having a sale. If the firm must raise prices, it should do it quietly and try to keep the customers from noticing it. Examples of goods having an elastic demand include furniture, automobiles, electronic goods, appliances, and houses.

If the demand is inelastic, the business firm can raise prices without losing many customers, resulting in higher sales revenue and less cost. There is no point in having a sale for inelastic goods because the result will be to sell the products to the same customers who would have continued to buy them at the original price. Examples of goods having an inelastic demand are chewing gum, street drugs, cigarettes, insulin, gasoline, and toilet paper.

One interesting violation of this response to an inelastic demand is when a supermarket advertises milk at a low price. Milk is obviously an inelastic good. The store is tempting the customer to come to their store for the cheaper milk, hoping they will do all their other grocery shopping while in the store. **We call this ploy a loss leader.**

Is There an Elasticity of Supply?

Just for completeness, let us consider the elasticity of supply. The concept of elasticity applies to supply as well as demand. Imagine a tomato grower who sells his tomatoes in the city's farmer's market. He loads up a truck each morning and goes to the market. One morning, he is surprised to find out that tomato prices are higher than before. At higher prices, he would like to sell more tomatoes. Sadly, he has only one truckload and cannot get anymore today.

When the time to react is zero, he cannot respond at all to the higher prices. He has a **perfectly inelastic supply.** However, he can call back to the farm and notify his workers to prepare two truckloads for the next day. With added time, the seller can respond to the price increase. His **supply becomes more elastic as time increases.** If he thinks tomato prices will continue to be high for a long time, he may decide to plant another acre or two of tomatoes for the next season. **The more time the producer has to respond, the more elastic his response.**

Who Bears the Burden of a Tax?

Retailers become tax collectors for the state when a tax is placed on the sale of a product. When the tax is imposed on a product, the retailer immediately raises its price to get the buyer to pay added money so that money can be sent to the state. How successful the retailer is in doing this depends on the elasticity of demand for the product being taxed.

It is important to recognize that no product ever pays the tax. Either the buyer of the product or the seller of the product pays the tax, or it may be a combination of both. **The burden of a tax is always on people, never on products or corporations.** For example, when Congress increased the tax on cigarettes, opponents of smoking loved it, saying that the tax was a punishment on the tobacco companies. In fact, the tobacco companies simply raised the price of cigarettes to its distributors and therefore the tax was passed on to the smoker, who paid the tax.

Taxing Inelastic Goods. If a good has an inelastic demand, the increased price due to adding the tax will reduce the amount purchased by a smaller percentage than the price increase. Inelastic products exhibit a small response to a big price increase. Because of this, buyers still buy the product in amounts nearly as big as before the tax but pay higher prices due to the tax. Total sales revenue goes up and the added revenue will be used by the retailer to pay the tax to the state. **The burden of the tax falls mainly on the buyers.**

It is because of this reason that we have large taxes levied on products such as cigarettes, alcoholic beverages, and gasoline. Retailers actively lobby state legislatures to place taxes, if at all, on products with inelastic demand.

Taxing Elastic Goods. If a good has an elastic demand, the increased price due to adding the tax will reduce the amount purchased by a larger percentage than the price increase. Elastic products exhibit a large response to a small price increase. Because of this, buyers reduce purchases after the tax is added. Total sales revenue decreases and the retailer must pay the tax to the state out of reduced revenues. **The burden of the tax falls primarily on the sellers.**

In the 1990s, Congress decided to raise taxes, but only on the rich. They did this by placing a tax on products only the rich can buy, like limousines, small private aircraft, yachts, and furs. Each of these goods has an elastic demand. As the retailers added the tax to the price, sales of the items dropped off sharply. The retailers saw their sales revenues decrease, but they still had to send the tax dollars to the Treasury for the remaining sales. As sales fell, orders to the factory also fell and production of these goods decreased. There were layoffs of factory workers and sales personnel. Some retailers and manufacturers saw so much decrease in business that they closed their doors. The rich simply avoided paying the tax by not buying the products. Who carried the burden of this tax? It was the ruined retailers and factory owners, and the unemployed salespeople and factory workers. It took several years for Congress to see the consequences of their tax, but finally, they repealed it. However, the ruined businesses did not reopen.

SUMMARY

1. **Determine what kinds of goods consumers spend their income on.**

   Consumers spend over $8 trillion annually on durable goods, nondurable goods, and services.

2. **Describe diminishing marginal utility.**

   Marginal utility is the added satisfaction the user gets out of using the next item in a succession of items. However, as we consume successive amounts of the same item, we find that our satisfaction diminishes. If it is food, for example, our hunger is going away rapidly. For most items, as we consume successive units of one item, the added utility received is less than it was for the previous one. Ultimately, marginal utility could drop to zero, and we will not accept that item unless it is free. Marginal utility could become negative, meaning we will be worse off if we consume that item.

3. **Describe how consumers maximize utility over a range of products.**

   The next unit of each candidate good to purchase has a marginal utility to price (MU/P) ratio. The consumer chooses the candidate with the largest MU/P ratio each time. As the consumer continues selecting, the MU/P for the next item diminishes. Ultimately, the MU/P for all candidate items become equal and the consumer stops buying items. The consumer has reached consumer equilibrium. At this point, the consumer has maximized utility over the several products from which he or she has selected.

4. **Identify the difference between inelastic demand and elastic demand.**

   A good has an inelastic demand if the customers respond very little to a change in the product's price. In other words, a large price change generates only a very small quantity change. Products with inelastic demand are necessities, items with a small price tag, and items with no good substitutes.

   A good has an elastic demand if the customers respond greatly to a change in the product's price. In other words, a small price change generates a large quantity change. Products with elastic demand are not needed immediately, items with large price tags, and items that have good substitutes.

5. **Determine the main factor affecting the elasticity of supply.**

   Time is the main factor affecting the elasticity of supply. The longer the supplier has to adjust his response to a price change for his product, the greater the response can be. No time to adjust? There is an inelastic response. As time available lengthens, the response becomes more elastic.

6. **Determine why both retailers and government policymakers prefer taxes to be levied on inelastic goods rather than elastic goods?**

   Retailers wish to pass the tax on to the consumer by increasing the product's price. If the product is inelastic, there will be a small response to the price increase, and the tax can be paid out of the added sales revenue and more taxes are collected for the government. The opposite is true if the product is elastic.

Homework Chapter 3

DESCRIPTIONS

Match the key terms with the descriptions.

_____ Selling land, labor, capital, and entre-preneurship resources.

_____ Consumer's after-tax income or take-home pay.

_____ Items that are expected to last three years or more.

_____ Items to be used up in <3 years.

_____ Activities that consumers pay some-body else to do for them.

_____ The pleasure, satisfaction, or useful-ness we get from consumption.

_____ The added utility we get from con-suming one more unit of a good.

_____ The sum of all the utility we obtain when we consume a series of goods.

_____ The added cost of obtaining one more unit of a good.

_____ Additional units of a good consumed in one setting each gives us less satis-faction or pleasure.

_____ A state where the ratio of value to cost is the same over the entire range of goods for consumption.

_____ A measure of the intensity of con-sumer response to a price change.

_____ % Change in quantity/% change in price.

_____ The ultimate bearer of the cost of a tax, rather than who writes the check.

_____ A demonstration of the fact that some products have higher marginal utility and lower total utility.

_____ The purchase of goods and services by consumers.

_____ A measure of the intensity of producer response to a price change.

_____ Substitutes readily available, large price tag compared to income, item not needed right away.

_____ No substitutes available, small price tag compared to income, item needs right away.

_____ Lowering the price of a good to get consumers "in the store."

KEY TERMS

1. Who bears the burden of a tax
2. Characteristics of goods with elastic demand
3. Characteristics of goods with inelastic demand
4. Consumer equilibrium
5. Consumption spending
6. Diamond-water paradox
7. Disposable income
8. Durable goods
9. Elasticity of demand
10. Elasticity of supply
11. Formula for elasticity
12. Law of diminishing marginal utility
13. Loss leader
14. Marginal cost
15. Marginal utility
16. Non-durable goods
17. Services
18. Sources of purchasing power
19. Total utility
20. Utility

EXERCISES

1. How do consumers obtain purchasing power?

2. Why is the durable goods category more volatile than nondurable goods?

3. What lesson is learned from the diamond-water paradox?

4. How does one achieve consumer equilibrium?

5. What are some practical uses of elasticity measures?

6. What is the main determinant of elasticity of supply?

7. Who ends up bearing the burden of a tax on a good or service that has an inelastic demand?

8. Who ends up bearing the burden of a tax on a good or service that has an elastic demand?

4

The Economics of Business Firms: Costs, Profit, and Decision-Making

In this chapter and the next chapter, we examine business firms and the economics of operating a business. Keep in mind that business firms exist for the purpose of making a profit. Non-profit firms should seek a profit, also. The difference is that a non-profit firm does not distribute any of the profit to the owners.

Profit occurs when the amount of sales revenue a firm receives as payment for the goods and services it produced and sold or for services rendered an amount of sales revenue that is large enough to pay all the costs of operating the business, producing or acquiring the product or service, and delivering it to the customer and to generate at least a minimum acceptable return on their investment to the business owner(s). In other words, the consumers have to like the goods or services the firm offers for sale so well that they are willing to pay enough for them to cover the complete cost of bringing the goods or services to market. If the consumers do not have the goods or services enough to do this, the firm will suffer losses and may begin to reconsider whether they wish to stay in this business.

In this chapter, we will cover costs, profit, and losses, which lead to an analysis of decision-making in the short run and in the long run. In the next chapter, we will investigate business organizations and industry market structures.

After studying this chapter, you should be able to:

1. Identify the difference between fixed costs and variable costs.
2. Fit average variable costs (AVC), average fixed costs (AFC), average total costs (ATC), and marginal costs (MC) together to form a production model.
3. Outline the profit maximization rules.
4. Describe the difference between accounting, economic, and normal profit.
5. Tell how a firm can exploit economies of scale.

How Do Businesses Use the Income Statement?

Business firms track and monitor their performance in order to identify how the business is doing and to determine if a profit has been made. Accountants use the income statement to do this.

The **income statement** shows the results of operating a business over a period of time. It lists **revenues** (money coming into the firm), **costs** (money and nonmonetary costs of inputs, services, and operation, also called expenses), and **profits** or **losses.** The difference between revenues and costs determines whether there is a profit or a loss:

Revenues > Costs = Profits

Revenues < Costs = Losses.

Total revenue (TR), also called sales revenue, documents what has been received from selling the firm's product. In a one-product firm, TR is price (P) of the product times, the quantity (Q) of the product sold, or:

TR = P x Q

If the firm sells multiple products or services, the total revenue for the firm is the sum of total revenues for each product.

Economists use the term **marginal revenue (MR)** to determine the profit-maximizing level of output. MR is defined as the additional revenue received when the firm sells one more unit of its product.

MR = (change in revenue)/(change in output)

Most markets have downward-sloping demand curves, requiring firms who want to sell more, that is, to increase output (Q) and to lower their price (P). Thus, as output (Q) increases, MR decreases. In fact, the slope of MR is twice as steep as the demand curve. **Figure 4-1** shows this in data and on a graph.

Q	P	TR	MR
0	10	0	
1	9	9	+9
2	8	16	+7
3	7	21	+5
4	6	24	+3
5	5	25	+1
6	4	24	−1

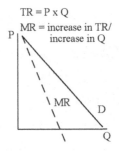

FIGURE 4-1. Demand and Marginal Revenue

Since most demand curves slope downward, marginal revenue (MR) decreases as output (Q) increases. In fact, it slopes downward at twice the rate of the demand curve. You can see that in the data: For each Q increase of one, P decreases by one but MR decreases by two.

Source: Mikel Cohick.

In the Short Run, What Are the Costs?

The costs of a firm can be described in several ways for different purposes. For our purpose, consider a set of costs as follows: **fixed costs (FC), variable costs (VC),** and **total costs** (TC). See **Figure 4-2** for a table of these three costs. Then **Figure 4-3** shows how the three costs appear on a graph.

Fixed costs (FC) are payments for the fixed inputs. FC are costs that do not change when the level of output changes. FC are payments for the inputs used by the firm that do not change during the production period. Examples are payments for rent, insurance, utilities, and administration.

Your car is a production system. It produces forward motion. It has FC. The insurance payment and the car payment are fixed, monthly costs. Those payments are the same each month no matter how many

As output (Q) increases:

Fixed Costs (FC) do not change.

Variable Costs (VC) increase at an irregular rate.

Total Costs (TC) = FC + VC.

Q	VC	FC	TC
0	0	120	120
10	85	120	205
20	150	120	270
30	240	120	360
40	350	120	470
50	550	120	670

FIGURE 4-2. FC, VC, and TC

Notice that when output (Q) equals 0, variable costs (VC) equal 0 but fixed costs (FC) exist. The consequence is that, even when the firm is not operating, it has costs that must be paid.

Source: Mikel Cohick.

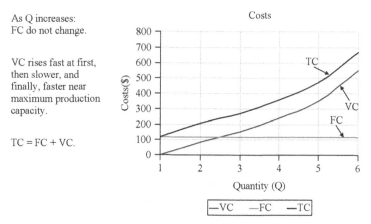

FIGURE 4-3. Graph of FC, VC, and TC

As output (Q) increases, total costs (TC) rise due to increased variable costs (VC). Note that fixed costs (FC) are constant as output increases.

Source: Mikel Cohick.

miles you drive in the month. They are the same if you drive 1000 miles that month or do not drive the car at all during the month.

Variable costs (VC) pay for variable inputs. VC are costs that continue to increase as the level of output increases. VC are payments for the inputs used by the firm that may increase or decrease in number during the production period. Examples are payments for raw materials and labor.

The main variable input for your car is gasoline. You use up the gasoline to produce the main product, which is forward motion. Drive many miles during the month and this cost is high. Drive fewer miles and this cost is lower. If you do not drive at all, this cost is zero. At low levels of production, at start-up, you consume gasoline faster than you do when you get the car up to speed in the desired range of production. When you drive in the tachometer's red zone, gasoline consumption is again high. This means, for your car as well as for any other production activity, variable costs at start-up and at maximum capacity are rising fast as production increases. VC rise at a slower pace in between in the production range.

Total costs (TC) include all the costs of producing a specific amount of output or service, both those costs that require a money outlay and the opportunity costs of the owners. They are the sum of the fixed costs and the VC:

TC = FC + VC.

What Does a Production Model Look Like?

Firms develop a model of their production process using costs per unit of production, or average costs. There are three average costs, one each corresponding to the costs above:

AFC equal the FC divided by the number (Q) of units being produced.

AFC = FC / Q.

Figure 4-4 shows you how the data is calculated and the typical shape of the AFC curve. In a typical firm, AFC are high at low levels of production and decreases continuously as production increases. This is because FC does not change but Q increases. FC are also called overhead, so increasing output is sometimes referred to as "spreading out the overhead."

AVC equal the VC divided by the number (Q) of units being produced.

AVC = VC / Q.

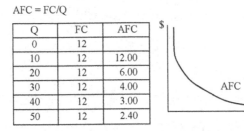

AFC = FC/Q

Q	FC	AFC
0	12	
10	12	12.00
20	12	6.00
30	12	4.00
40	12	3.00
50	12	2.40

FIGURE 4-4. Average Fixed Costs (AFC)

Since FC do not change as output increases, AFC decreases continuously.

Source: Mikel Cohick.

Figure 4-5 shows you how the data is calculated and the typical shape of the AVC curve. In a typical firm, AVC are high at low levels of production, decrease as production increases, but begin to increase as production levels approach the firm's maximum capability. The AVC curve is bowl-shaped with a well-defined minimum point.

ATC equal the total costs divided by the number (Q) of units being produced.

ATC = TC / Q.

Figure 4-6 shows you how the data is calculated and the typical shape of the ATC curve. In a typical firm, ATC are high at low levels of production (dominated by the FC), decrease as production increases, but begin to increase as production levels approach the firm's maximum capacity, where they are dominated by the variable costs. The ATC curve, like the AVC curve, is bowl-shaped with a well-defined minimum point. The ATC curve is always above the AVC curve. The ATC curve's minimum point is at a higher level of output than the AVC curve. Also,

ATC = AFC +AVC.

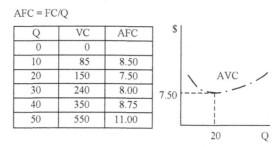

AFC = FC/Q

Q	VC	AFC
0	0	
10	85	8.50
20	150	7.50
30	240	8.00
40	350	8.75
50	550	11.00

FIGURE 4-5. Average Variable Costs (AVC)

In start-up mode, where output (Q) is low, average variable costs (AVC) are high. They decrease as output increases into the production range, and reach a minimum. In this example, the minimum occurs at Q = 20 units. As output increases above 20 units, AVC increases as maximum productive capacity is approached.

Source: Mikel Cohick.

ATC = TC/Q = AFC + AVC

Q	TC	ATC
0	120	
10	205	20.50
20	270	13.50
30	360	12.00
40	470	11.75
50	670	13.40

FIGURE 4-6. Average Total Costs (ATC)

Average total costs (ATC), being the sum of AFC and AVC, start off by decreasing as output (Q) increases. It reaches a minimum point and then begins to rise again as maximum capacity is approached. The minimum point occurs at Q = 40 units. ATC reaches its minimum at a higher cost and at a larger output than does AVC.

Source: Mikel Cohick.

One more cost of importance to the production model is **MC**. MC is the added cost the firm incurs when it increases production by one unit. **Figure 4-7** shows you how the data is calculated and the typical shape of the MC curve. For example, increasing Q from 10 to 20 causes TC to increase from $205 to $270, an change of $65. Divide $65 by 10 and you get $6.50. Since fixed costs do not increase when production is increased, the MC is all VC.

MC = (change in TC) / (change in Q) = (change in VC) / (change in Q)

The MC curve is related to the AVC and ATC curves. After a brief decrease at start-up levels of production, MC reaches a minimum and then rises continuously as production increases. When MC is at a lower level than AVC, AVC decreases. When MC is at a higher level than AVC, AVC increases. MC intersects AVC at the AVC minimum point. The same is true relating MC and ATC. When MC is at a lower level than ATC, ATC decreases. When MC is at a higher level than ATC, ATC increases. MC intersects ATC at the AVC minimum point. **Figure 4-8** shows the interrelationship of MC to the other cost curves. This is the **production model**, applicable to all firms.

Q	TC	MC
0	120	
10	205	8.50
20	270	6.50
30	360	9.00
40	470	11.00
50	670	20.00

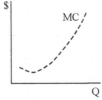

FIGURE 4-7. Marginal Cost (MC)

To calculate MC, divide the increase in TC by the increase in Q. Let us do the first calculation above as Q increases from 0 to 10: MC = ($205–$120) / (10–0) = $85/10 = $8.50.

Source: Mikel Cohick.

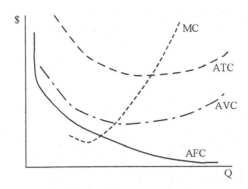

FIGURE 4-8. The Production Model

All firms experience this production model. The MC curve passes upward through the minimum point of both the AVC curve and the ATC curve. The AFC curve has no minimum point.

Source: Mikel Cohick.

What Are the Goals of Running a Business?

A business has many goals. One goal is to provide a product that best satisfies customers' wants or needs. A second goal is to do it using a production process that minimizes the use of scarce resources and keeps costs as low as possible. A third goal is to generate at least an acceptable return on their investment (a normal profit) to the business owners.

Firms aspire to maximize profit. In the short run, a firm can use benefit-cost analysis to find the level of output (Q) that maximizes its profit. They use the MR—MC approach. The firm compares MR (the increase in revenue) with MC (the increase in cost of producing and selling) for each additional unit of output they plan to produce. For each added unit of production where MR > MC, more profit is added to the total profit. For each unit of added production where MR < MC, profit is removed from the total profit. Since MR decreases as output increases and MC increases as output increases, there is a profit-maximizing quantity (Q) where all available profit is added, and none is removed. That occurs at an output where MR = MC. At this level of output, profits are maximized.

If MR > MC, expand production and profits rise.

If MR < MC, decrease production and profits rise.

If MR = MC, this is the level at which profits maximize.

Figure 4-9 shows the process of choosing the profit-maximizing level of output (Q) and the profit-maximizing price (P) to charge.

In the Long Run, How Are Costs and Profits Determined?

The bottom line of the income statement shows whether a firm made a profit or a loss during the time period being examined. Accountants and economists define profit differently because they look at costs differently. The accountant works for the owner(s). Accountants consider only **explicit costs**, which are actual out-of-pocket payments by the firm, plus depreciation. Economists also consider explicit costs, but also consider **implicit costs**, which are not money payments, but are the opportunity costs of the

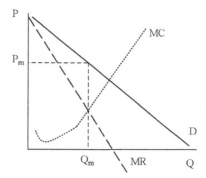

FIGURE 4-9. MR, MC, and Profit Maximization

The output (Q) that will be selected by profit-maximizing firms is always defined by the intersection of MR and MC. Thus, the supplier increases and decreases output by moving along the MC curve. Therefore, MC is the firm's short-run supply curve. This is one reason supply curves slope upward.

Source: Mikel Cohick.

owner's use of his or her time, talent, assets, and effort in running the firm. In the analysis of the firm, only the owner(s) can evaluate the size of the implicit costs.

Accounting profit is defined as total revenue less explicit costs. Accountants follow the "paper trail," that is, they collect all the receipts from sales and the payments of the bills. They also calculate depreciation on the capital goods. Accounting profit is used to compare firms in the same industry for investment purposes. Also, the Internal Revenue Service uses accounting profit to determine the tax due.

Economic profit is defined as total revenue less both explicit costs and implicit costs. Economists are concerned about how the owner(s) make decisions. Owners will include all costs, including their opportunity costs, in their decision-making.

Another name for implicit costs is **normal profit.** Normal profit is the **minimum return on investment necessary for the owner to decide to continue to operate the business**. If the owner does not earn normal profit, he or she could close the business and redeploy his or her time, talent, assets, and effort to an alternative that now looks like it is the better choice for the owner. This could be another business or a job with an employer.

Figure 4-10 shows the difference between accounting profit, economic profit, and normal profit.

In the Long Run, How Are Decisions made?

Let us consider what the owner would do if **economic profits were greater than zero**. In this situation, the owner is enjoying a return on his or her investment that is **greater than the minimum necessary to continue in the business**. Customers obviously like the product and are willing to pay more for it than it costs to bring the product to market. The owner may consider expanding the business in response to the consumer demand. If this owner does not expand, other owners, perhaps those stuck in businesses or industries that have no economic profit may redeploy their assets into this industry in search for economic profit. Either way, this industry will expand, drawing in more resources to produce more of the products customers like.

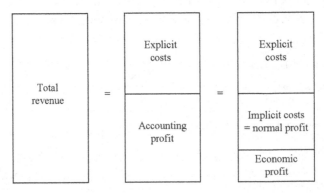

FIGURE 4-10. Relating Accounting, Economic and Normal Profit

Accountants consider only explicit costs to compute accounting profit. Economists also take into consideration implicit costs because they are equally as important when the entrepreneur must make decisions whether to start-up, expand, continue, shrink, or end a business. Subtracting both explicit costs and implicit costs (also known as normal profit) from total revenue gives you economic profit.

Source: Mikel Cohick.

If **economic profits equal zero**, the owner is receiving **exactly the minimum return necessary to continue to operate the business** and will indeed continue to operate in the same way. If economic profit equals zero industry-wide, firms in the industry earn a normal profit, and the industry will remain the same size.

If **economic profits were less than zero**, the owner is no longer receiving a normal profit, **the minimum necessary to keep him or her interested in continuing to operate the business**. Customers no longer are willing to pay enough to cover all the costs of bringing the product to market. The owner has an incentive to cut back production or to exit this industry altogether. Resources used to make these products would be redeployed to other industries where better opportunities to earn a normal profit (or more) exist. This industry will shrink.

To summarize,

> **Economic profit > zero: owner may consider expanding business.**
>
> **Economic profit = zero, owner will continue to operate.**
>
> **Economic profit < zero, owner may consider closing the business.**

In competitive industries, economic profits and economic losses will not persist. They will return to a where economic profits equal zero, and only normal profit remains.

Here are the dynamics of **industry expansion**. Customers like the product and pay more than the costs of bringing it to market. Firms enjoy economic profits as price exceeds ATC. Firms expand and new firms enter this industry, shifting the supply curve to the right. This causes the price to decrease. Supply will continue to shift right, and the price will continue to decrease until the price equals ATC. At that point, economic profits reach zero and industry expansion stops. The market for this product stabilizes at a new, lower price and a greater quantity supplied.

Here are the dynamics of **industry decline**. Customers no longer like a product as much as they used to. Some firms have economic losses as the price is less than their ATC for the product. These firms cut back production or leave the industry, shifting the supply curve to the left. This causes the price to increase. Supply will continue to shift left and the price will continue to rise until the price equals ATC. At that point, economic losses disappear, and firms stop departing the industry. Industry shrinkage stops. Economic losses reach zero. Industry decline leads to zero economic profits for the remaining firms. The market for this product stabilizes at a new, higher price and a smaller quantity supplied. Resources that are removed from this declining and shrinking industry are reallocated by entrepreneurs to expanding industries.

What Are Some Other Cost Considerations?

Breakeven analysis

The goal of a firm is to maximize profits. However, the first step is to become profitable, that is, to reach and surpass the breakeven point. This is incredibly important to the start-up entrepreneur. If you are interested in starting any form of business, you first should do a paper exercise to see if there is a reasonable chance that your intended market is big enough to deliver enough revenues to cover all your FC and your variable costs. You can do this by making judicious estimates and doing a breakeven analysis.

Here are the steps to take in breakeven analysis. First, estimate the price (P) at which you will sell your product. Second, make a list of all the variable inputs you will need to operate your business. Figure out the AVC per unit of product produced. Compute the contribution the sale of each unit of product will have toward paying the costs. It is equal to P–AVC. Third, add up all the fixed costs to get total fixed costs (FC). Fourth, divide fixed costs by this contribution. That determines the quantity (Q) you need to sell to pay all the variable costs and all the fixed costs. This is the breakeven quantity. Fifth, seriously think about whether you can sell that many consistently at the price you mentioned. Remember to include normal profit (your minimum return for your time, effort, and assets) as a fixed cost.

Here is the math of breakeven analysis:

TR – TC = Profit = 0 at breakeven.

P x Q – (FC + VC) = 0

P x Q – FC – AVC x Q = 0

(P – AVC) x Q – FC = 0

(P – AVC) x Q = FC

Q = FC / (P – AVC) is the breakeven quantity.

Sunk costs are expenses that have been paid and cannot be recovered. Owners should not include sunk costs when deciding. Imagine the owner is trying to decide whether to replace a truck. He paid $5,000 for his old truck three years ago and it has little or no trade-in or sales value. If he decides to buy a new truck, that $5,000 was paid. If he decides not to buy a new truck, that $5,000 was paid. The $5,000 is not recoverable and, therefore, it is not relevant to the decision. The owner should only consider relevant costs and relevant benefits when making the decision. For example, what are the changes in operating expenses he can expect? What are the changes in reliability he can expect? These are relevant; a cost paid in the past is not.

What Is the Goal of Long-Run Decision-Making?

The difference between the short run and the long run is that, in the short run, at least one input is fixed while in the long run all inputs can be increased or decreased. In the short run, as described above, there are fixed inputs and fixed costs. Typically, the fixed input is the physical capacity of the firm: the size of its facility, the amount of equipment, and the like. Since capacity is fixed, diminishing marginal returns set in and this fact is responsible for the shape of the curves in the production model. Therefore, the principal decision a firm makes in the short run is a daily decision of **how much to produce** today. A wise firm will choose the output that maximizes profit.

The period for the long run is the time it takes to go from deciding to expand the facility until that moment when the expansion is complete and ready to be made operational. This time varies from industry to industry and may take a year or more. The decision to be made in long-run is **how large a facility should be built.**

The economic concept to be implemented in this decision is **economies of scale.** "Scale" refers to size. As capacity to produce increases, ATC decrease. There are several reasons for this. Most significant are the switch from batch mode operation to assembly line operation, specialization of the employees and machinery, and buying inputs in bulk.

In batch mode, one product is completed before the next one is begun. All workers work on the one product, then switch to the next. In assembly line mode, each worker specializes in a specific task and is placed along the assembly line. Products move down the assembly line, achieving increasing stages of completion as they do this. Several products are in various stages of completion at the same time. The results of the assembly line process are specialization of workers, who get more proficient at their tasks and thereby more productive, and more products are completed in a period of time. As the operation grows, more inputs are needed. These inputs can be purchased from suppliers in larger quantities at lower per-unit prices.

The supermarket replaced the smaller, "mom and pop" grocery stores because it achieved economies of scale and provided groceries to the consumers at lower prices due to the lower costs that accompanied economies of scale. Rearranging the layout of the store provided each consumer with an assembly-line method of selecting the groceries she wanted, employees specialized in check-out, carry-out, produce, meats, shelf stocking, bakery, and the like. The larger store can purchase inputs from suppliers in larger quantities and lower per unit costs than "mom and pop" could.

ATC decrease as scale, or size, increases for nearly all industries. However, there is a limit to how much costs can decrease. After reaching a particular size of a firm's facility, ATC will begin to rise as **diseconomies of scale** set in. If the facility gets too large, one manager cannot manage it. He will appoint assistant managers to run parts of the operation. This is the first step toward the creation of a bureaucracy. Thus, administrative costs rise. The manager may, however, retain decision-making authority. Therefore, the decision-making point is removed from the production floor, causing delays in deciding what to do in the event something goes wrong. Costly mistakes could be perpetuated, or defective products could be produced. Rework of defective products, not to mention liability problems, increases ATC.

Therefore, the long-run decision is to increase the size of the facility to achieve all the economies of scale but not to expand beyond the size where diseconomies of scale set in. The firm operates at **constant returns to scale** where the long-run average cost does not change with an increase in output and is at a minimum. The size of the facility that accomplishes this is called the **ideal-sized plant.**

SUMMARY

1. Identify the difference between fixed costs and variable costs.

In the short run, one input, usually capital, is fixed. All other inputs are variable. If no output is produced, the amount of variable input used is zero and variable costs are zero. However, the fixed input still must be paid for, so fixed costs exist even when output is zero. As output increases, fixed costs stay the same while variable costs increase rapidly at first in the start-up range, then slower in the production range, and finally rapidly as maximum capacity is approached.

2. Fit together AVC, AFC, ATC, and MC to form a production model.

AFC continually decrease as output increases. As output increases, AVC decrease at first to a minimum point then increase beyond that. ATC are the sum of AFC and AVC. As output increases, ATC follows a pattern similar to AVC, except at higher values and the minimum point occurs at a higher level of output. Marginal cost (MC) is the increase in cost that occurs when output is increase by one unit. Marginal cost pushes upward through the minimum points of both the AVC and the ATC curve.

3. Describe the profit maximization rules.

Step by step, the businessperson will compare marginal revenue (MR), the added revenue received from selling one more unit of the product, to the marginal cost (MC), the added cost of producing that unit. If MR > MC, the firm receives more dollars than it pays out and profits grow. In this case, the firm should produce one more unit of the product and check again. The firm continues to do this as long as MR > MC. Profits increase each time. When the output where MR = MC is reached, all possible profit has been obtained and increases in production should cease. If the firm goes beyond this profit-maximizing level of output, MR < MC, and each added unit produced costs more to make than it can be sold for, which decreases profits.

4. Describe the difference between accounting, economic, and normal profit.

Accounting profit is the difference between total revenue and explicit costs. Economic profit recognizes that there are implicit costs, not identifiable by a paper trail, which are significant to the entrepreneur or business owner. Another term for these implicit costs is normal profit. Normal profit is the minimum necessary return to the owner for the commitment of the owner's time, talent, assets, and effort to the business. Economic profit, therefore, is the difference between total revenue and both explicit costs and implicit costs added together. Another way to say this is that economic profit equals accounting profit minus normal profit.

5. Tell why the existence of economic profit lead to industry expansion.5.

If an industry is enjoying economic profit, that means revenues exceed the minimum return necessary to keep the owners interested in staying in the business. This is usually due to the customers liking the product being made. When economic profit exists, the owners in the industry already have an incentive to expand to produce more of the popular product. Also, owners of other businesses outside the industry, who might not be making enough to cover their expected normal profit, may switch into this industry where opportunity is greater. Either way, the industry will expand.

6. Tell how a firm can exploit economies of scale.

A firm can exploit economies of scale by choosing a plant size that takes advantage of all the sources of economies of scale and none of the sources of diseconomies of scale. With economies of scale, as plant size increases, ATC decrease. The most significant sources of economies of scale are switching from batch mode operation to assembly line operation, specialization of employees and equipment, and buying inputs in bulk at lower input prices. With diseconomies of scale, as output increases, ATC also increase. This is due to the inefficiencies due to bureaucratization. With constant returns to scale, as output increases the ATC do not change.

Homework Chapter 4

Name_____

DESCRIPTIONS

Match the key terms with the descriptions.

_____ What a firm receives from selling its products.

_____ Money and nonmonetary cost of inputs, services, and operation.

_____ Revenues minus costs

_____ The additional revenue received when the firm sells one more unit of its product.

_____ Costs that do not change when the level of output changes.

_____ Costs that change as the level of output changes.

_____ Increase in production leading to no change in long-run ATC.

_____ Fixed costs plus VC

_____ FC. VC or TC divided by the quantity produced.

_____ Total revenue less explicit costs.

_____ Total revenue less explicit and implicit costs.

_____ Actual out-of-pocket payments of the business, plus depreciation.

_____ Increase in production leading to a decrease in long-run ATC.

_____ Opportunity cost of the owner's assets, time, and efforts used in a business.

_____ Expenses that have been incurred and are unrecoverable.

_____ Minimum return on investment necessary for the owner to continue to operate the business.

KEY TERMS

1. Accounting profit
2. Average costs (FC, VC, or TC)
3. Costs
4. Economic profit
5. Explicit costs
6. Fixed costs (FC)
7. Implicit costs
8. Marginal revenue (MR)
9. Normal profit
10. Profits or losses
11. Revenues
12. Constant returns to scale
13. Sunk costs
14. Total costs (TC)
15. Variable costs (VC)
16. Economies of scale

EXERCISES

1. Describe the significant goals of running a business.

2. What is breakeven analysis and why is it important for a start-up entrepreneur?

3. Should sunk costs be considered in business decision-making? Why or why not?

4. Can economic profit ever be greater than accounting profit? Why or why not?

5. Why does AFC continuously decrease with increased production?

6. Describe the ideal-sized plant. Why does it operate at constant returns to scale at the lowest ATC?

5 The Economics of Business Firms: Business Organization and Market Structure

In this chapter, we start by analysing how firms can be organized. Then we turn to markets in general for products. We look at the four market structures: perfect competition, monopolistic competition, oligopoly, and monopoly. Each has its specific characteristics which dictate how participants in each market must act. Also, we look at how newly created businesses, if successful, will evolve from a start-up firm through its growth phase in monopolistic competition into its mature stage, possibly as an oligopoly.

After studying this chapter, you should be able to:

1. Outline the differences in the three forms of business organization.

2. Identify and contrast the four market structures

3. Define market power.

4. Tell why regulated monopolies come into existence.

5. Describe how a monopolistic competition industry expands.

6. Describe how an industry in monopolistic competition can evolve into an oligopoly.

7. Describe how preserving market share affects the behavior of an oligopoly.

8. Outline the difference between a cooperative and noncooperative game in oligopoly markets.

How Can a Business Be Organized?

There are three main types of business firm organization: sole proprietorship, partnership, and corporation. Details of each type are outlined below and expanded upon in Chapter 14.

A **sole proprietorship** has one owner. It is possible that the owner is also the entire workforce, and this one person supplied all the assets of the business. About three-fourths of all business firms in the United States are sole proprietorships. Most businesses started out as sole proprietorships. They are a primary source of creativity and entrepreneurship.

The owner faces unlimited liability for all the debts of the firm and for any judgment against the firm in a court of law. It is possible that the personal belongings of the owner could be seized to pay the firm's debts or to satisfy a legal judgment against the firm. On the other hand, it is easy to start a sole proprietorship. Most new businesses start out this way.

A **partnership** has two or more owners. It is important that partnership papers are prepared to specifically outline the rights of each partner, how the partnership will operate, how profits will be determined and distributed, and how the partnership will be terminated. This is much like a pre-nuptial agreement in marriage. The outcome of a marital divorce is much more orderly, and with less animosity and arguments, if there has been a pre-nuptial agreement. It is the same for the termination of a partnership.

The advantage of a partnership is that there can be a pooling of diverse talents needed in the firm. For example, a person who is good at sales could partner with a person who is good at production. Partnerships face the same liability for the debt and legal judgment as the sole proprietorship, a significant disadvantage of this form of organization.

A **corporation** is legal entity that owns the assets and is obligated to pay the liabilities of a firm. It is owned by its stockholders. Each stockholder is shielded from liability for debts of the firm and legal judgments against the firm. Each owner of stock can only lose the total value of the stock held, that is, if the stockholder bought $1,000 worth of stock in a corporation that ultimately goes bankrupt, the shares would have no value and the stockholder would have lost his $1,000 investment.

The advantages of a corporation are that its stockholders are shielded from liability and that the corporation can raise large amounts of capital by issuing stock to the public. Almost all large business firms in the United States are corporations.

What Is Market Structure and Market Power?

An industry includes all of the firms that produce a particular (or closely related) product or service.

Market structure refers to the characteristics of an industry. There are four market structures, listed in the order of increasing **market power**:

> **Perfect competition (no market power)**
>
> **Monopolistic competition (some market power)**
>
> **Oligopoly (considerable market power)**
>
> **Monopoly (total market power)**

Market power comes from a **firm's ability to manipulate the market price**. Firms in perfect competition have no market power. They are too small relative to the entire market. A monopoly has complete market power in that this firm is the sole supplier. The other two structures lie in between. Nearly all businesses and companies fall into these two structures. Firms in monopolistic competition are small and have some market power while firms in an oligopoly are large and have considerable market power. We will analyze each structure.

What Are the Characteristics of Perfect Competition?

Perfect competition has the following characteristics: **many small firms exist, identical products are sold at the same price, and it is easy to enter and exit the industry.**

Many agricultural commodity producers face perfect competition. Agricultural producers take their crop to a marketing board where it is graded and standardized, making sure that all products are identical. The agricultural producer receives the market price of the day for his crop. Each firm is a **price taker.** They must accept the price determined by the market. No firm can lower their price to gain an edge on the competition, nor can it alter its product or service to do so.

The only decision left for a firm in this type of industry is to determine how much to produce. They would do so using the profit-maximization technique described in the previous chapter. Any economic profit or loss would rapidly move toward zero in this structure due to the ease of entry and exit.

Other than several tightly controlled agricultural industries, there are very few industries that comply with the characteristics of perfect competition. Imagine you want to shop for a pair of shoes. If shoe stores were in perfect competition, there would be several shoe stores., each selling shoes that would be the same style at the same price. The quality of each vendor's shoes would be the same. You would not need to visit more than one shoe store. Just choose the most convenient one. That is not much of a competition in the shoe business. Ironically, competition in a perfect competition industry is not much competition at all.

What are the Characteristics of Monopoly?

A **monopoly** sits at the other extreme. A monopolist has complete market power. A monopoly is characterized by having **only one firm producing the product and having a total barrier to other firms entering the industry.** One firm, therefore, controls the entire supply curve of the industry's market. By determining its output, which it would do using the profit-maximizing technique, the monopoly determines the quantity supplied to the market. By looking at the market's demand curve, the monopolist's quantity produced determines the price the monopolist will charge.

The monopolist will charge the price corresponding to the profit-maximizing quantity. It would not charge a higher price than that, thereby "gouging" the customers, because its profits would be lower. Also, the monopolist would have no reason to increase output and lower the price, because its profits would fall.

The monopoly makes an economic profit as long as customers buy its product, which they will do as long as they need it and have no alternative way to satisfy this particular need. Even though economic profits exist, the barrier to entry prevents new firms from entering this industry. The barrier might be a patent, a government license requirement, a franchising requirement, extraordinarily high start-up costs, economies of scale, or a government regulation.

Most monopolies in existence today are government-regulated industries. Examples are electric, water, telephone, cable, and other utility distribution systems. In these cases, a government agency permits only one firm to operate in a geographically distinct market. The government rate-setting board regulates the price charged by the utility to ensure economic profits are zero. A normal profit is the maximum allowed by the regulator.

In industries with high fixed costs of production and distribution, it is possible that only one firm can grow large enough to bring down costs by achieving economies of scale. Multiple firms operating in competition would operate at higher costs and necessarily would have to deliver the product or service to the customer at a higher price. **A regulated monopoly serving the entire market will deliver the service at a lower price.** Government entities will establish a regulated monopoly to serve the entire market. Many utilities—electricity, gas, water, sewer, trash collection, recycling—are provided to customers by regulated monopolies for this reason.

In a non-regulated industry, one firm may attempt to become a monopoly by taking action to restrict competition. The Antitrust Division of the Justice Department is continuously on the lookout for business practices that restrict competition, such as collusion between firms to act together as if one firm owns an industry. They act in concert with each other to eliminate the possibility that newcomers cannot enter the industry to compete. These practices have been made illegal in the United States. Other countries do not have as stringent an outlook on monopolistic practices.

Which Categories Contain Most Businesses?

Most industries fall into one of the two other categories: monopolistic competition and oligopoly. The business you encounter every day most likely fall into one of these two categories. Based on the amount of market power, monopolistic competition is closer to perfect competition and oligopoly is closer to monopoly. As industries are created and grow, they operate in monopolistic competition. As they mature, they evolve into oligopolies.

What Are the Characteristics of Monopolistic Competition?

An industry in **monopolistic competition** is characterized by **having many intensely competitive firms, each with a slightly different version of the product, selling at slightly different prices. There is an easy entry into and exit from the industry.** Most local outlets, small businesses, and start-up operations, such as fast-food restaurants, gasoline stations, and software development firms are examples of monopolistic competition. Their operating arena is incredibly dynamic, and each firm strives to maximize its profits by employing the profit-maximizing technique. Each firm tries to get ahead of the competition by slightly differentiating its product from the ones of the competition. Successful product differentiation gives the firm some market power. Advertising is one of the tools used to drive product differentiation. Innovation is another tool used to drive product differentiation.

Imagine an entrepreneur with a new idea on how to satisfy the customer's particular need better than it is currently being done. The entrepreneur opens a shop and offers an innovative product. Customers discover this product and flock to the shop to buy it. For a brief period of time, this shop is a monopoly; since it is the only place the customer can acquire this version of the product. Previous sources where the consumer could get this satisfaction note a steep decline in business. It is possible that the innovative entrepreneur is enjoying huge economic profits and decides to expand. Others see these high profits, and they enter this profitable industry by copying the successful product. This is called cloning the idea. Now, instead of being a monopoly, the first firm faces intensive competition as the industry expands.

Prices will fall as the industry expands with these new entries, but the real competition comes from each participant constantly modifying its product to make it more appealing to the customer. Each time one firm does this, it resembles, for a short time, a monopolist, enjoying economic profits. However, it is easy for other firms to add the new feature to their product, and everyone is back to square one again.

As this competition occurs, supply shifts right and prices fall. Many of the more inefficient, higher-cost operators encounter economic losses. They may be forced to discontinue operation. Others are more efficient and operate at a lower cost structure and, with economic profits, they want to expand. They will do so by buying out the failing firms and redeploying those assets into their firm. Also, they will hire the resources freed up by firms closing their doors. As this industry grows, a few successful firms expand rapidly while many of the failing firms fall by the wayside.

Ultimately, this innovative product is no longer "new." The typical buyer is no longer a first-time buyer. Most sales are replacement sales. The industry has evolved from a growth industry into a mature industry. Since there are now a few, successful, very large firms dominating this industry (with possibly some smaller firms as niche players), it has evolved into an oligopoly.

What Are the Characteristics of Oligopoly?

An **oligopoly** is characterized by **a few large firms dominating the industry, significant price-setting power, and significant barriers to entry**. Examples include automobiles, breakfast cereals, personal computer manufacturers, and tires. Most large, name-brand producers are members of an oligopoly. An oligopoly market is formed out of a growing monopolistic competition market as a few efficient, low-cost survivors of the industry shakeout expand and less efficient, higher-cost companies shrink or close. The survivors do this by buying out their less efficient competitors and by acquiring more resources as failing competitors exit the industry. The prefix "olig" means "a few."

The products sold in an oligopoly are mature brands. Repeat customers rely on the perceived quality that the name brand implies. Once products become mature, **brand-name loyalty** by repeat customers becomes highly significant to the firm. Because of this, firms in an oligopoly are huge advertisers. Their advertisements are designed to reinforce brand-name loyalty in their existing customers and to draw customers from a rival firm to their firm.

Mature industries will continue to exist as long as the customer likes the product and keeps coming back for more. However, when a new product appears on the market, it is possible that this new way of satisfying the customers' wants or needs will lead to industry decline in the old products industry. This is what happened to the typewriter market when the personal computer came along. However, the ketchup industry reached maturity in the 1870's and is still going strong. It will continue to do so until something comes along to replace ketchup in the hearts and minds of the customers (and on their French fries).

Why Do Oligopolists Protect Market Share?

Firms in an oligopoly strive to maximize profits, like all firms. To do so, they would employ the profit-maximizing technique. However, of great significance to each firm is the size of their **market share**. Assume Coca-Cola has 50 percent of the sales in the soft drink market, Pepsico has 35 percent, and Dr. Pepper has 10 percent (smaller firms have 5 percent). These percentages are each firm's market share. The firms are very protective of their market share. They know if they lose market share that means one of their rivals has gained market share. No firm wants this to happen. Therefore, each firm will play the "What if?" game. They will not take significant action without evaluating what their rivals would do in retaliation.

For example, PepsiCo could strive to gain market share by lowering its price. If they do, they will decrease profit, however. Coca-Cola, noting that PepsiCo dropped its price, would retaliate by dropping its price also, thereby denying PepsiCo's bid to increase market share at Coca-Cola's expense. Now both firms will have decreased profits. Preserving market share becomes more important than maximizing profit. This reliance on the "What if?" game by oligopolistic firms leads to a loss of independence in decision-making. One of the firms cannot make a big decision without knowing what the rival members of the oligopoly will do, Thus, the firms are interdependent.

What Is Game Theory?

This interdependence situation is called **strategic dependence**. No oligopoly firm can make a decision about its own pricing strategy, product advertising, product quality, production quantity, and new sales locations without taking into account how their own decision-making will be strategically counteracted by other firms in the market. Firms behave strategically in oligopoly markets. This is possible because of the existence of only a few firms in the market.

As part of behavioral economics, **game theory** is the analytical framework utilized to describe the strategic behaviors of firms in oligopoly markets. Games are either cooperative or noncooperative. In a **cooperative game**, firms can negotiate to improve their outcomes. In a **noncooperative game**, firms are not able to negotiate or cooperate in any way.

In many countries such as the United States cooperation between firms such as price-fixing is illegal. Firms analyze their outcomes in terms of positive, negative, or zero payoff rewards. Firms have different strategies at their disposal. A strategy is defined as a decision rule. The strategy that produces the highest payoff reward for a firm regardless of what other firms decide to do is called the **dominant strategy** of the firm.

An example of a noncooperative game is the **Prisoner's Dilemma**. Firms are not able to negotiate and collaborate to improve their payoff rewards. Firms pursue their respective dominant strategy regardless of what the other firms do. Each firm does so. The result is an inferior payoff reward for each firm compared to a cooperative game. The prisoner's dilemma is typical for decision-making in oligopoly markets.

An example would be two oligopoly cybersecurity firms competing for small business clients to provide their information technology (IT) security. The first firm, CyberIT, considers offering a security plan containing up to $1 million in damage reimbursement to its clients if potential hackers break through CyberIT's security services to damage a client. If CyberIT does offer it and advertises this plan heavily, it will gain the majority of clients in the market and reap high profits. However, CyberIT knows that the second firm, SecureIT, will not just sit on the sidelines and do nothing in response.

If CyberIT offers up to $1 million reimbursement plan for potential damages and SecureIT does not, then CyberIT corners the market and reaps profits from IT security sales of $50 million while SecureIT loses market share and makes profits of only $10 million.

If SecureIT offers this plan but CyberIT decides not to, then SecureIT corners the market and reaps profits of $50 million and CyberIT profits only $10 million due to the loss in market share.

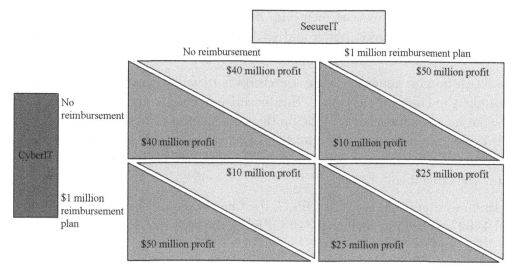

FIGURE 5-1. A Cybersecurity example of the Prisoner's Dilemma

Prisoner's Dilemma. The two cybersecurity companies will receive different profit depending on which reimbursement plan each chooses.

Source: Mikel Cohick.

If both offer the plan, then they both end up with $25 million in profits each. However, if they both could hypothetically cooperate and reach an agreement that neither one of them offers the plan, then they both would end up with $40 million in profit. In the prisoner's dilemma firms are not allowed to cooperate.

Both firms will individually pursue their dominant strategy. The dominant strategy is to offer the plan because it is the strategy that is associated with the highest payoff reward of $50 million in profit regardless of what the other firm does. Both, CyberIT and SecureIT, end up offering the plan and will make $25 million in profit each.

This is far less in profits compared to the situation in which they would have cooperated and not offered the plan. This result is called Nash equilibrium after Economics Nobel prize-winning mathematician turned economist John Nash who developed this concept.

The prisoner's dilemma is a dilemma because firms may end up worse off pursuing their dominant strategy compared to cooperating with each other. The prisoner's dilemma is a one-time game. In real life, when firms face the threat of retaliation from other firms in repeated games, the payoff result may improve when firms voluntarily follow the market-leading firms without directly cooperating with such other firms.

How Do Cartels Operate?

An example of a cooperative game would be a **cartel**. Firms can negotiate agreements and collude to improve their payoff rewards. Examples are agreements on assigning sales territory to specific cartel members, price and output fixing, and exclusive cartel member bid rotation lists for public sector project bidding.

Cartel members cooperate to increase their joint market power. They act like a monopoly. Successful cartels can maximize their market power and set quantity and pricing just like a profit-maximizing monopoly would do. Cartel members then share the profits.

Cartels are illegal in most countries. Many cartels do not last long because of the inherent incentive of cartel members to cheat on each other. This incentive to cheat comes from the fact that the cartel restricts the output of its members to drive up the market price. Cartel members know that they can individually lower their own price to certain clients (sometimes secretly at first) and sell more output to make more profit. The market price will then drop if enough cartel members cheat and output expands substantially. The cartel then collapses.

The most famous cartel in the world is OPEC, the Organization of Petroleum Exporting Countries, founded in 1960 and still in existence today. OPEC is a special case of a cartel because it consists of sovereign nations and not individual firms.

SUMMARY

1. **Outline the differences in the three forms of business organization.**

   A sole proprietorship has only one owner, has limited access to talent and capital, and has unlimited liability concerning debts and taxes. A partnership is much like the sole proprietorship, except that it has greater access to talent and capital. A corporation creates shares of stock that can be sold to multiple owners who will have limited liability. It can raise large amounts of capital by selling shares or by issuing debt instruments called corporate bonds.

2. **Identify and contrast the four market structures.**

   Perfect competition has the following characteristics: many small firms exist, identical products are sold at the same price, and it is easy to enter and exit the industry. A monopolist has complete market power. A monopoly is characterized by having only one firm producing the product and having a total barrier to other firms entering the industry. An industry in monopolistic competition is characterized by having many intensely competitive firms, each with a slightly different version of the product, selling at slightly different prices. There is an easy entry into and exit from the industry. An oligopoly is characterized by a few large firms dominating the industry, significant price-setting power, and significant barriers to entry.

3. **Define market power.**

   Market power is a firm's ability to manipulate the market price of the product or service it sells. Perfectly competitive firms have no market power because they sell identical products or services at the same price. They are price takers and must take the market price as their own price. A monopoly has complete market power as it is the only firm in the market. Monopolistic competitive firms may acquire some market power depending on how successful they are in differentiating their products from their competitors. Oligopoly firms may have considerable market power depending on how successful they are in building up the brand loyalty of their customers to charge higher prices.

4. **Tell why regulated monopolies come into existence.**

   Regulated monopolies come into existence because a government agency permits only one firm to operate in a geographically distinct market.

5. **Describe how a monopolistic competition expands.**

   A monopolistically competitive industry expands through successful product differentiation. Such product differentiation includes product innovations. Successful firms reap higher economic profits. These economic profits serve as incentives for other firms to enter the industry and copy the successful products. More firms enter this industry and the market supply curve shifts to the right. The industry expands.

6. **Describe an industry in monopolistic competition evolve into an oligopoly.**

   Many small firms enter a new industry where a new idea has captivated the consumer and economic profits exist. Competition is intense and the best way to get ahead of the competition is to innovate or improve the product. The firm that does this becomes the only one doing so and, for a moment, resembles a monopolist. Quickly, others clone the new innovation or improvement, and all are the same again until another firm jumps ahead by innovation. As this continuous improvement process goes on, some firms can succeed in producing the product at lower costs while others have high costs. As prices fall, the high-cost companies either go out of business or sell out to the low-cost firms that want to expand. Ultimately, as the product matures, many of the original firms are long gone while a few successful firms expand to dominate the industry. This result is called an oligopoly.

7. Describe how preserving market share affects the behavior of an oligopoly.

Oligopoly firms are very protective of their market share. Losing market share means that a rival firm has gained this market share. Oligopoly firms will not take significant action without first strategically evaluating what their rivals would do in this "What if?" game. This leads to strategic dependence in the behavior of oligopoly firms. Game theory describes this strategic behavior.

8. Outline the difference between a cooperative and noncooperative game in oligopoly markets.

A cooperative game is a situation where firms can negotiate with each other to come to agreements in terms of coordinating with each other in their pricing strategies, for their production quantities, for their advertising strategies, on which markets to penetrate, etc. A noncooperative game is a situation where firms are not allowed to negotiate with each other. Each firm then chooses to do the best they can given their own circumstances regardless of what the other firm chooses to do.

Homework Chapter 5

DESCRIPTIONS

Match the descriptions with the key terms

_____ A one-owner business where the owner faces unlimited liability for the debts of the business.

_____ A two or more-owner business with each facing unlimited liability for the debts of the business.

_____ The ability of a firm to influence the market price of the product or service it sells.

_____ A legal entity owned by shareholders, who are shielded from liabilities. The legal entity owns the assets of a business and is obligated to pay the liabilities.

_____ The number of firms in a market and their relative size.

_____ A market structure consisting of many small firms producing identical products.

_____ A few firms negotiate with each other on a new pricing strategy.

_____ A market structure consisting of one firm producing a unique product and other firms are blocked from entering the industry.

_____ A market structure consisting of many small firms producing differentiated products.

_____ Investors are only liable to lose their original investment in a corporation (stock purchase) but are not liable with other personal assets for the losses of the corporation.

_____ Firms are not allowed to negotiate with each other to agree which market each firm may exclusively sell to.

_____ A firm that must accept the price as determined by the market.

_____ Several firms cooperate to act like a monopoly.

_____ A market structure consisting of a few large firms producing either identical or differentiated products.

_____ A firm selects the strategy associated with the highest payout regardless of what other firms do.

KEY TERMS

1. Market power
2. Cooperative game
3. Price taker
4. Dominant strategy
5. Corporation
6. Market structure
7. Oligopoly
8. Monopolistic competition
9. Monopoly
10. Noncooperative game
11. Partnership
12. Perfect competition
13. Cartel
14. Limited liability
15. Sole proprietorship

EXERCISES

1. What is market power, and which of the four market structures has it? Why?

2. Why does economic profit or loss eventually revert to zero in perfect competition?

3. Why can't monopolies charge any price they want and still maximize profit?

4. Why do cartels usually not last a long time?

5. What forms do product differentiations take in monopolistic competition?

6. Why does a firm pursuing its dominant strategy in a prisoner's dilemma earn less profit compared to a situation where the firm could cooperate with other firms?

7. Why are perfectly competitive firms price takers?

6 The Economics of Government

Government plays a significant role in the economy. Primarily, it is the **agent of society**. Members of a society expect their government to do things that make their society function more smoothly and efficiently. Society calls upon its government to be the referee in the economic game. Government passes laws that govern the conduct of its member as they pursue their daily activities. When conflict arises between participants, government is called upon to adjudicate and resolve the conflict.

Society also calls upon its government to aid the needier members of society. Another role of the government is to provide or arrange to provide goods and services for the use of its members. Government is also a consumer and, therefore, it has a budget. Since the government is not a producer, it must impose taxes upon the members of its society to pay its bills.

All these roles require making decisions by elected officials, bureaucrats, and voters. The economics of decision-making applies to each of these roles.

In this chapter, we will examine government's several roles: providing goods and services, government budgeting and tax policy, decision making in the public sector, and providing for those living in poverty.

While the market economy is a highly efficient mechanism to provide goods and services, distribute resources and generate incomes, there are certain situations for which the market has a less than perfect solution and government steps in to provide the good or service. We shall examine government's role in the economics of the creation and provision of **public goods** and goods that generate **externalities.**

After studying this chapter, you should be able to:

1. Describe public goods and outline the role of government to insure they are available to society.

2. Describe a negative externality and the role of government when dealing with one.

3. Describe a positive externality and the role of government when dealing with one.

4. List four activities where government acts as the agent for society.

5. Contrast a progressive tax system with a regressive tax system.

6. Describe the use of a transfer payment.

7. Relate the government budget to the national debt.

8. Contrast decision-making in the voting booth with decision-making in the marketplace.

9. Contrast running a bureaucracy with running a business.

10. Tell how the government defines the poverty line.

11. Describe the conflict between the two economic goals of equity and efficiency.

What Is the Government's Role When Dealing with a Public Good?

To better understand what a public good is, we first must look at the definition of a **private good** and then compare the two. Food is a good example of a private good. A private good is rival in consumption, which means that one person's consumption means another person cannot consume the same good. What you had for dinner is gone. Once you have eaten it, no one else can. A private good is also exclusionary, which means the producer can stop someone from consuming it without paying for it. Someone had to pay for your dinner, either at the supermarket or at the restaurant, or you wouldn't have been able to eat it.

A **public good**, on the other hand, is non-rival in consumption. National defense is the classic example of a public good. If one person is being protected by the national defense, it doesn't stop anyone else from being protected by national defense. A public good is also non-exclusionary. It is nearly impossible to stop anyone from being protected by the national defense, short of deporting them from the country.

Another example is the streetlight at the corner in your neighborhood. Not only you, but all your neighbors have access to the light being emitted. You enjoy its light, but you would have great difficulty precluding others from enjoying it also. Another example you use every day is the city streets. Notice that you are not the only one using the street. You cannot use up the street, either.

Would you be willing to voluntarily write a check each year specifically for your "fair share" of national defense? Most people would say "No, I will just prefer to let the rich pay for it, because they have more to lose than I do." This is called the **free rider problem**. Why should we pay for something if someone else will pay for it and we get to use it for free? Most of us would choose to be free riders and let someone else pay.

A private-sector market fails to provide for these things that society clearly wants. Why? In a strictly private sector market, the producers can see no way that they would be paid to produce a public good. Nobody steps up and offers to buy it. Therefore, government, as agent for society, steps in and becomes the buyer and assures the producer that he will be paid to produce the good. Government then compels us to pay for this good indirectly via taxes.

Other examples of public goods are not quite as pure. They may satisfy one of the non-rival, non-exclusionary descriptions but not the other. City streets are non-rival in consumption, except during rush hour when there are too many drivers on the street. During those times, the city could charge the many drivers a toll to use the street, but usually does not. That would be too disruptive, and entry and exit would have to be limited.

Fire protection may be non-rival in consumption, but the Fire Department could exclude people who didn't buy a subscription for fire protection. As a practical matter though, a fire from a non-paying citizen's home or business could spread and ignite a paying citizen's home or business. The solution is to have government furnish most of these goods and then charge taxes and user fees to pay for them. Examples of public goods like these are the zoo, roads and highways, libraries, sidewalks, and streetlights.

Is a good or a service a public good? Once provided for by the government, do the members of society get to use the good for free or a token user fee? If not, it is not a public good.

Is a pro football stadium a public good? Is it true that the only way the city can have a pro football stadium is for the government to provide it and pay for it out of taxes and user fees? The test is whether the citizenry of the city will get to use the pro football stadium to watch games for free or a token fee, instead of the full ticket price. If so, then the government, as agent of society, should provide the stadium. If not, then tax dollars are being directed to the benefit of a special interest group (the team's owners) at the expense of the taxpayer.

What Is the Government's Role When Dealing with Externalities?

An externality is a cost or benefit arising from an activity that falls on a third party, that is, someone other than the producer or the consumer. An externality can be either negative or positive, depending upon whether a cost or a benefit falls upon the third party.

A **negative externality** might arise because of a neighbor who doesn't mow his lawn, has a car jacked up on blocks in the front yard, paint is peeling off the house and he slaughters animals in the back yard. Other people on the block suffer (pay a cost) because of this behavior.

A **positive externality** might arise because of a neighbor whose lawn is manicured like a golf green, the house is kept up well and repainted when necessary and it has a beautiful flower garden that is visible from the street. Others benefit from this person's behavior.

Which house would you rather have in your neighborhood? In one case, the other people living on the street suffer a decrease in their house's value, In the other case, they enjoy an increase in their house's value. We shall examine the externalities more closely.

Negative Externality

The classic example of a negative externality is the producer who, rather than treating the pollution that is a byproduct of an inefficient manufacturing process, dumps it in the river, killing the fish and making the children sick downstream. The people living downstream from the polluting factory are suffering the external cost. The actual production costs incurred by the producer are private costs. The damage caused by the pollution when it is dumped into society is an external cost. The private cost and the external cost are both borne by society and together are the social cost.

These goods get overconsumed and therefore are overproduced. For example, if private costs (including normal profits) to produce a particular item are $10 and the externalized cost is $2, then the cost to society (social cost) is $12. If the good is produced without cleaning up the pollution, then it can sell for $10. If the producer must spend $2 cleaning up the pollution, then the goods must sell for $12. Remember the law of demand which says that as the price falls, more quantity is demanded. Consumers will buy more of the good at $10 than at $12, so the good is overconsumed and overproduced.

How does society deal with externalized costs like pollution? While economists believe that markets are highly efficient, the market decision-making mechanism only takes into consideration the benefits and costs of the buyer and seller. Third- party costs do not get considered in a market decision. Because of this, the market fails to deal well with externalities. Therefore, there is a call for government to intervene.

There are three basic methods to reduce externalities. The government can either force the party involved to **internalize the cost**, **prohibit** production that causes the external costs in the first place, or **reward** good behavior that does not impose social costs.

Internalize the Cost

The polluter is given a choice of cleaning up the pollution or face fines and penalties well more than the cost of cleanup. One form of coercion would be for the government to tell the polluter exactly how to clean up the pollution or tell the firm how to change the production process to minimize the pollution. Another form of coercion would be for the government to let the polluter choose the cleanup method which will satisfy the government inspectors when they check for compliance. Finally, the government could tax the product and use the tax money to clean up the mess.

Prohibit

The production process that caused the externality could be prohibited by law. Offenders would be subject to civil penalties like fines or even criminal penalties like imprisonment. This solution would raise the cost of the production, probably well above any money earned from the production itself.

Reward

This method is closer to a market-oriented approach. Examples would include giving producers rewards or other incentives to have pollution-free factories or giving good drivers subsidies if they select pollution-free vehicles.

Positive Externality

A positive externality is where a benefit, rather than the cost, from an activity falls on a third party. The bystander gains from the activity, rather than lose. An example of an activity with a positive externality is basic (K-12) education. Benefits to the teachers, the students, and their parents are private benefits. However, society also receives a benefit. Business firms want and need an educated workforce. An educated public is important for self-government to work and as a crime reduction measure. These are called social benefits.

These activities are underproduced by markets. If all families had to pay directly for the true cost of their children's basic education, far fewer children would get an education. This would be the case if all K-12 education took place in private schools. We made a political decision in this country that we want to encourage everyone to get a basic education. The government gets involved with two forms of encouragement: **subsidies** and **coercion**. The states developed the public K-12 education system to do this. The government subsidizes K-12 public education by enabling students to attend for free. The government also coerces children up to a certain age to attend school.

Subsidies

A subsidy can take the form of a direct payment or a reduction in taxes. In the case of basic education, we subsidize through the government's power to tax. In the case of basic education, state and local governments set certain requirements and provide the education itself.

Coercion

In other cases, the government may require certain activities that have external benefits. An example would be mandatory school attendance up to a certain age. Even if the parents and their children don't understand the benefits to themselves, society recognizes the benefits of lower crime, more educated voters, and the productivity that comes from a better-educated workforce. Other examples would include inoculation against infectious diseases and mandatory snow removal from sidewalks in winter.

How Is Government an Agent of Society?

Rules of Conduct

Anarchy means a state without any government. A market economy cannot operate in a state of anarchy. Government is necessary to provide the envelope of rules within which an economy can operate. That envelope consists of the civil and criminal justice systems that set the rules for the marketplace and for contracts, fraud, and property rights. Society chooses the constraints of the envelope so that, when operating within the envelope, daily activities function smoothly. Criminal activity takes place outside the envelope.

Law of Contracts

When business transactions become more sophisticated and move beyond the requirements of a simple "handshake deal," written contracts are necessary. Contracts set out in writing the basic terms of a transaction. Since a contract that contained a provision for every contingency that might happen over its life would be much too costly to implement, most contracts just describe the basic terms of a transaction.

Many times, however, there is either disagreement as to the meaning of the terms of the contracts or events happen that were not originally anticipated. These situations require interpretation by an arbitrator who is both independent and empowered to enforce its findings. The civil justice system, consisting of the courts, the uniform commercial code, and existing case law, provides the necessary independence to make decisions and the power to enforce them.

Fraud Laws

Fraud is any act, expression, omission, or concealment calculated to deceive another to his or her disadvantage. It is a knowing misrepresentation or concealment with reference to some fact material to a transaction. Fraud is done with the intent to deceive a party who is injured thereby. Markets are highly efficient mechanisms within which transactions can be completed. Not all actors in the economy bring the same degree of moral standards to the marketplace so certain provisions of the law are necessary to protect the unsuspecting from abuse. These provisions are called fraud laws.

Property Rights

Private property is the right of private persons and firms to obtain, own, control, employ, dispose of, and bequeath land, capital, and other property. Private property rights are one of the sacred tenets of the market system and are the essence of capitalism. People tend to take much better care of property they own as individuals, rather than in common through the government. In a state of anarchy, people must protect their own property rights with the use of force, which can be a drag on economic activity. The market system works much better if the institution of government protects property rights. No one wants to make an investment such as to build a factory in a country that doesn't protect private property rights.

The principal property right to be protected by government is the freedom of citizens from seizure of the property by government itself without due process of law. In the past, and in many societies in the present, this protection does not exist or is poorly defined. In societies like these, the ruling elite simply confiscate property from citizens, who have no legal recourse. This has a severe dampening effect on the citizens' motivation to accumulate property, to begin with. Why work hard, earn an income, and acquire goods that will improve one's life, if those goods will be seized by government agents for the use of the ruling elite?

The result of this absence of property rights protection is a two-tier class system: the very well-to-do ruling elite and the desperately poor. If the right to accumulate wealth is protected from seizure, many of the poor will exploit their talents and skills, begin to accumulate wealth, and move up the wealth ladder. In this way, a prosperous middle class is created as several poor people move up the ladder. A significant result of the protection of property rights is that there are substantially fewer people left at the bottom of the wealth ladder.

How Does the Government Collect Taxes and Fund Expenditures?

Government finance consists of two parts: funds coming into the government treasury, generally by taxation, and funds being disbursed by the treasury, generally to fund government purchases or to provide for transfer payments.

Taxes

Taxes provide an income stream for government. Taxes are paid by income earners. There are two main kinds of tax systems, a progressive tax system, and a regressive tax system,

Progressive Tax System

When the tax rate increases as incomes increase, the tax is called progressive. The higher-income taxpayers pay a higher portion of their incomes in taxes than lower- income taxpayers. An example of a progressive tax system is the U.S. Federal Income Tax System. Taxable income is grouped into tiers called **tax brackets** with the higher tax brackets subject to higher rates of tax. Here is what a portion of a tax table might look like:

Taxable Bracket	Tax Rate	Tax Incurred
Less than $ 18,450	10%	$ 1,845.00
$18,451 to $74,900	15%	$ 8,467.50
$74,901 to $151,200	25%	$19,075.00

Using the table above, a married taxpayer filing jointly with a taxable income of $100,000 would pay $16,587.50. That is the sum of 10% of the first $18,450; 15% of the next $56,450; and 25% of the amount remaining up to $100,000.

Regressive Tax System

When the tax rate decreases as incomes increase, the tax is called a regressive tax. Examples would include general sales taxes, social security taxes (FICA), and ad valorem taxes on personal and real property. Regressive taxes cause low-income people to pay a larger portion of their income in tax than high-income people do.

Many lower-income earners and those who live paycheck to paycheck spend all their money, saving none. They are likely to incur sales taxes on most or all of their spending, so the proportion of taxes paid to income (the tax rate) is higher than the high-income earner who might save half of their earnings and only incur sales taxes on the other half. Thus, general sales taxes are considered a regressive tax.

Social security taxes do not increase with income and, in fact, have an upper annual limit so that the very highest income earners quickly reach their annual limit and pay no social security taxes for the rest of the year. Since the social security tax rate on the income above the limit is 0 percent, social security taxes are regressive as well.

Taxes on property are also regressive. Picture the senior citizen on a fixed income whose home value is increasing each year at least as much as inflation and possibly more. Higher home values mean ever-higher property taxes incurred while their incomes are not increasing. Thus, the taxes paid on their homes become an ever-increasing portion of their incomes. Rents charged to tenants increase as property taxes increase. Many renters are low-income people who cannot afford to buy their own home. Since the percentage of income going to taxes increases while income stays the same, property taxes are regressive.

Many states have a lottery. Participation in a lottery is voluntary, however, most lottery players are in the lower income levels, so we believe the lottery is quite regressive.

Transfer Payments

A transfer payment is one in which a person or institution receives a payment from the government to which he or it is entitled by law, but for which there is no requirement for any product to be made or action to be taken in return. We have made a political decision in the United States to partially redistribute income, for a variety of reasons.

This is accomplished in two ways. First, the burden of paying for the Federal government is borne more by middle- and higher-income earners than by lower- income earners because of the progressive income tax system. Second, we provide a social safety net, consisting of various transfer programs described below for people who are down on their luck, make bad decisions, experience misfortune, or become disabled.

Cash Transfer Programs

Disability payments and Temporary Aid to Needy Families (TANF) are two examples of programs where cash is used as an income supplement for individuals and families who qualify.

In-kind Programs

These programs are designed to ensure that the funding goes for its intended purpose, rather than for something the recipient may want but not necessarily need. Three examples of in-kind payments are Food Stamps, Housing Assistance (vouchers and public housing), and Medicaid (health insurance for the indigent).

Entitlement Programs

An entitlement program gets its name from the fact that Congress can't necessarily limit the amount of funds spent by the program. The spending levels depend upon the number of people who become "entitled" to participate in the program by virtue of reaching a certain age or their incomes drop below a certain level. Two examples of programs whose costs are increasing faster than the overall price levels are Medicaid and Medicare.

You are entitled to Medicaid when your income drops below a certain level and your use of it depends upon the state of your health and how much time you can spend obtaining the care. Medicaid affects both the Federal government and all state governments. The program is designed by the Federal government and administered by states. States pay a substantial portion of the cost and Medicaid has become one of the largest categories of state spending.

Medicare is health care insurance for the aged and is a federal program paid for by the Federal government (the taxpayers). You are entitled to Medicare when you reach a certain age, around 65. Your use of Medicare depends upon your health and your willingness to spend time obtaining the care. The problem with Medicare is that the population is aging and at the same time health care costs are increasing faster than the overall price level is increasing.

Interest Groups

In reality, not all transfer payments go to the low-income earners. The U.S. Government provides many subsidies to industry, including but not limited to agriculture, housing, and health care. These subsidies were established and are maintained by extensive lobbying efforts and political contributions focused on the U.S. Congress. Members of Congress are fond of living in Washington and maintaining political power. Lobbying efforts are sponsored by both individuals and interest groups representing like-minded individuals and business firms. Payments and political contributions from interest groups become a significant incentive to members of Congress and therefore impact their decisions about who gets access to the members.

Government Expenditures

Government expenditures are payments by the government for specific goods and services. They differ from transfer payments in that there is definitely an expectation by the government for the recipient of the payment to provide a product or a service in return.

Goods and Services

All three levels of government (local, state, and Federal) spend money for goods and services, just like individual households and business firms. For example, local governments purchase items like fire trucks, school textbooks, and streetlights; state governments purchase vehicles for the state police, computers, and highways; and the Federal government purchases aircraft carriers, radar systems, and health care services.

Resources

All three levels of government employ labor of all types. Local governments hire sanitation workers, police officers, and clerks. State governments hire teachers, tax collectors, and clerks. The Federal government hires border patrol agents, Navy Seals, and clerks. In addition to labor, the government consumes large amounts of land and capital.

What Does the Federal Government Budget Look Like?

This discussion is confined to the Federal government. Most state governments require the operating budgets of the state and the local governments to be balanced each year, so surpluses and deficits are not an issue.

Deficit and Surplus

Governments generate revenues from sources like taxes and fees and generate expenditures for a variety of resources, goods, and services.

> **A surplus occurs when revenues are greater than expenditures.**
>
> **A deficit occurs when expenditures are greater than revenues.**
>
> **A balanced budget occurs when revenues equal expenditures.**

It is rare to have a federal government budget that is either balanced or in a surplus condition. A deficit is the usual result because that is the most politically palatable avenue for politicians to take. A politician running for office who promises higher taxes on the voters probably will not get elected. Similarly, advocating decreased government funding on the voters' projects is also a losing campaign promise. Winning campaigns stress lower taxes and more government-provided goodies, both of which increase the deficit.

Debt

If an individual or a business has a deficit they must either tap into savings or, if none exist, borrow to fund the deficit. The Federal government is no different. It must increase its borrowings to finance budget deficits. The individual goes to a bank or a variety of consumer financing sources to borrow money. The business borrows money from a bank or a variety of commercial financing sources. The Department of the Treasury finances the Federal government's budget deficit by issuing securities called Treasury Bills (short-term obligations), Treasury Notes (intermediate-term obligations), and Treasury Bonds (long-term obligations). These securities are sold to dealers who turn around and resell them to other governmental agencies, banks, other financial institutions, and individual investors.

A budget deficit or surplus is for a specific period, such as one fiscal year.

The national debt is the total amount owed by the Federal government as of a particular date, say, at the end of the fiscal year.

The national debt is an accumulation of all the deficits and surpluses since the newly created Federal government assumed the revolutionary war debt of the 13 states upon their ratification of the U.S. Constitution in 1789. In 2022, the national debt passed $30 trillion.

The Treasury Securities listed above are in demand by buyers who want to make an investment with little risk of default. The Federal Reserve System, the Social Security Administration, other Government agencies, and many foreign central banks also purchase and hold Treasury Securities. Private investors, government entities, and foreign holders participate in extensive buying and selling of previously issued Treasuries in the secondary market.

As the deficit grows, the government needs more financing and the demand for funds increases, which results in higher interest rates. Higher interest rates tend to stifle spending by business firms on capital goods and by consumers on durable consumer goods. The Treasury Department taps the same sources of funds to borrow as businesses and consumers, so when the government needs to borrow more, there will be less to borrow by anyone else.

This phenomenon is known as **crowding out** because government borrowing tends to crowd out private sector borrowing. Crowding out can be reduced by an increase in the money supply by the Federal Reserve System and by the extent that foreign entities buy the securities.

With a seemingly never-ending string of budget deficits adding to the national debt each year, what happens when the securities mature and must be paid? The credit of the United States government is very good, and many individuals, institutions, and foreign governments are more than happy to extend it. Therefore, when an individual Treasury Security matures and must be repaid, a new Treasury Security is issued to obtain the funds to pay off the one that is due. This is **rolling over the debt.**

Interest Payments

Each Treasury Security, being a debt instrument, must pay its holder an interest payment. Interest is like any other current operating expense and must be paid out of current revenues. As the national debt increases due to continued deficit spending by the Federal government, the interest payment burden grows. Interest on the national debt is substantial and accounts for a growing portion of the Federal budget.

Who Carries the Burden? Taxpayers, of course, carry the burden of all government spending. The real question is who pays the taxes? The U.S. has a basic "ability to pay" system, which means that as one's income rises, the tax burden should rise as well and does so in many cases.

Here are a couple of "equity" or fairness perspectives:

Horizontal equity means that either two persons or two families with the same income would pay roughly the same amount of tax.

Vertical equity means a higher-income person or family would pay more tax than a lower-income person or family. The U.S. income tax code is theoretically designed to achieve this but, like anything else subjected to the political process gets perverted, so does the tax code.

Not all high-income earners pay the highest rates of taxes. Our federal income tax code contains many special provisions called **loopholes** that may exempt certain kinds of income from being included in taxable income. Those with enough wealth and income can afford to lobby the U.S. Congress for special tax breaks, so the middle-income earners usually end up paying the most taxes. Many **special interest groups** are formed exactly for this purpose.

How Are Decisions Made in Government?

All participants in the government are people and, therefore, make decisions exactly like other people do. Each one uses his value system to evaluate the benefits and the costs of the next decision to be made.

The problem comes when it is realized that, in government, the benefits and costs of a decision do not all accrue to the decision-maker but will fall on others. Therefore, a government decision-maker, either an elected official or a bureaucrat, cannot possibly know the preferences of all the people who will be affected by the decision. He relies on his own value system and tries to do "the right thing." It follows that, in government decision-making, not everyone affected is going to get his or her wishes filled. Benefits accrued by one group of people could be offset by costs accrued by another group of people.

The Voting Booth vs. the Market

Public choice theory is the name given to a school of thought that believes that voters express their preferences for public goods in the voting booth in a similar fashion to the way they express their preferences for goods and services in the marketplace. In other words, voters research each candidate's position on the issues and then select the candidate that best suits their preferences.

There are several difficulties with this approach. First, at the supermarket, a shopper can pick each individual fruit and vegetable, can make the meat selections of their choice, and then opt for the bread they like. At the voting booth, the choice may be between a candidate that the voter agrees with on two issues out of five and a candidate that the voter agrees with on three issues out of five. It's like getting the meat and fruit selections of your choice but having to accept vegetables and bread that you would never buy as individual items. To further complicate our shopping trip, suppose you must visit the supermarket with many of your neighbors, everyone gets to vote on what to buy and majority rules. If you end up on the losing side, you may have to pay for groceries that fit other people's preferences but not your own. That result happens very often in the voting arena.

Often, other factors outweigh candidate's positions on issues. In a general election, most candidates try to blur their position on controversial issues, because taking a stand usually means making a big portion of the voters angry. Also, factors such as a candidate's looks, charisma, experience, sound, name identification, and party label sometimes play a larger role than positions on the issues.

Finally, there is **rational ignorance**. Preparing to vote is yet another claim on a person's already crowded agenda. If its priority is low relative to the importance of other things he must do with his time, he will not devote much time investigating the issues or the candidates. It is, therefore, rational for him to remain ignorant. For such a person, is it a rational act to spend the necessary time researching each candidate's positions, and then spend the time it takes to vote? Does one vote make a difference? In contrast to this very real view, we are admonished that we should all vote because it is our civic duty. Participatory democracy works best when citizens actively participate.

Elected Officials

Just as consumers seek to maximize their utility and producers seek to maximize their profits, career politicians seek to maximize their chances for reelection or a chance to move up to a higher office. On the state and local level of government, there are many "citizen legislators"—people who have a law practice or a business or another life in which to return after briefly serving in public office. Most members of the U.S. Congress, however, are known as career politicians who wish to remain in office, having chosen politics as a profession.

Maximizing one's chances for reelection means doing things that may not completely be in the long-term best interest of society. A perpetual reelection campaign for a member of Congress starts with their first acceptance speech upon winning their first election and continues until they are finally defeated or retire to become a public affairs director for a trade association (commonly known as a lobbyist). Getting reelected may mean that one must make many promises to please the voters, trade promises for campaign funding, and support things that have visible results now, even though the long-term costs far outweigh the benefits.

Interest Groups and Lobbying

The United States is a nation of interest groups. We join associations to be with people who have a common interest with ourselves. A most effective way to influence the government at any level is through interest group activity. If one citizen contacts his elected representative, he may get a three-minute introduction but most likely will only be able to meet with a member's staff. If a representative of a special interest group representing hundreds or thousands of members with the potential to make multiple campaign contributions contacts the elected representative the interest group will get a hearing. Campaign contributions buy access. If an articulate spokesperson has access and the other side doesn't, who do you think will win the debate?

Why doesn't the public rebel about all these special favors? It is a matter of concentrated benefits and widespread costs. Those receiving the benefits know it. Those paying the extra taxes don't realize it. An example would be tariffs on imported goods to protect a domestic industry. Every manager in the industry, as well as every union member in the industry, knows about the protective tariffs and how a protective tariff benefits their firm or their workers. The millions of consumers who pay extra for the products don't notice the extra cost or don't realize they are paying more because of the tariffs.

Bureaucracy

Bureaucrats are necessary for large organizations to work effectively. Someone must be able to follow the rules and carry out the organization's mandate in an orderly, unbiased way. Our encounters with government bureaucrats may not be fun because of their necessarily rigid enforcement of rules and procedures.

People that move up the bureaucratic ladder and become managers of government agencies and departments are the most skilled in the ways of a bureaucracy. These bureaucratic managers are human, and seek to expand their power, influence, and funding just as corporate managers do. But while a corporate manager may be judged by their division's increase in revenues and profits, a bureaucrat is judged by the size of their department's budget and their number of employees. Thus, there is a constant need to expand the scope of the department by taking on more responsibility. In the public sector, taking on more responsibility usually means more regulation of private sector activity and providing more public goods at the expense of private goods.

The incentives for efficiency are also perverse. If a corporate manager loses money or overruns their expense budget, a reprimand or worse is usually in order. If a public sector manager doesn't complete their responsibilities or overruns their budget, they usually end up with a larger budget the following year. If a corporate manager increases profits, a bonus, raise or promotion could follow. If a public sector manager fulfills their responsibilities and doesn't spend all their budgeted funds, their budget is usually reduced the following year.

There is little or no incentive for cost-cutting. Cost-cutting means losing employees, budget, and thus status. Cutting government programs is even harder. Every government program has a constituency who will fight to keep it. The constituency consists of all of its employees and their families, all of the clients who benefit from the program and their families, and the politicians whose reelection chances are enhanced by the program, and all of the politician's supporters.

In Chapter 4, we introduced the long-run concepts of economies of scale, diseconomies of scale, and the ideal sized facility. **Figure 6-1** shows how the average total cost (ATC) changes under these conditions. Since government agencies are bureaucratic, costs continue to rise, and any bureaucracy will ultimately expand beyond its ideal size and continually achieve diseconomies of scale. Not only will the costs of providing the agency's services continue to rise, but also inefficiency of doing so will also rise. All of this will occur while the agency consumes more tax dollars to fund itself.

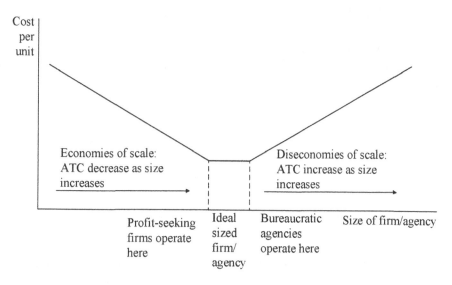

FIGURE 6-1. Profit-Seeking Firms and Bureaucratic Agencies

Profit-seeking firms try to lower unit costs. One way is to expand and achieve savings due to economies of scale. If this firm grows so large that it experiences diseconomies of scale (rising unit costs), it will usually downsize. Bureaucracies measure success by increasing their size. Ultimately, they experience diseconomies of scale and increasing unit costs of providing their service. They are not profit-seeking, so they request a larger budget.

Source: Mikel Cohick.

How Is Income Distributed?

Income distribution refers to how much income each person receives from selling the resources they own, primarily their labor resources. The markets distribute income in a highly efficient manner. If what one does for a living (talents and skills) is in demand by others, they will receive a high rate of pay. The more desirable talents and skills receive higher pay. The larger the market for the talent or skill, the higher the pay. Why does Oprah Winfrey or make so much money? What she does is very much in demand by her fans and television allows her to reach a very wide audience. Do professional athletes do more for society than elementary school teachers? If not, why do they seem so overpaid in comparison? Before there was television, many professional athletes had off-season jobs to support themselves and their families. Now television allows them to reach much wider audiences and in effect sell their talents to many more people.

Poverty

Since the 1960's the United States has defined poverty in terms of income levels. **The poverty line is defined as three times the cost of nutritiously feeding a family.** The Department of Agriculture found that expenses for non-food items among poor people were twice as high as for food items, leading to the multiple of three. In 2022, the **poverty line** was $26,500 for a family of four in the U.S. (except for Hawaii and Alaska, where it was much higher because of the costs of living there). Families with incomes lower than the poverty line were "in poverty" and eligible for various public assistance programs.

Determinants of Income

Incomes are distributed unequally in the U.S. by the market. The top 20 percent of the people make over 50 percent of the income. The lowest 20 percent of the people make less than 5 percent of the income. There are a multitude of reasons why incomes are unequal: education level, family structure, work ethic, talents and skills availability, age, experience, health, willingness to take risks, discrimination in hiring, and even luck.

Characteristics of Low-Income Families

Some characteristics of low-income families include low educational attainment, low skill development, a broken family structure, and elderly members. Education is one of the determinants of income, therefore up to a point, the higher a family's educational attainment, the greater a family's income. High school dropouts are at the bottom of the ladder while MBA's, law, and medical school graduates are close to the top.

Despite the decline of American manufacturing relative to the expansion of services, those selling their skilled labor (machinists, mechanics, plumbers, electricians, software developers, and welders, for instance) still have an open door into the middle class. Those unable to develop one of these or similar skills are faced with a lifetime of being at the bottom of the income ladder. As entry-level and low-skill jobs continue to disappear, opportunities to acquire experience, and on-the-job skills development also disappear.

While there are many heroic stories of children from broken homes making it big, the average is not so good. A stable home life contributes to the ability of one to get an education and develop skill sets.

Finally, income varies with age. Earned income is usually starts low for the young, increases as educational levels, skill development and experience increases and then drops off as workers reach retirement age or completely retire.

Equality vs. Efficiency

These two economic goals are clearly in conflict. While the market distributes incomes in a highly efficient manner, the distribution is as unequal as it is efficient. In the U.S., we have made a political decision to partially redistribute incomes through the income tax system and through government transfer payments like unemployment compensation, Medicaid, food stamps, and housing assistance.

The Federal Income Tax system is progressive, in that those with higher amounts of income get taxed at a higher rate than those with lower amounts of income. The burden of paying for the Federal government is borne by the high- and middle-income earners more than the low-income earners. Since the Federal government is such a large portion of our economy, the progressive income tax system is a form of redistribution.

The transfer payments to the lower-income earners somewhat decrease the inequality of a market distribution. Unemployment compensation is temporary and aids those losing their jobs for something other than cause. Medicaid is a government insurance program for the indigent. Food stamps assist the indigent in obtaining food and housing assistance could be in the form of government-furnished housing and vouchers to help tenants pay rent in non-government furnished housing.

Why not just raise the taxes on the higher income earners and raise the levels of assistance to low-income earners, thereby gaining more equality? The problems with well-meaning moves like these are the unintended consequences. The level of taxes required to equalize incomes would remove or reduce incentives to get an education, to develop good skill sets and to work harder. Why work hard and try to improve one's lot in life if the government takes most of the money you make and redistributes it to others? Equal outcome schemes (socialism, communism, and other welfare states) have been tried throughout the twentieth century and the results have been dismal failures.

SUMMARY

1. **Describe a public good and outline the role of government to insure public goods are available to society.**

   Since public goods, such as a highway, can be used by anyone as soon as they are available, nobody wants to pay for them. If you do pay for a public good, everybody else gets to use it for free (they are "free riders"). If nobody wants to pay for a public good, the producer of the goodwill not produce it. Government steps in to become the buyer of the public good, by contracting with the producer to produce it. To acquire the funds to pay for the public good, government levies taxes on the general public and/or charges a fee for each user.

2. **Describe a negative externality and the role of government when dealing with one.**

   A negative externality occurs when some party other than the buyer and the seller suffers a cost because of the transaction. An example is when pollution is created in the disposal of waste products. That keeps costs down for the producer (and price down for the buyer), but the pollution imposes costs on those who must live in the pollution. Since the external costs are not included in the market deliberation, there is too much of this type of good produced. Government, as agent of society, steps in and gets the producer to internalize the external cost, say, by handling the waste so that is does not pollute. Therefore, less of this goodwill be produced because it must sell at a higher price.

3. **Describe a positive externality and the role of government when dealing with one.**

   A positive externality occurs when some party other than the buyer and the seller gains a benefit because of the transaction. An example is the schooling of children. If education were purely a private sector activity, fewer children would get an education and each family would pay a significant amount for that education. There would be not enough education produced. Since educated people are a benefit to society, education has positive externalities. Government, as agent of society, steps in and arranges to have all children educated at no substantial cost to the parents, by subsidizing the education. Therefore, more education is produced, and it is provided at zero direct cost to parents. The government acquires the funds to provide for the subsidy by levying taxes on its citizens.

4. **List four activities where government acts as the agent for society.**

   Government establishes the arena where daily economic activity can take place without fear by establishing the rules of conduct, laws of contracts, fraud laws, and the protection of private property rights.

5. **Contrast a progressive tax system with a regressive tax system.**

   In a progressive tax system, as your income increases, the percentage of your income going to taxes increases. In a regressive tax system, as your income increases, the percentage of your income going to taxes decreases.

6. **Describe the use of a transfer payment.**

The function of a transfer payment is to transfer purchasing power from taxpayers to a group or to individuals who, by legislation, are qualified to receive the payment. Government payments to welfare recipients and to interest groups, as well as subsidies to businesses and organizations, are transfer payments.

7. **Relate the government budget to the national debt.**

The government budget consists of dollars coming into the Treasury (mainly taxes (T)) and dollars going out of the Treasury (mainly government expenditures (G)). If tax collections are not high enough to pay for all the government expenditures, that is $T < G$, a budget deficit occurs. This is the typical annual situation at the Federal level. To pay the bills, the government must borrow to cover the deficit. This added borrowing adds to the national debt.

8. **Contrast decision-making in the voting booth to decision-making in the market-place.**

In the marketplace, everyone decides what he or she wishes to buy and buys only that. In the voting booth, the voter must choose between a few candidates. He or she will decide on one of the candidates, even though that candidate might favor policies the voter does not like. However, the choice is the best of the options available. If the voter's candidate wins the election, the voter has an elected official that most closely favors the voter's position. However, if the voter's candidate loses the election, the voter must accept the winning candidate. If this happened in the marketplace, whatever the majority of shoppers in the store wanted would be what you had to buy, whether or not you liked or wanted any of those goods. The marketplace is, therefore, more democratic than the voting booth!

9. **Contrast running a bureaucracy to running a business.**

The principal difference has to do with costs. A business has incentive to reduce costs while maintaining a salable product or service, in order to improve its profit position. Success in business is measured by profit. In contrast, a bureaucracy has incentive to increase its budget, that is, increase its costs, while it has no incentive to maintain high-quality service. The success of a leader in a bureaucracy is measured by the size of the bureaucracy's budget.

10. **Tell how government identifies the poverty line.**

A family is living in poverty if its income is less than three times the cost of a nutritional diet.

11. **Describe the conflict between the two economic goals of efficiency and equity.**

In order to maximize efficiency, it is necessary to reward people for high productivity. This necessarily leads to unequal incomes. Since purchasing power comes from income, families will not experience equity in access to satisfying goods and services. To maximize equity, high productivity must be rewarded no more than low productivity. This destroys the incentive of those who are productive to perform up to their maximum ability, thereby destroying efficiency.

Homework Chapter 6

Name_____

DESCRIPTIONS

Match the key terms with the descriptions.

_____ A good that is non-exclusionary and non-rival in consumption.

_____ A good that is exclusionary and rival in consumption.

_____ Our unwillingness to pay for something if someone else will pay for it and let us use it for free.

_____ A cost arising from an activity that falls on a third party.

_____ A benefit arising from an activity that falls on a third party.

_____ Coercion by the government on the polluter, forcing them to clean up pollution.

_____ A direct payment from the government or a reduction of taxes paid to the government.

_____ The right of private persons and firms to obtain, own, control, employ, dispose of, and bequeath land, capital, and other property.

_____ System where the rate of tax increases as income increases.

_____ System where the proportion of tax paid to income decreases as incomes increase.

_____ A person or institution receives a payment from the government to which they or it is entitled by law, but for which there is no requirement for any action in return.

_____ Rather than cash, a specific good or service is delivered directly to the recipient.

_____ Spending exceeds revenues.

_____ Revenues exceed spending.

_____ The amount owed by the Federal government as of a particular date.

_____ High-interest rates because of government borrowing tend to stifle private sector spending by business firms and consumers.

_____ A professional advocate for a political cause or position.

_____ The name was given to a school of thought that believes that voters express their preferences in the voting booth in a similar fashion as the marketplace.

_____ Given the time it takes to research the candidates and vote, it is rational not to be a voter.

_____ An association of individuals or firms with a common political agenda.

_____ A benchmark to determine whether a family is eligible for public assistance programs.

KEY TERMS

1. Budget deficit
2. Budget surplus
3. Crowding out
4. Free rider problem
5. In-kind payments
6. Interest group
7. Internalization
8. Lobbyist
9. National debt
10. Negative externality
11. Positive externality
12. Poverty line
13. Private good
14. Progressive tax system
15. Property rights
16. Public choice theory
17. Public good
18. Rational ignorance
19. Regressive tax system
20. Subsidy
21. Transfer payments

EXERCISES

1. What does the government do when acting as an agent of society?

2. Why is public (K-12) education a positive externality instead of a public good?

3. What would happen if the Fire Department in a particular city tried to exclude people from fire protection who had not paid their fees, charges, or taxes?

4. Briefly describes a society without a government to establish and enforce the rules of conduct.

5. Why are each of these forms of revenue raised by government considered regressive?

   a. General sales tax (no exemptions).

   b. Property taxes.

   c. Lotteries.

6. Contrast the difference between voting for candidates and shopping for groceries.

7 International Economics

Check the labels on your clothes. Check out the electronic gear you use all the time. Scan the parking lot. You will find that many of the products you see and use every day—your clothes, your communications and entertainment devices, your vehicles—were produced, completely or in part, in a foreign country. International trade is a fact. International trade is growing and will continue to grow.

There are two ways that international trade is different from trade between, say, a buyer in Texas and a seller in Oklahoma. First, there are two governments, not just one, that could become involved and impose restrictions on the trade. Second, there may be two currencies involved, which would require the use of a separate market to deal with the exchange of currencies. This is the foreign exchange market. Other than that, trade between people living in different countries is no different from trade between people living in the same country.

After studying this chapter, you should be able to:

1. Grasp the significance of international economics.
2. Define a trade deficit or surplus.
3. Identify the results of organizing, both domestically and internationally, based on comparative advantage and specialization.
4. Determine who wins and who loses in free international trade.
5. Identify the two principal ways trade is "protected."
6. Determine who wins and who loses in "protected" international trade.
7. Describe how free international trade affects jobs and the standard of living in the trading countries.
8. Describe outsourcing.
9. Describe how a floating exchange rate system works.

Why Trade with Other Countries?

There are three basic reasons for international trade:

First, there are some goods and services that we cannot produce at all or cannot produce in sufficient quantities in this country. We must import these items from other countries where they can be produced. Things we do not or cannot produce here include bananas, rubber, coffee, tea, cocoa, rum, and Guinness.

Second, when we trade with other people, we get benefits from specialization. Does your family grow its own vegetables, or do you buy them in the grocery? Do you sew your own clothes or buy them at the boutique? Do you raise livestock for meat or buy it in the butcher shop? We search out specialists in our country and we also search out specialists in other countries.

Over a century ago, people were more self-sufficient than they are now. Why don't we do these things for ourselves anymore? People have become specialists. We pick a vocation, trade, or profession and get good at specializing in doing one thing. The more we practice what we do, the better and more productive we become. The more productive we become, the more income we can earn and have available to buy the other things in which we do not specialize.

We buy those things from others who are specialists in producing them. When people do this, their standard of living improves greatly because they become more efficient. Countries are the same way as well. Countries specialize in what they do best, get better at it and trade for other goods and services.

In summary, trade allows us to specialize. Specialization allows us to be more efficient. Efficiency means more production. By trading, we end up producing and consuming more than we could possibly do otherwise. This is true for individuals, for businesses, and for countries.

Third, trade gives us more choices. We can purchase autos produced in the U.S., but we also purchase autos produced in Japan, South Korea, England, Germany, Sweden, France, and Italy. Without international trade, our consumption of autos would be limited to brands produced hereby General Motors, Ford, and Chrysler. With trade, we can buy brands such as Toyota, Nissan, Honda, Mitsubishi, Hyundai, Jaguar, Volvo, Mercedes-Benz, BMW, Audi, Volkswagen, Peugeot, and Fiat. Some people prefer Fords. Some prefer Fiats. With trade, we all get to express our preferences.

What Are Imports and Exports?

When we buy a good or service produced in another country, we are buying an import. **American imports are made in a foreign country and bought by Americans**.

When we sell a good or service produced in the U.S. to someone in another country, we are exporting. **American exports are made in America and bought by foreigners.**

We import autos, consumer electronics, clothes, and commodity semiconductors. We export aircraft, software, telecommunications products, grains, and powerful semiconductors. We also export a lot of high-end services, such as accounting, engineering, information technology, architecture, and financial. Another large category of American exports is entertainment: movies, music, books, television shows, and Internet-delivered products.

What Is a Trade Deficit and a Trade Surplus?

A trade deficit exists when imports of goods and services exceed exports of goods and services.

A trade surplus exists when exports of goods and services exceed imports of goods and services.

We have balanced trade when we export just as much as we import. With only a few exceptions, we have had trade deficits every year for the last 30 years.

If our country runs a trade deficit, it has the effect of increasing our standard of living. It allows us to consume more than we produce. In other words, for the same amount of effort on our part and the same consumption of resources, we can satisfy more of our wants and needs. If we buy more from foreigners than they buy from us, the foreigners end up with dollars left over. They deposit those dollars in a bank. That bank loans those dollars out to people who want to buy U.S. assets. Thus, the trade deficit gets financed when governments, business firms, and individuals in foreign lands buy assets in the United States. These assets can be government debt, the assets of business firms, or real property. As a result, the number of dollars leaving the U.S. roughly equals the number of dollars returning to the U.S.

How Does Free International Trade Begin?

In free, unrestricted international trade, there is no government involvement. Let us start with a market in America in which only American firms produce the product for domestic sale, as shown in **Figure 7-1**.

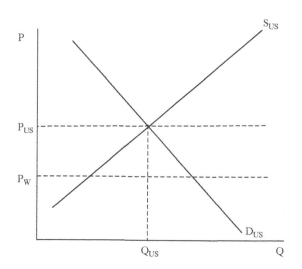

FIGURE 7-1. The American Market Before Imports

Assume the American producers are high-cost producers relative to the rest of the world. Thus, in the American market (with no imports), the American consumer must pay a higher price, P_{US}, than consumers in other parts of the world must pay, P_w. This is necessary to cover the higher costs of production of many of the American firms.

Source: Mikel Cohick

Now, imagine that a firm from the European Union (EU) is selling this product elsewhere in the world and can bring this product into the American market at a lower cost of production and delivery and, therefore, can offer it for sale to Americans at the lower international price. This new foreign seller shifts the supply curve to the right, as shown in **Figure 7-2**.

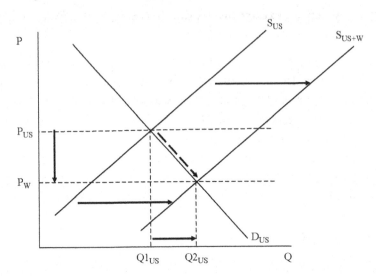

FIGURE 7-2. The American Market After Imports

Now let a foreign firm enter the American market. This new supplier shifts the market supply curve to the right. Prices fall. They will continue to fall until the price in the American market reaches the world price, P_W. At these lower prices, American consumers can afford to buy more of this product with the same amount of money as they spent before. Also, the American consumer enjoys a wider variety of this product from which to choose.

Source: Mikel Cohick

As supply increases, the American market price falls to the level of the international price asked by the foreign seller. At this lower price, American consumers buy more and have a wider variety from which to choose. However, at the lower price, some American firms suffer losses since they are high-cost operators. They reduce production or even quit producing the product altogether, as shown in **Figure 7-3**. American firms lay off workers. American jobs are eliminated due to the importation of foreign goods.

Now let us go over this story again. This time it is a market for a product in the European Union and it is an American firm that can bring the product into the EU at a lower cost. The same result occurs. Supply shifts right. Price falls. EU consumers pay less and have a wider choice. Some EU firms, those who are high-cost operators, suffer losses, reduce production, or quit altogether. EU workers are laid off. EU jobs are eliminated due to the importation of certain American goods.

Therefore, international trade destroys jobs, right? Yes, it destroys jobs in high-cost, internationally uncompetitive industries. However, the low-cost, internationally competitive firms, both EU and American, expand sales, increase production, create new jobs, and hire more workers. Also, since these goods must be transported between the EU and America, the transportation industry expands and creates jobs. As a result, international trade creates more jobs than it destroys in both countries.

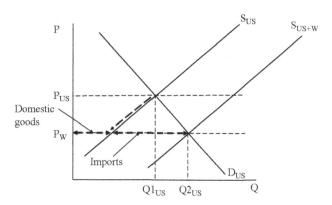

FIGURE 7-3. The American Market After Imports

The consumers are enjoying this new international market, but the American producers do not like it at all. Recall that they were high-cost producers, who charged the higher price, P_{US}, to cover these higher costs. Now the price in the market has fallen to P_W, and several firms are no longer profitable. They reduce production or close entirely and lay off workers. The total amount sold by domestic producers shrinks. The rest of the sales are imported goods.

Source: Mikel Cohick

Who Wins and Who Loses In Free International Trade?

Since the international price of an item must be lower than the domestic price to gain a foothold in the domestic market, then free international trade makes consumers a winner and the domestic high-cost producers a loser. Consumers get to buy the item at a lower price and incur a benefit equal to the difference in the prices, which they can use to buy something else, thereby increasing consumer satisfaction with the same expenditure as before. Domestic producers must now lower their prices to the international price and suffer a drop in revenues. The benefits and costs are not equal, however, because of the law of demand. The lower price results in greater consumption and therefore **benefit to consumers exceeds the cost to producers.**

There are other benefits. More choices for consumers result from the competition of foreign producers. Overall, this competition requires the remaining domestic producers to become much more efficient. Resources get allocated more efficiently. Also, countries whose economies are interconnected because of unrestricted free trade are less likely to go to war with each other.

The story is the same if we look at American exports. American firms can export to, say, the EU, when the domestic price is lower than the international price, the introduction of free trade results in a gain to the domestic producers. EU consumers can buy the goods at a lower price. American exporters expand their market and increase production, create jobs, and hire more workers.

As domestic producers serve a larger market, they get the benefit of being a larger producer and the resultant economies of scale. Economies of scale enable the producer to use resources (capital and labor) that are specialized and therefore more efficient. The larger firm also has an advantage in buying raw materials because of the leverage they get from their buying power. Overall, these benefits accrue to consumers in the form of lower prices.

Therefore, exports are not bad for America. Imports are not bad for America. They are also not bad for the countries we trade with. Both contribute to an improved standard of living for Americans, just as they improve the standard of living of America's trading partners.

How Does Comparative Advantage Fit In?

We previously mentioned that countries specialize in producing the goods and services that they do best. How do we determine what we do best? With what products does the U.S. have an advantage? How about Japan, China, and South Korea? Where does their advantage lie and how do we measure such advantage?

Comparative advantage is the underlying basis for international trade. Before we get to comparative advantage let us look at the definition of absolute advantage. If a country has an **absolute advantage** in a product, they can produce the product using fewer resources (lower wages for labor, lower interest payments for capital, and lower rent for land).

If one country has an absolute advantage in growing beef cattle and another country has an absolute advantage in writing computer software, it seems natural that the first country would specialize in growing beef cattle and the second country would specialize in writing computer software, and then there would be benefits to the two countries from specialization and trade.

But what happens if one country has the absolute advantage producing both products? Can there be gains from trade even if one country has an absolute advantage in both products? Yes, because of the concept of **comparative advantage**.

While absolute advantage means to produce using fewer resources, comparative advantage means to produce at a lower opportunity cost. If opportunity cost represents the highest valued foregone choice, then the opportunity cost of producing cattle would be what the country would have produced instead of cattle. To the extent that one country uses its resources to produce beef cattle, it cannot use those resources to write software. To society, the opportunity cost of producing beef cattle is the software not written.

We use comparative advantage to choose what we will do for ourselves and for a career, as well as to choose what we will rely on others to do for us. We specialize in doing tasks for which we have a comparative advantage (we can produce at a lower opportunity cost than others). Others become our customers. We become customers of others who have a comparative advantage over us in producing other goods.

For example, even though your family's kitchen is well suited to baking bread, we recognize our opportunity cost of baking bread is high compared to the bakery that supplies the local supermarket. So, we buy our bread at the supermarket and use our time and other resources to do things in which we have the comparative advantage.

Take this logic and apply it to an international scenario. It explains why Costa Ricans specialize in banana production and order personal computers from Dell. American consumers buy Costa Rican bananas and Costa Rican consumers buy American-made computers. Costa Rica has a comparative advantage over the U.S. in banana production The U.S. has a comparative advantage over Costa Rica in computer production.

Why are so many of our clothes produced in Asian countries rather than here in the U.S.? The conventional wisdom is that since wages are lower in Asia, it is less expensive to make clothes there, compared to the cost of making them in the U.S. What would be our full cost of making clothes here in the U.S.?

Our opportunity cost of making clothes might be the aircraft that we do not make. What is the opportunity cost of making clothes in Asia? Quite possibly it would be subsistence farming, a very inefficient way of eking out a bare living farming a small plot of land. That is why we make aircraft here in the U.S. and buy clothes made in Asia. Also, Asian countries buy American-made aircraft. We have a comparative advantage in aircraft and Asian countries have a comparative advantage in clothes.

Why Does Government Get Involved in International Trade?

The domestic high-cost producers do not like losing sales, decreasing production, laying off employees, and being faced with going out of business. They appeal to their representatives in Congress to "do something." Fearing that high unemployment in their districts might jeopardize their re-election chances, members of Congress collaborate with other members who are in the same fix to pass legislation to "protect" the high-cost American producer from competing with imported goods. The **Congress members say they are "protecting" the American consumer, but in reality, they are "protecting" high-cost, non-competitive producers.**

Free international trade is the absence of trade restrictions. **Trade restrictions are imposed by governments on behalf of a special interest group or in response to political pressure.** Trade restrictions increase the domestic price of imported items. Free trade can only occur when the trade restrictions are removed, generally because of negotiations among countries. If Germany agrees to remove trade restrictions on tractors made in the U.S., then the U.S. will agree to remove trade restrictions on steel made in Germany. Since steel is used in the production of tractors, the deal described above lowers the cost of U.S. tractor producers while opening up foreign markets for them as well.

Trade restrictions are actually protection of domestic producers from foreign competition. Trade restrictions can come in many forms and have several justifications, few of which have any merit.

The two main methods of used to restrict imports are the imposition of a tariff or a quota on the imported good. Tariffs and quotas directly affect the marketplace by increasing the price.

A protective **tariff is a tax on imports** to increase their price to consumers, thereby discouraging their consumption.

A **quota is an absolute limit on the number of imports** of a particular product.

There are other techniques used to reduce imports. One is creating bureaucratic red tapes like licensing requirements and product specifications that can restrict free international trade. A prospective trader might hear something like: "Of course you can sell your products in our country but first you need a license to do so. We will start taking applications for these licenses in a few months and the processing time is several more months. Then we will get back to you and tell you if your application passed or needs more explanation. And, the product must meet these particular specifications in order to be sold here."

Another is a Voluntary Restraint Agreement. One country agrees to voluntarily limit their exports to another country. Why would they do that? They are worried that the other country will impose a quota on their products.

Rather than simply telling the truth about why they are imposing trade restrictions, advocates of restricted trade come up with several stories to attempt to justify trade protection. Most are fallacious. Some are:

Self-Sufficiency

Should we be dependent upon another country to furnish us with military equipment in lieu of subsidizing domestic producers? It is not practical to be relying on the continuation of foreign trade if a war breaks out. While it might be safe to depend upon Canada, whose proximity to the U.S. and history of cooperation has been good, for some defense-related items, we might not want to depend upon Iran for crude oil or Russia for military boots.

This also applies to the reliance on importing vital components needed in the domestic manufacture of goods., including medical supplies This aspect of the problem showed up during the supply chain disruption that occurred during the COVID-19 turmoil. Of all the justifications for trade protection, this one has the most merit.

Increased Domestic Employment

This one has the most political merit. "Free trade costs American jobs." "Let's save American jobs." These statements are frequently heard during an election year and are excellent sound bites for the television news.

That doesn't make them right, though. By protecting one industry we could be hurting another. We protect the domestic sugar industry, saving a few jobs in that industry. However, many candy producers have moved from the U. S. to Canada, which has no domestic sugar industry to protect. When the producers move to Canada, the jobs go with them.

Usually, protective actions taken by one nation results in retaliation by another. As was shown above, international trade creates more jobs than it eliminates in both trading countries.

Infant Industry

The mantra goes this way: "Let's protect our newly formed industries from foreign competition until they get big and strong enough to protect themselves." The infant industry argument was used to justify protective tariffs on industrial goods at the birth of our nation, after the Revolutionary War ended. Here is the problem. Many of these protected industries were still protected 200 years later. When is an industry sufficiently grown-up to stand on its own two feet? How do you wean the protected industry off the tariffs? Since the government selects the favored industries to protect, the process is left open to political manipulation.

Dumping

Dumping is defined as selling goods in a foreign market at a price below the cost of production. Dumping is illegal in the U.S. The arguments used to justify making dumping illegal were something like this: The government of Japan is subsidizing the Japanese auto industry so they can sell autos in the U.S. below cost and drive all the domestic manufacturers out of business. The reality is: first, American consumers benefit from the dumping; second, the Japanese automakers are outselling the American automakers without the dumping; and third, do we really believe that the government of Japan would overtax its citizens and give the money to their auto industry so they could give American consumers inexpensive goods?

Cheap Foreign Labor

The argument goes something like this: If we trade with any country whose wages are lower than wages in our country, eventually wages in the U.S. will fall to the same amount as those in the foreign country. The problem with this argument is that the level of wages is determined by productivity. Wages are higher in the U.S. because productivity is higher. Productivity is higher because our workers have access to more capital goods and are educated, trained, and experienced in how to use them. Once workers in the lower wage countries have the same access to capital, education, training, and experience as do workers in the U.S., then their productivity will increase and their wages will rise to the same level as ours, rather than ours falling to the same level as theirs.

If the cheap foreign labor argument had merit, then it would be folly for any high-income earner to make a transaction with a low-income earner, because his income would begin to fall. That would mean you would have to mow your own grass.

Who Wins and Who Loses in Restricted International Trade?

The winners in free international trade—domestic low-cost producers and consumers in both countries—lose when trade is restricted by protectionist legislation.

The losers in free international trade—domestic high-cost producers in both countries—win when trade is restricted by protectionist legislation.

Protected international trade rewards the inefficient and wasteful industries and punishes the efficient, competitive industries. Also, the consumers get hammered by higher prices. Society loses because its standard of living goes down in both countries.

Trade restrictions benefit high-cost domestic producers. The competing import is now more expensive. Also, usually the domestic goods price rises to the new price on the imported good. Trade restrictions raise the price of both domestic and imported goods to domestic consumers.

The increased prices paid by domestic consumers are not the only problem with trade restrictions. Trade restrictions increase resource costs to domestic producers. A tariff on imported steel increases the price of steel to each domestic manufacturer who uses steel. Autos, trucks, tractors, and commercial building frames all have a high content of steel.

Trade restrictions also interfere with the market's allocation of resources. The market without restrictions reallocates resources from inefficient failing industries to more efficient industries on the upswing. When trade restrictions prop up an inefficient domestic industry they increase the cost of those resources to other industries.

If free trade benefits consumers more than it costs producers and trade restrictions costs consumers more than it benefits producers, why does the U.S. Congress enact legislation that restricts trade? There are at least two reasons:

First, the benefits are concentrated in one industry and both labor and management understand where they came from and who voted for and against them. The costs, however, are widespread. The consumers do not realize that the increase in the price of a good, whether domestically produced or imported, is due to the trade restriction.

Second, in a political argument, the side with the short, catchy, easy to understand argument like "save American jobs" usually beats the side whose case usually takes several paragraphs to make.

What Is Outsourcing?

Outsourcing has been around for a long time. **Outsourcing is hiring an outsider to take over a particular function of a business.** The outsider usually specializes in that function and can do it better and more efficiently than the original business. Earlier we described how you "outsourced" your family's bread production to the bakery for exactly these reasons.

An American cell phone company may create, design, and engineer the phone in America. They may market the unit to countries across the world. However, they may outsource most of the final manufacturing of the individual phones to another country if that country has the comparative advantage over American in parts fabrication and product assembly. It simply costs less to do that in the other country.

The new model for business is to decide what activities a business firm has a competitive advantage, concentrate on those functions, and outsource the others. If the competitive advantage is in product design and marketing but not in manufacturing, then the entire manufacturing function could be outsourced. If the competitive advantage is in manufacturing, then concentrate on manufacturing other firm's products. This firm can outsource to another specialty business in its own country, or it can outsource to another country, called "offshoring."

The political problem and public outcry come from "offshoring." Offshoring can result in a loss of jobs in the U.S. It can also create jobs. Picture a machine tool company in the U.S. whose main competitor is in Germany. If the U.S. company can become the low-cost producer by offshoring its manufacturing function to Mexico, then its sales will increase at the expense of the company in Germany. Yes, manufacturing jobs will be lost in the U.S. but the increase in sales will mean that more workers are needed for all the other functions of the company, most of which are higher- paying.

Insourcing is when a company in another country engages a U.S. company to do certain functions. Since the U.S. economy is becoming a service-based economy, most of the work that is insourced is high-end work such as computer services, engineering services, architectural services, and financial services. Even a lot of manufacturing is insourced into the U.S. There are almost as many "foreign" model autos and trucks made in the U.S. as domestic models. Toyota, Nissan, Honda, Mercedes-Benz, BMW, and Volkswagen all have manufacturing plants in the U. S. for autos and trucks. Alcatel has extensive manufacturing of telecom equipment in the U.S. According to U.S. Chamber of Commerce estimates, more jobs are insourced into the U.S. than are outsourced or offshored out of the U.S.

How Does a Foreign Exchange Market Work?

An exchange rate is the domestic price of a foreign currency. An example of an exchange rate is U.S. Dollar $1.20 = U.K. Pound 1.00. The U.K. Pound costs $1.20. Conversely, the U.S. Dollar costs 0.8333 U.K. Pounds to buy. One price must always be the reciprocal of the other (0.8333 = 1 / 1.20).

Exchange rates (prices of foreign currencies) can be determined in two ways at the choice of the country issuing the currency. With **fixed exchange rates,** the government of the issuing country picks a major country's currency and fixes the value of its currency to the major currency.

Assume that Saudi Arabia fixes its currency to the dollar at the rate of US$0.2666 = Saudi Arabia Riyal 1.00 or US$1.00 = Saudi Arabia Riyal 3.7509. If there are excess Riyals in the foreign exchange market, the Saudi government agrees to buy up those excess Riyals with their reserves of foreign currency. If there are excess dollars in the foreign exchange market, then the Saudis agree to buy up the excess dollars.

If a government decides that the fixed exchange rate that they have chosen is inappropriate (usually because they start running out of reserves supporting that rate), they can change the official rate and support the new rate. If there is an excess supply of their currency in the foreign exchange market and they have depleted their foreign exchange reserves, they can formally **devalue** the currency and support the new rate. If there is excess demand for their currency in the foreign exchange market, they can formally **revalue** their currency to have a higher exchange rate. The main problem with this is that devaluation immediately causes the holders of the currency to be poorer.

Alternatively, a government could allow its currency to float. **With floating exchange rates, the exchange rates are simply determined by supply and demand in the foreign exchange market**, just as prices for wheat and corn are determined by supply and demand in the grain markets. In a floating exchange system, the exchange rates fluctuate every day.

If the supply of a currency decreases or the demand for a currency increases, its price goes up in the market. It gains value. This is **appreciation**.

If the supply of a currency increases or the demand for a currency decreases, its price goes down in the market. It loses value. This is **depreciation**.

We know that, in any market, an increase in demand or a decrease in supply pushes the price up and a decrease in demand or an increase in supply pushes the price down. This is true in a foreign exchange market.

Currencies trade 24 hours a day in the foreign exchange markets. The foreign exchange market is a highly decentralized marketplace with every major bank participating. If you wish to engage in a transaction in another country, you must go through the foreign exchange market and change your money.

In the foreign exchange market between Euros and dollars, there are many small daily increases in demand and decreases in demand for both dollars and Euros, as well as many small daily increases in supply and decreases in supply of both dollars and Euros.

Who participates in an exchange market? American exporters to Europe have a supply of euros and a demand for dollars. European exporters to America (American imports) have a supply of dollars and a demand for Euro. American tourists in Europe have a supply of dollars and a demand for Euro. European tourists in America have a supply of Euro and a demand for dollars. This is the basis of the foreign exchange market.

It is conventional to say that when the price of the dollar (in terms of how many Euros it takes to buy a dollar) decreases, the dollar is weakening. Also, when the price of the dollar (in terms of how many Euros it takes to buy a dollar) increases, the dollar is strengthening. Note that, in the foreign exchange market between Euros and dollars, when the dollar weakens the Euro strengthens and vice versa.

What Is the Balance of Payments?

The balance of payments has three parts: the current account, the capital account, and the reserve account.

The **current account** includes trade, income from investments and unilateral transfers, or items such as foreign aid to other countries. The largest part is due to trade and tourism. For example, An American firm buys Euros to pay for German machinery. An Italian farmer buys dollars to pay for an American-made tractor. An American tourist buys Euros to be able to eat a good meal at a Paris restaurant.

The **capital account** includes investments made in other countries and foreign investment here. It documents the purchase and sale of assets. For example, A French bank may buy dollars to pay for U.S. Treasury bonds. An American firm buys Euro to build a factory in Ireland. A German firm buys dollars to acquire an American fertilizer company.

The **reserve account** is a reserve of foreign currencies used to take some of the volatility out of currency exchange rates.

A deficit in the current account (imports and exports) implies a surplus in the capital account (investments), with any differences being offset in the reserve account. Thus, a trade deficit is offset by an increase in investments in the U.S. In the first part of this Chapter we mentioned the fact that the United States has had mostly trade deficits over the last 30 years. What caused these deficits? We can answer this question by looking at the determinants of each component of the balance of payments.

Why are imports greater than exports? Among other things, U.S. incomes are higher than those of our trading partners. That means Americans can buy more, both American-made and foreign.

Why are foreign investments in the U.S. greater than U.S. investments overseas? Savings rates are much higher in other countries than in the U.S. Our government has a history of enforcing the rule of law. We have an adequate amount of economic freedoms (freedoms from excessive taxation, regulation, and trade barriers) to provide a good return on investment, so the risk-return ratio is more favourable for American investments than for foreign investments.

Are Trade Deficits Good or Bad?

There is continuous political and media concern about the size of the United States' trade deficit. According to the media, a large trade deficit is "bad." In fact, as described earlier in the chapter, Americans achieve a higher standard of living when the U.S. runs a trade deficit.

There is an inverse relationship between the United States' trade deficit and the American business cycle. The trade deficit shrinks in recessions, reaching almost zero at the trough. As recession turns to recovery and recovery turns into prosperity, the trade deficit grows.

The obvious reason is connected to American income. At the trough, with high unemployment, incomes are at their lowest for the cycle and spending, including spending on imports, is at its lowest also. In recovery and prosperity, incomes rise and so does spending, including spending on imports.

What is the surest way that politicians could eliminate a "bad" trade deficit? Have the economy plummet into a deep recession! Of course, like castor oil, the remedy would be worse than the symptom.

Our ability to continue to buy imported goods also depends on the strength of the dollar. As the dollar weakens, the imported goods cost our consumers more dollars. A way to understand the cause of the trade deficit is this. The East Asian economies are awash in cash from high savings rates. The United States is a relatively low risk, high return place to invest. As the excess cash gets invested in the United States, it maintains the value of the dollar relatively to the currencies of countries in East Asia, allowing us to continue to buy goods made in those countries at a relatively inexpensive price.

SUMMARY

1. **Grasp the significance of international economics.**

   Without international trade, the United States would have to be self-sufficient. That is, the United States would have to produce every good and service needed to satisfy the millions of wants and needs of its people. In many cases, this is simply impossible. An example is the production of bananas. In many other cases, people in other countries can produce a better product at a lower cost and at a lower consumption of resources than we can in America. Similarly, Americans can produce certain goods and services that others find simply impossible to produce or find that they cannot produce as good a product or would have to produce it at significantly higher cost and at a higher consumption of resources to do it themselves. Thus, it is less expensive and more efficient to engage in international trade.

2. **Define a trade deficit or surplus.**

   A trade deficit is defined as the volume of imports exceeding the volume of exports (measured in dollars). A trade surplus is the opposite.

3. **Identify the results of organizing, both domestically and internationally, based on comparative advantage and specialization.**

   A person, a firm, or a nation has the comparative advantage in producing a good or service if they can produce it at a lower opportunity cost than others. If this is the case, the person, firm, or nation should specialize in producing that good or service. They should produce more than they need for their own use and sell the rest to others who have a comparative disadvantage. This requires specialization in producing that good or service. The advantages of specialization are improved efficiency, production with a smaller consumption of scarce resources, and product improvement. These goods and services then can be brought to market at lower prices, enabling more wants and needs to be satisfied, and this raises the standard of living.

4. **Determine who wins and who loses in free international trade.**

   Consumers and low-cost producers in both trading nations win, while high-cost producers in both countries lose.

5. **Identify the two typical ways trade is "protected."**

   The two most typical methods of protection are to impose a tariff, a tax on the imported goods, or a quota, a restriction on the amount of goods allowed to be imported.

6. **Determine who wins and who loses in "protected" international trade.**

   Consumers and low-cost producers in both trading nations lose, while high-cost producers in both countries win.

7. **Describe how free international trade affects jobs and the standard of living in the trading countries.**

In free international trade, there is a net job increase. Although high-cost domestic producers eliminate jobs, the low-cost producers, who are expanding into foreign markets, create jobs. Also, transportation of goods between countries expands and that industry creates jobs. Free international trade lowers prices to consumers in both trading countries. Therefore, their incomes go further, and they can satisfy more wants and needs with the same income. Also, low-cost producers increase production and high-cost producers decrease production. Therefore, more goods and services are produced at a lower cost, that is, at a lower consumption of scarce resources. Society gets more wants and needs satisfied from fewer resources consumed. This is the very definition of an increase in standard of living.

8. **Describe outsourcing.**

Families, firms, and nations identify tasks in which they have competence. They concentrate on accomplishing those tasks. They seek experts who are good at accomplishing certain other tasks and hire them to do those tasks. This is called "outsourcing." When American firms outsource tasks to firms outside the United States, politicians, labor unions, and the media take note that American jobs are "being sent overseas." This is not a one-way street. Many foreign firms outsource tasks into the United States. The most significant example is all the automobile assembly plants in the United States operated by foreign brand automobile companies. Politicians, labor unions, and the media do not seem to note that, in the case of Toyota, Japanese jobs are "being sent overseas," but enthusiastically welcome such events.

9. **Describe how a floating exchange rate system works.**

Each international trade of goods and services is accompanied by a simultaneous trade in the currencies of the trading countries. There are millions of trades made daily, from gigantic ones—China buying Boeing's jets—to small ones—an American buying a beer in Munich. Currencies are exchanged in a foreign exchange market. The floating exchange rate system takes note of each increase or decrease in demand for each currency as the many international trades occur. The market adjusts the exchange rates to account for these changes in demand and supply.

Homework Chapter 7

Name_____

DESCRIPTIONS

Match the key terms with the descriptions.

_____ Goods or services produced in another country and bought in the U.S.

_____ Goods or services produced in the U.S. and sold to someone in another country.

_____ Imports exceed exports.

_____ Exports exceed imports.

_____ Being able to produce using fewer resources.

_____ Being able to produce incurring less opportunity costs.

_____ The absence of trade restrictions.

_____ A tax on imports.

_____ An absolute limit on imports of certain products.

_____ A argument for trade restrictions that stresses being able to domestically produce all the products need for the military.

_____ An argument for trade restrictions that stresses protecting newly formed industries from foreign competition.

_____ Selling of excess goods in a foreign market at a price below the cost of production.

_____ Hiring an outsider to take over a particular function of a business.

_____ Outsourcing functions to a firm in another country.

_____ The net of all foreign trade, investment, and other transactions.

_____ Those countries in the European Union that adopted the Euro as their currency.

_____ When a firm in another country outsources a function to a U.S. company.

_____ Domestic price of a foreign currency.

_____ Exchange rates are determined by supply and demand.

_____ That part of a country's balance of payments that includes trade, income from investments, and foreign aid.

_____ That part of a country's balance of payments that includes investments made in other countries and foreign investments in the domestic country.

KEY TERMS

1. Having an absolute advantage.
2. Balance of payments.
3. Capital account.
4. Having a comparative advantage.
5. Current account.
6. Dumping.
7. Euro area.
8. Exchange rate.
9. Exports.
10. Floating exchange rates.
11. Free international trade.
12. Imports.
13. Infant industry.
14. Insourcing.
15. Military self-sufficiency.
16. Offshoring.
17. Outsourcing.
18. Tariffs.
19. Quotas.
20. Trade deficit.
21. Trade surplus.

EXERCISES

1. Why do companies outsource certain functions to other companies?

2. What are the benefits of free international trade?

3. What are the costs of trade restrictions?

4. Does our current trade deficit pose a problem for the United States? Why or why not?

5. Why would the U.S. Congress enact trade restrictions if the costs to society exceed the benefits to society?

6. What are the benefits of foreign investment in the U.S.?

7. What are the major determinants of imports?

8 The Economics of Resource Markets

Just as there are markets for goods and services, in which business firms produce the goods and services and make them available for sale to consumers, there are also markets for the resource inputs that the business firms need to produce those goods and services.

In a market capitalist society, resources are privately owned by those residing in households, who make them available to the resource markets. This is where those resources earn income for their owners.

All the basic ideas of the product market's law of supply and the law of demand that you have already learned also apply to the resource markets. In this chapter, we first look in-depth at the labor market, and then we will examine the market for land resources, the market for capital and the capital formation process, and, finally, at the entrepreneur.

After studying this chapter, you should be able to:

1. Identify the connection between a firm's demand for labor and the demand for the firm's product.

2. Identify the connection between a firm's demand for labor and worker productivity.

3. Understand why an increase in the minimum wage causes an increase in unemployment among low-skill workers.

4. Describe how a firm decides how many workers to hire.

5. Tell why firms offer higher pay for overtime work.

6. Discuss why the labor supply curves for low-skilled workers and high-skilled workers are so different.

7. Define economic rent.

8. Describe how interest rates are determined.

9. Tell how a firm decides whether to pursue investment in capital goods.

10. Tell why an entrepreneur is unlikely to be risk-averse.

How Are Resource Markets and Product Markets Connected?

The circular flow connects the product market for finished goods and services and markets for resources. In the resource market, consumers living in households own and sell resources to business firms that need them to produce goods and services. In the product market, business firms produce and sell products to consumers who need them and are willing and able to pay for them.

Consumer spending becomes business sales revenue. The costs paid by business firms to acquire the resources become income to the resource owners. A key point is that no part of this flow exists in isolation. Any attempt by political forces to "fix" one part will result in changes in all other parts. **Figure 8-1** shows a basic circular flow model, consisting only of business firms and households.

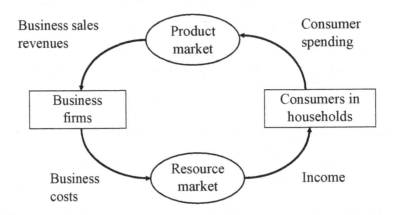

FIGURE 8-1. Basic Circular Flow

Consumer spending in product markets becomes sales revenue to businesses selling the products. Businesses use the sales revenue received to pay the costs of acquiring the resources—land, labor, capital, and entrepreneurship—used in the production of the products. These payments are income to the owners who put their resources up for sale in the resource market. They live in the households on the right. Consumers in those households now have earned purchasing power to purchase goods and services in the product market.

Just as in product markets, resource markets have a supply of the resource (made available by the resource owners) and a demand for the resource (by the business firms needing the resources as inputs to production).

What Is the Demand for Labor?

The **labor market** consists of a **demand for labor** and a **supply of labor**. First, we shall speak of a labor market in general and then differentiate that market into specific markets for specific skills.

Several factors determine how many workers an employer will want to hire. Of great significance is the demand for the product that labor will produce, and the revenues received from selling that product. Also, the productivity of the workers hired is significant.

We measure labor productivity by the number of units of the product a worker can produce in a period of time.

Labor productivity is constrained by the amount of capital goods made available at the worksite. **As the employer increases the number of workers hired without increasing the amount of capital goods available, marginal productivity, the added amount of product produced as another worker is hired, decreases.** This concept is similar to the diminishing returns we saw when you eat more and more of an item and stuff it into your fixed-size stomach.

The number of workers hired also depends upon the **wage** paid to the workers.

The wage includes the total costs to the firm of hiring the worker, not just the take-home pay of the worker.

Think of the wage as the price (P) paid by the firm for a worker and the number of workers hired as the quantity (Q). Then the relationship between wages and the number hired is a downward sloping demand curve for labor.

Product demand and **labor productivity** are determinants of the demand for labor. A change in product demand or a change in labor productivity will shift the labor demand curve.

The demand for labor is not independent. It is derived from the product demand. No firm hires workers just for the fun of having people around. If a firm's product demand increases, that firm will increase its demand for workers to make more of that product. If a firm's product demand decreases, that firm will decrease its demand for workers since they need to produce fewer products. Because of this, **labor demand is a derived demand**. It is derived from the product demand. This is true for the demand for any resource.

How Do Firms Determine the Number of Workers to Hire?

The firm must pay the costs of hiring the workers. They obtain the funds to do so by selling the products the workers make. A firm adds more workers to make more products and sells those products, increasing sales revenue (additional dollars coming in). The firm pays the added workers (additional dollars going out). Therefore, a cost-benefit analysis can be done to identify how many workers to hire. In deciding whether to hire the next worker, the firm compares the additional sales revenue it will receive from selling the additional products to the additional cost of hiring the worker to make the added products.

The benefit, the additional sales revenue coming from selling the additional output due to hiring the worker, is **Marginal Revenue Product (MRP).** We calculate MRP by multiplying Marginal Revenue (MR, added dollars/added unit of output) times Marginal Product (MP, added output/added worker).

> **MRP (dollars in/worker) = MR (dollars in/output) x MP (output/worker)**

> **The cost (dollars out/worker) = added wages paid out to hire the added worker**

Now we can do a cost-benefit analysis as shown in **Figure 8-2**. In fact, it is a variant of profit-maximization decision-making. Compare MRP (dollars in/worker) to wage (dollars out/worker):

> **If MRP > wage, hire one more worker, and profit rises.**

> **If MRP < wage, lay off one more worker, and profit rises.**

> **If MRP = wage, this is the ideal number of workers and profit maximizes.**

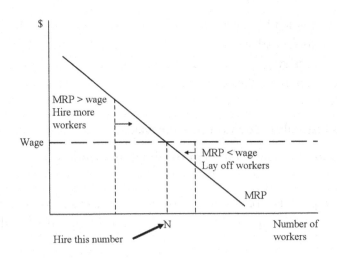

FIGURE 8-2. MRP-Wage Cost-Benefit Analysis

If a firm has hired too few workers and MRP > wage, the firm should increase the number hired and profits will rise. If a firm has hired too many workers and MRP < wage, the firm should decrease the number hired and profits will rise. Profits will be maximized when the firm hires the number of workers corresponding to the intersection where MRP = wage.

Source: Mikel Cohick.

When product demand increases, MRP shifts right (**Figure 8-3**). At the original hire, MRP > wage, signaling the firm to increase the number hired. The firm will increase the number of workers hired until MRP = wage for the latest person hired.

When product demand decreases, MRP shifts left (**Figure 8-4**). At the original hire, MRP < wage, signaling the firm to decrease the number hired. The firm will decrease the number of workers hired by laying off workers until MRP = wage at the new hire.

When wages rise with no change in productivity (**Figure 8-5**), the firm will also decrease the number of workers hired by laying off workers. This is the typical result in low-skill, low-experience labor markets when Congress increases the minimum wage. Because of this, you can expect the unemployment rate for low-skill, low-experienced workers to rise when the minimum wage is increased.

What Is the Supply of Labor?

The factors that affect how many people wish to work in a particular occupation include the wages paid, the skills required to perform the work, the ease or difficulty of acquiring those skills, the rigors and dangers associated with the occupation, and the degree of job satisfaction or dissatisfaction one might have in the occupation.

The labor supply for any occupation is the relationship between the wage and the number of people willing and qualified to work in that occupation. If wages rise, the number of qualified workers who want to work rises and if wages fall, the number of qualified workers who want to work falls.

A peculiarity of labor is that working uses up available hours and each worker has only 24 hours in one day to do everything the worker wishes to do, including work. If you are already working 8 hours a day,

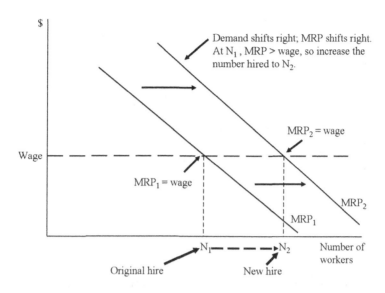

FIGURE 8-3. Product Demand Increases

The firm's product demand increases, so its MRP increases from MRP_1, to MRP_2. At the number hired N_1, now MRP > wage. The firm should increase hiring to N_2, where MRP = wage.

Source: Mikel Cohick.

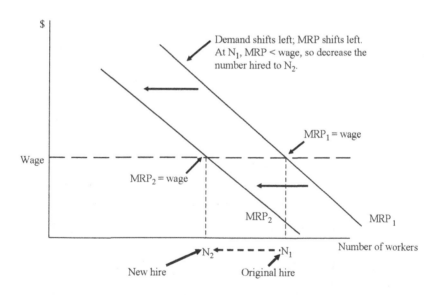

FIGURE 8-4. Product Demand Decreases

The product demand for the firm has decreased. Therefore, MRP has decreased from MRP_1 to MRP_2. At the number hired, N_1, wage > MRP, and the firm should lay off workers until only N_2 are employed.

Source: Mikel Cohick.

you must cram everything else you want to do in the other 16 hours. If your boss wants you to work overtime, your **opportunity cost** of working extra hours is the value you place on the foregone opportunity to use those hours for leisure activities.

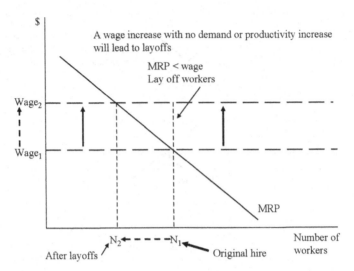

FIGURE 8-5. Wage Increase with no Productivity Increase

If the firm is forced to increase wages with no corresponding demand or productivity increase, the firm will find that now MRP < wage at the original number hired, N_1. The firm will lay off workers to cut back to N_2, where MRP = wage. This is what happens when the Congress raises the minimum wage.

Source: Mikel Cohick.

The opportunity cost of working an extra hour is the value of the leisure time lost.

Leisure activities include sleeping, eating, errands, family time, and entertainment. The more hours you are expected to work, the higher value you place on those foregone hours. This is the **labor-leisure trade-off**. It is the reason the employer offers higher pay for overtime work, to compensate you for those higher valued hours of lost leisure.

Separate labor supply into two categories: the supply of **high-skilled labor** and the supply of **low-skilled labor**. The interaction of the demand for labor and the supply of labor will determine the equilibrium price (the wage or salary) for each market and the number of workers that will be hired.

Note that each line of work or profession will have a separate labor market, with its own supply of labor (workers qualified to do the task) and its own demand for labor (firms who need that task completed). When a person is looking for a job, it is unlikely, for example, that a welding specialist would apply for a job in the nursing profession. Each specialty has its own pool of potential hires.

High-skilled Labor Market

To qualify for a high-skilled position, the worker usually must go through a formal training program which includes several years in undergraduate and graduate college programs, or an apprenticeship in a skilled trade. The path is difficult and the pipeline to completion and qualification is long. When this process is complete, the newly minted high-skilled worker usually has little trouble entering the profession. Few unemployed but qualified workers exist, except in unusual circumstances. Because of this, an increase in demand for these workers is met by a small response. The response to a wage increase for skilled positions is highly inelastic. There is a small response to even a big price (wage) increase. Higher wage offers are accepted by applicants who already have positions in other firms. Only a few unemployed people exist. The profession can help a bit by accelerating trainees out of the pipeline. Thus, a demand increase in a skilled labor field sharply increases wages with only a few more people added to the workforce.

Low-Skilled Labor Market

It does not take much effort to qualify for a low-skilled position. The worker usually needs only make himself available. Training is minimal, usually a short on-the-job event. Therefore, the pipeline to completion and qualification is short. New qualified people arrive continuously. The newly qualified low-skilled worker usually finds the competition to be great and might find it difficult to get a job. Many unemployed, but qualified, low-skill workers exist. Because of this, a slight increase in demand for these workers is met by a very large response. There is a large response to even a very small, if any, price (wage) increase, the response is highly elastic. Thus, a demand increase in a low-skilled field does not generate much of a wage increase.

Figure 8-6 contrasts the labor market for high-skilled workers and low-skilled workers.

Here is the reality in the modern labor markets. Labor demand for high-skilled workers is indeed shifting right, causing high-skilled wages and salaries to rise rapidly. At the same time, the labor demand for low-skilled workers is stagnant or shifting to the left. For that reason, wages for low-skilled workers are stagnant and would fall if minimum wage laws did not exist. Because minimum wage laws do exist, firms simply reduce the number of low-skilled workers they hire when the labor demand for these workers decreases.

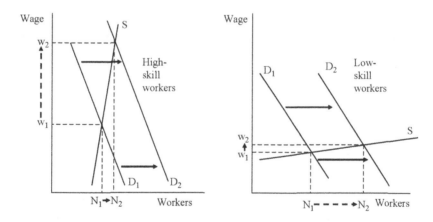

FIGURE 8-6. Low-Skilled vs. High-Skilled Labor Markets

High-skill workers (left) have a steep supply curve indicating the difficulty one has in acquiring the high skill. Low-skill workers (right) have a shallow supply curve indicating the ease at which one can qualify for a low-skill job. When demand increases, therefore, wages for high-skill workers rise rapidly while wages for low-skill workers barely budge. In reality, demand for high-skill workers is indeed increasing but demand for low-skill workers is and will continue to decrease.

Source: Mikel Cohick.

The workers who enter the low-skilled labor market are those with little or no formal education or training, or those with little on-the-job experience. A low-skill job is a good place to acquire on-the-job experience and get on-the-job training. However, as the costs to hire workers to continue to rise, firms reorganize their processes to reduce the number of workers needed by replacing them with machinery. They change the process to automate the workplace. Alternatively, firms might outsource many of these jobs, if possible, to other countries where the skill exists but the cost of labor is lower. The result is that the demand for low-skill workers in the United States is decreasing and will continue to do so.

How Does a Market for a Land Resource Operate?

A market for a **land** resource operates like a product market, except that the firms are the buyers who need a particular resource (gravel, wheat, chickens, lithium, or crude oil) as inputs to their production process. The resource owners are members of households and who offer the land resource they own in return for income.

As the business firm's product demand increases, their demand for the land resources increases, and vice versa. When the cost of acquiring the land resource rises, the firms' profits are squeezed and usually, they will pass the cost increase on to their customers, or switch to lower-cost inputs. When crude oil prices rise, for example, refiners pass the increase on to the gasoline purchaser. When crude oil prices fall, the retail price of gasoline usually begins to fall also.

What Is So Special About Acreage?

One land resource is, of course, acreage. The supply of acres of land is fixed. Therefore, the price of an acre of land is determined entirely by the demand for that piece of land. **Figure 8-7** shows this. As demand increases, the price goes up, and vice versa. Rent is the name of the payment for a land resource, after the French term *rente*.

Normal rent is the minimum necessary payment the landowner will accept to allow his land to be put into use. If demand for the land increases and the price rises above this normal rent, the difference

- Acreage is in fixed supply as shown by a vertical supply curve.

- The price of one acre increases as demand increases, and vice versa.

- If price P_2 yields normal rent to the owner, any price above P_2 will generate economic rent.

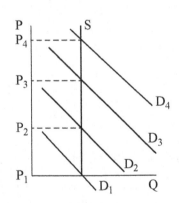

FIGURE 8-7. Economic Rent

As demand for the land increases (shifts right), the price per acre of the land goes up. If the owner would receive only a normal rent at price P_2, he will not sell or lease the land at any price below P_2. However, if the price rises above P_2, to P_3, for example, he will receive more than the minimum needed for him to sell or lease the land and he would enjoy economic rent.

Source: Mikel Cohick.

received by the landowner is economic rent. **Economic rent is a payment over and above the minimum necessary to get used of the land.** These terms are perfectly analogous to the notions of normal profit and economic profit outlined in Chapter 4. If the landowner cannot receive what he considers to be normal rent, he will let his land lie unused until such time demand picks up. This is the reason you might see several acres in rural areas offered for rent or sale, but not sold. The owner is waiting for a bid at least as big as the normal rent.

How Does a Market for Capital Operate?

Capital (capital goods) includes all the human-made products used in the production of goods and services. Examples include factories, lathes, vehicles, computers, sewing machines, milking machines, and the like.

A firm finances the acquisition of capital either internally by using the profits it earned or externally by borrowing funds. Funds can be borrowed directly from a bank or by selling notes or bonds, which are obligations to pay back the holder in the future. Let us concentrate on the external funding source.

Anyone who wants to borrow funds (or wants to sell bonds) has a demand for funds. Those who save generate a supply of funds. Together, they create a market for funds. On a graph, this market looks like any other market. The demand curve slopes downward, and the supply curve slopes upward.

As in any market, the demander must pay the supplier for the good. In this case, the borrower will pay **interest** (an amount of dollars) for the use of the lender's funds.

The Interest Rate is Expressed As a Percent of the Loan

For example, the borrower receives a loan of $1,000 and agrees to pay it back in one year plus an interest payment of $80. The interest rate is, therefore, 8 percent (= 100 x $80 / $1,000).

The Interest Rate is The Price in The Funds Market

It is determined by the interaction of the supply of funds and the demand for funds. The law of demand applies: Borrowers will wish to borrow more if interest rates are lower and less if interest rates are higher. The law of supply applies: Lenders will wish to save (and make available for lending) more if interest rates are higher and less if interest rates are lower.

Firms who want to borrow funds to finance capital goods do a cost-benefit analysis:

The **benefit of acquiring capital goods** is the added production and the added sales revenue (or reduced costs) that develops by using the new capital goods. Firms estimate this by calculating a **return on investment (ROI)**. If adding $1,000 worth of new capital goods generates a $100 increase in sales revenues, the return on investment is 10 percent (= 100 x $100 / $1,000).

The **cost to acquire these capital goods** is the interest rate of the borrowed funds. If the interest rate is 8 percent, the benefit exceeds the cost, and the firm will proceed to borrow the funds and acquire the capital goods.

As demonstrated in **Figure 8-8**, as interest rates decrease, the amount of investment in capital goods will increase, and vice versa, all other things unchanged.

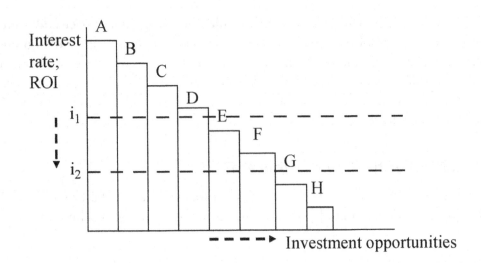

FIGURE 8-8. The Investment Decision

Rectangles A through H represents several projects in which the firm can invest. The height of the rectangle represents the expected return on investment (ROI). The firm must borrow funds to finance the projects at interest rate i_1. Only projects with ROI > i_1 will be approved. Projects A through D will be approved. If interest rates fall to i_2, then projects E and F would also be approved.

Source: Mikel Cohick.

How Is Entrepreneurship Compensated?

What do entrepreneurs do? **Entrepreneurs create, organize, and operate the production process.** Entrepreneurs are not necessarily the inventors of new products or processes. They are the ones who can recognize the potential and carry it to commercial success. It is because of them that resources are transformed into goods and services that satisfy our unmet wants. They identify a want that is being satisfied inadequately and create a new process or an innovation that better satisfies that want. They look for changes in the process that lowers costs, reduce the consumption of resources, and generate less waste by operating more efficiently. They assume the risk of being wrong in their estimation of the market by putting at risk their time, talent, assets, and effort. If they are indeed wrong, they shoulder the burden of the loss.

The reward for their success is profit. In Chapter 4 we differentiated between normal profit and economic profit. **The entrepreneur must earn at least a normal profit to justify continuing to operate the firm. Earning economic profit may trigger an expansion of the firm.** The prospect of profit encourages the entrepreneur to take the risks involved and generate the changes to products in the marketplace.

Since assuming risk is central to the entrepreneurial effort, it follows that if you are risk averse, that is, you do not like to take risks, then you might not be entrepreneur material. Do not despair! Most people are risk averse. The consequence is that these people will end up working for the entrepreneur.

SUMMARY

1. **Identify the connection between a firm's demand for labor and the demand for the firm's product.**

   A firm's demand for labor is derived from the demand by consumers for its goods and services. Labor is an input to produce the goods and services. Increase the consumer demand and the firm will increase its labor demand, and vice versa. There is no independent demand for labor by a firm.

2. **Identify the connection between a firm's demand for labor and worker productivity.**

   More productive workers are in greater demand than less productive workers. However, the marginal productivity of the next worker to be hired diminishes because of the fixed amount of capital goods. This has less to do with the quality of the worker than the quantity of workspace and equipment provided by the firm to the worker.

3. **Understand why an increase in the minimum wage cause an increase in unemployment among low-skill workers.**

   An increase in the minimum wage, with no corresponding increase in product demand or worker productivity, will raise the wage above MRP. This is the signal to the firm to lay off workers, who then become unemployed.

4. **Describe how a firm decides how many workers to hire.**

   Firms use a cost-benefit analysis where MRP is the benefit of hiring a worker and the wage is the cost of hiring a worker. If MRP > wage, the firm will increase hiring. If MRP = wage, the firm will not hire any more workers. At this number, the firm has the ideal number of workers. If MRP < wage, the firm will lay off workers.

5. **Tell why firms offer higher pay for overtime work.**

   To convince a worker to agree to work extra hours, the firm must make it worthwhile to the worker. The opportunity cost to the worker of working additional hours is the foregone use of those hours for leisure activities. Since there are only 24 hours in a day, working additional hours impose higher and higher opportunity costs. Thus, the firm offers higher pay for overtime work to induce the worker to choose working over leisure activities.

6. **Tell why the labor supply curves for low-skilled workers and high-skilled workers are so different.**

   The pipeline to qualify for a high-skilled job is long and hard. Fewer people start and fewer people succeed. On the other hand, the pipeline to qualify for a low-skilled job is short and easy. More people start and more people succeed. Therefore, the response time to enter a high-skilled workplace is much longer and more difficult than to entering a low-skilled workplace. This is shown by a steep labor supply curve for high-skilled workers and a shallow supply curve for low-skilled workers.

7. Define economic rent.

Economic rent is a payment over and above the minimum payment necessary to get the owner to allow use of his asset, such as an acre of land. The price for the acre of land, which is in fixed supply, is determined by the demand for the land.

8. Describe how interest rates are determined.

An interest rate is the price in a funds market. Lenders (suppliers) receive the interest payment corresponding to the interest rate for the use of their funds. Borrowers (demanders) pay the interest payment corresponding to the interest rate to obtain the use of these funds. The intersection of the demand for funds and the supply of funds will determine the interest rate.

9. Tell how a firm decides whether to pursue investment in capital goods.

A firm usually has several projects it could choose to invest in capital goods. Each project is analyzed with the intent to predict an expected rate of return on investment (ROI). ROI is expressed as a percent of the funds needed to finance the investment project. Each ROI is then compared to the interest rate at which the funds must be borrowed. Those projects with ROI > interest rate will be approved and funded, the others will not. If interest rates fall, more projects could be funded. If interest rates rise, fewer projects could be funded.

10. Tell why an entrepreneur is unlikely to be risk-averse.

Taking risks is a trait that sets entrepreneurs apart from other people. The entrepreneur must be willing to risk failure and loss of funds in his proposed venture if it does not succeed. Risk-averse people—and that includes most of us – are unwilling to take that risk.

Homework Chapter 8

Name_____

DESCRIPTIONS

Match the key terms with the descriptions.

_____ Demand for a resource is determined by the demand for the product that resource produces.

_____ The more hours one is expected to work, the higher value one places on those foregone hours.

_____ Price is determined by the interaction of the demand and supply of labor.

_____ The responsiveness of workers' willing to work for higher wages.

_____ Payment for a land resource.

_____ Minimum necessary payment the land-owner will accept to get their land put to use.

_____ Payments over and above normal rent.

_____ The human-made products used in the production of goods and services.

_____ Interaction of the demand and supply of funds.

_____ The price for the use of lenders' funds.

_____ Benefits (increased revenue or decreased cost)/cost of investment.

_____ The process of identifying unsatisfied wants, organizing production, and of taking risks.

_____ The return to entrepreneurship.

_____ The reluctance to take risks.

_____ The relationship between the wage and the willingness of employers to hire workers.

_____ Number of units of a product a worker can produce in a period of time.

_____ The added sales revenue comes from selling the added output due to the additional worker.

_____ The relationship between the wage and the number of people willing and qualified to work in that occupation.

KEY TERMS

1. Capital goods
2. Demand for labor
3. Derived demand
4. Economic rent
5. Entrepreneurship
6. Equilibrium wage
7. Interest
8. Labor productivity
9. Labor supply elasticity
10. Labor-leisure tradeoff
11. Marginal revenue product
12. Market for funds
13. Normal rent
14. Profits and losses
15. Rent
16. Return on investment
17. Risk aversion
18. Supply of labor

EXERCISES

1. The cost of a new widget-making machine is $100,000, fully installed. Use of the new machine will result in a savings of operating and maintenance costs of $15,000 each year. What is the percentage return on investment for the new machine?

2. Draw a basic circular flow model showing the product and resource markets as well as consumers in households and business firms. Point out consumer spending, income to consumers, business cost, and business revenues.

3. The demand for autos made in the U.S. by Ford, G.M. and Chrysler decreases. All other things being equal, what will be the effect of the decrease on the demand for auto workers by these three companies?

4. What factors go into the hiring decision (whether to add workers to a plant)?

5. The productivity of workers in a particular firm increases 5 percent in one year. All other things being equal, what effect will that productivity increase have on the number of workers demanded by the firm? What if the wage rate goes up by the same amount?

6. Why do low-skill workers have a shallow supply curve and high-skill workers have a steep supply curve?

9 Macroeconomic Measurements: Gross Domestic Product and Economic Growth

The national economy is a large and complex entity. To describe it, several measurements must be made. The participants have been introduced: consumers (in Chapter 3), business firms (in Chapters 4 and 5), government (in Chapter 6), the international sector (in Chapter 7), and employees and employers (in Chapter 8).

The macroeconomic goals are to achieve a low inflation rate, a low unemployment rate, and an economic growth rate greater than population growth. These goals can be conflicting and have been difficult to achieve.

To keep track of whether the goals are achieved (or achievable), several measurements must be made. The standard measure of the total output of a nation is Gross Domestic Product (GDP). After we correct this measurement for inflation, its year-to-year change is a measure of economic growth. The short-run variations in inflation-corrected GDP comprise the business cycle. We will examine GDP, economic growth, and the business cycle in this chapter. We will cover inflation and unemployment in the next chapter.

After studying this chapter, you should be able to:

1. Define GDP.
2. Describe the expenditures components of GDP.
3. Tell why Nominal GDP must be corrected for inflation.
4. Describe how economic growth is calculated.
5. Outline the difference between growth, stagnation, and decline.
6. Describe the phases of the business cycle.

What Is Gross Domestic Product?

GDP is the dollar market value of all final goods and services, produced within a nation's borders, in one year. GDP is also a measure of the total expenditures of the nation. It also measures the total income of the nation. This must be true because for each dollar spent by someone, there is a dollar in income received by someone else.

Let us look at each part of the definition to help us understand it. We measure GDP in dollars, that is, the quantity of all goods and services produced as measured by their market value, that is, their price. The term market value means the price at which the goods and services sell, not the price that may be on a price tag or sticker.

The term "final goods and services" means we only include production once, when the end-user buys, not after each stage of production. For example, the farmer grows wheat and sells it to the flour mill. The mill turns the wheat into flour and sells it to the baker. The baker uses the flour to bake bread, which he sells to the grocer. The grocer sells the bread to the end-user and the price of the bread captures the cost of growing, milling, baking, and distributing the bread to a location convenient to the end-user. At each point value is added. If we counted each sale, we would be double counting, or more. We include only the sale to the end-user to avoid double counting. The last price reflects all the value-added at each intermediate stage of production and distribution.

We count only goods and services produced in the U.S. as part of the U.S. GDP. Toyota is a Japanese company with a plant in San Antonio, Texas that assembles pickup trucks. The workers are employed in the U.S., so the output from that plant is included in the U.S. GDP, even though Toyota is a Japanese company. If Ford builds a plant in Canada, Canadian workers will be employed so the output would be part of Canada's GDP.

Finally, for our answer to be meaningful we must measure it over a period of time. One year is the normal period used to calculate GDP. We calculate GDP each quarter, then it is annualized to compare to the goal of growing at least as much as the population increases each year.

What Is Not Included in Gross Domestic Product?

Three broad categories of transactions are excluded from GDP: transfer payments, unreported income, and work for which no money changed hands.

Transfer payments, for example, payments of social security to retirees, are excluded because nothing was produced. The government simply sends a check to the retiree.

Unreported income is excluded because there is no way to measure it. Unreported income is income earned. However, the earner does not report this income for income tax purposes. It could include legal activities, like paying your neighbor's kid in cash for raking the leaves from your yard. It could also include illegal activities, like the proceeds from running a meth lab or selling street drugs. There is no way for the government to know about it to count it as part of GDP.

There is also work done and products produced where no money changes hand. This includes volunteer work, like building houses for Habitat for Humanity, and products produced in the family for which there is no formal, reportable payment.

What this indicates is that the official calculation of GDP underestimates the actual amount of goods and services produced in the country in one year. Studies indicate the unmeasured part of production grows at about the same pace as reported GDP. The most important use of GDP is to identify year-to-year economic growth. The percent increase in reported GDP, therefore, is a good indicator of this growth.

What Does the Basic Circular Flow Model Show Us?

Figure 9-1 shows the basic circular flow model. People living in the households own all the factors of production (land, labor, capital, and entrepreneurship) and they sell these factors to businesses in the resource markets. Payments for the factors (rents, wages, interest, and profits) represent income (Y) to households. For this basic model, we shall assume that all income earned is spent in the product market as consumer spending.

Business firms use the factors of production they buy in the resource market to produce goods and ser-

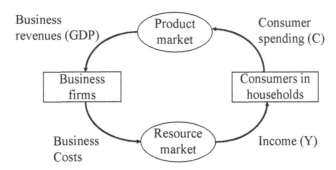

FIGURE 9-1. Basic Circular Flow

The basic circular flow deals with only the domestic private sector (no government or international elements).

Source: Mikel Cohick

vices. The businesses then sell these goods and services in the product markets. For this basic model, we shall assume that consumers in households buy all goods and services.

Sales revenues received by businesses represent total expenditures. Thus, it measures GDP. The firms must pay for all factors of production. These are business costs and become the income of the households who sold the factors to the firms. Therefore, the GDP measured by sales revenue equals the income received by households.

All economic activity interconnects in this way. One activity, such as household income (Y) cannot be isolated and dealt with alone. Dealing with household income will cause all other activities in the circular flow to adjust. For example, higher household income raises business costs, which causes the firms to either accept lower profit (less income to owners) or to raise prices. It is more likely that prices will be raised. That will require consumers to increase the dollar amount of spending to purchase the same amount of goods as before. The outcome is that, collectively, households will be no better off than before their incomes were made higher

What Are the Expenditures Components of GDP?

The usage of resources is determined by the level of total spending. Total spending consists of the sum of the following components:

C – Consumption spending

It is also called consumer spending. This is spending for goods and services by their end-user (the consumer). Consumption goods are what we eat, wear, drive, and entertain ourselves with. In Chapter 3, we identified goods, like cars and pickups that are expected to last longer than 3 years as durable goods. Other goods were identified as non-durable goods. Services were identified as purchased activities like dry cleaning, getting a tattoo, and doctor visits. The amount of C is determined by the size of our income and our expectation of the future.

Plus

I – Investment spending. This is spending, primarily by business firms, for physical capital (capital goods). Goods used in the production of goods and services are capital goods The increase in spending on equipment, delivery vans, tools, industrial ovens, and factories are examples of investment in capital goods. This category also includes new housing construction and changes in business inventories. The determining factors for I are interest rates (the cost of borrowing funds to finance the purchase of capital goods), the expected return on that investment, and the firms' expectation of future business activity.

Plus

G – Government spending. This is spending at all three levels of government: Federal, state, and local. Included in this category is spending for goods and services in the product market as well as for resources in the resource market. The principal determining factors for G are politics and unexpected external events, like natural disasters and wars.

Plus

X – Exports: This is the sale of American-produced goods, services, and factors of production to buyers living in foreign countries. The determining factors are the income of the foreign customers and the comparative advantage of the American-made products.

Minus

M - Imports: This is the purchase by Americans of foreign-made goods, services, and factors of production. The determining factors are the income of American customers and the comparative advantage of foreign-made products. M must be deducted from GDP because the purchases of imports are counted along with domestic products when we count C, I, and G.

What Is Macro Equilibrium?

Macro equilibrium in the economy occurs when **the quantity of total spending on goods and services equals the production of goods and services.** At macro equilibrium, all the production of goods and services is bought. There is no unexpected increase or decrease in inventories. Total spending equals total output. Ideally, macro equilibrium occurs at an output level where the economy uses all its capacity to produce goods and services. This is an economy that is operating at a full-employment level.

Macro equilibrium can occur at times when all the capacity to produce is not used. We have idle factors of production, particularly labor and capital goods. This means workers and plants are unemployed. This is a situation where the economy is **underperforming.** The public casually calls this a **recession.**

At other times, macro equilibrium can occur where total spending exceeds the capacity of the economy to produce. There are more buyers of goods than sellers. This situation causes shortages in both the product and the resource markets. Shortages lead to rising prices across the board, which leads to **inflation.** This is a situation where the economy is **overheated.**

Since the macro economy is dynamic, it can change from one macro equilibrium to another. Next, we will consider examples of what can cause the changes and what can shift the macro equilibrium.

What Are Leakages and Injections?

We will now complicate the basic circular flow a bit. Consumers in households must pay taxes out of their income. Also, they purchase foreign-made products (imports). Households also save part of their income. These three activities reduce the amount of income going to consumer spending and are **leakages** from the circular flow.

Meanwhile, the government spends funds on goods and services in the product market. Banks lend out the savings to business firms to fund their purchase of investment goods from other businesses. Foreigners use the money received from selling consumers imports to purchase exports in the product market. These three activities increase sales in the product market are **injections** into the circular flow.

To summarize, the **leakages** out of the circular flow are **saving (S), taxes (T), and imports (M).** The **injections** back into the circular flow are **investment spending (I), government spending (G), and exports (X).** Leakages and injections are added to the basic circular flow in **Figure 9-2.**

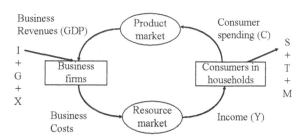

FIGURE 9-2. Basic Circular Flow Leakages and Injections

Since consumers in households do not spend all their income (Y) on consumer goods (C), income leaks out of the circular flow. These leakages are savings (S), taxes (T), and imports (M). On the other side, it is not just consumers who purchase goods and services in the product market. Businesses spend for investment purposes (I), governments spend (G), and there are exports (X). These are injections into the circular flow. When the economy is in macro equilibrium, leakages equal injections, or S + T + M = I + G + X.

Source: Mikel Cohick

The economy is in macro equilibrium when leakages equal injections:

$$S + T + M = I + G + X$$

If there is an imbalance of spending and output, macro equilibrium will change. The imbalance can occur when leakages exceed injections and there is a decrease in total spending. This could lead to an underperforming economy. Also, an imbalance can occur when injections exceed leakages and there is an increase in total spending. This could lead to an overheated economy.

It may seem logical to you that each leakage should pair up with an injection. Taxes (T) should match government spending (G). Saving (S) should match business investment spending (I). Imports (M) should match exports (X). This is rarely the case. For macro equilibrium to occur, the following requirements are needed: total production = total spending; inventories do not change; and total leakages = total injections, which is:

$$S + T + M = I + G + X$$

How Do Recessions Begin?

Inventories are a necessary item to do business, especially for a retail store or a wholesale distributor. Businesses plan their desired level of inventory to have a desired amount of product available to satisfy their customers. Too little means some customers will not find their desired purchase. Too much means the firm has money tied up in the excess inventory that could have been used for better purposes. To maintain this ideal level of inventory, they arrange for their distributors to routinely deliver new inventory to match the amount sold. Therefore, a change in inventory levels is an early signal that the macro equilibrium is changing.

If all the output of the economy is not purchased, then the level of inventory increases. This is an unplanned increase in investment in inventory. When retailers see their inventory levels increase (sales falling off and unsold goods piling up), they reduce orders from their distributors and lay off salespeople. When the distributor notifies the factory of reduced orders, the factory cuts back production and lays off workers. Thus, an unexpected inventory increase is one of the first indications of the onset of a recession.

The chain of events for a recession can happen this way. Recessions usually begin with a decrease in total spending. When spending is less than production, not all the produced goods and services are sold and consumed, and inventory begins to pile up. When inventories go unsold, this sends a signal to retail firms to reduce or cancel factory orders. Business firms cut back on production and reduce or cancel orders from their supply chain. Less production means lower resource use and the first reductions usually come from labor. Employees lose their jobs and have trouble finding new ones because business firms are not hiring. Fewer jobs mean less income for households. Less income for households means less spending; this starts the cycle all over again. In addition, when a recession starts, businesses are very reluctant to make investments in capital goods, which lowers spending even more. GDP, instead of increasing, decreases as spending and incomes drop. This cycle continues until production decreases enough to catch up with decreased spending and we reach macro equilibrium at a much lower level of GDP.

The characteristics of a recession include decreased spending, falling production, higher unemployment, lower inflation, less tax collections, and more government spending on transfer payments such as unemployment compensation and welfare. Unpaid bills, bad debts, and personal and business bankruptcies increase. Since expectations of business firms worsen, they are reluctant to make capital investments or add new employees. Investment spending usually decreases quickly as the recession deepens. Since consumer expectations worsen, they defer spending on items that can be deferred, especially durable goods. Households that are still working tend to save more during recessions because workers fear they will lose their jobs and not be able to find another one.

Recessions can spread from country to country. If total spending decreases in one country, then the ability of its consumers to buy imported goods will decrease as well. A decrease in one country's imports of goods and services from its trading partners means that the exports of those trading partners decrease as well, starting the chain of events that can lead to a recession in the other country.

Using the leakages and injections model, a recession can begin with decreases in injections or increases in leakages. Lower expectations by households result in more saving (S) and less consumption (C). Lower expectations by business result in less investment (I) in capital goods. Result: **S > I**. Another cause could be an increase in taxes (T) by government, resulting in greater leakages. The same result would happen if government decreased spending (G) without lowering taxes (T). Result: **T > G**. Finally, if imports (M) increase and/or exports (X) decrease because of changing international trade patterns, then leakages would increase and/or injections would decrease. Result: **M > X**. Each would upset the balance between leakages and injections and reduce spending.

What Is a Business Cycle?

A business cycle demonstrates these periodic changes in macroeconomic conditions, but the changes are not as regular as the word cycle may suggest. Over the long term, the economy grows on average at a rate of 2.5 to 3 percent a year. Over the short-term, however, there are periods where output can grow faster or slower than the 3 percent average. In recessions, output can decrease. The periods of growth and decline tend to occur in the four phases of the business cycle. **The four phases are: (1) peak, (2) recession/ contraction, (3) trough, and (4) recovery/ expansion/ prosperity.**

Figure 9-3 shows a stylized business cycle and locates the four phases. The long-run trend is upward at about 3 percent. In recent times, the reality has been that an expansion phase can last for several years and the contraction phase for only a few months.

Peak: At the peak, economic activity is at its highest. Unemployment is low and transfer payments by the government (unemployment compensation and welfare payments) are also low. Incomes are at their highest, so income tax collections are high. During the peak phase, there is a danger of increasing inflation because total spending can exceed the economy's capacity to produce. Shortages arise, pushing up prices and causing inflation. This strong demand means that business sales and profits are at their highest point. The period is referred to as an economic boom and the expectations of both consumers and producers about the future are good. This is the real prosperity phase of the business cycle.

Contraction/ Recession: In this phase, economic activity is slowing as is total spending. Businesses experience an unexpected increase in inventory levels. They react by decreasing their level of production. When production decreases, fewer employees are needed. Some employees lose their jobs and the rate of unemployment increases. Tax collections fall and transfer payments (unemployment compensation and welfare payments) begin to increase. Consumers without jobs cut back on their spending so aggregate demand or total spending slows down even more. Expectations of both consumers and producers about the future worsen. Both postpone the economic activity until conditions look brighter.

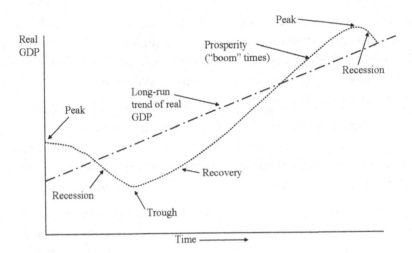

FIGURE 9-3. A Stylized Business Cycle

Around the long-run trend, there are short-run fluctuations. In a recession, real GDP decreases. In recovery and, later, in prosperity, real GDP grows faster than the long-run trend. The peak is the highest level of real GDP attained in any one business cycle. The trough is the lowest level of real GDP reached in any one business cycle. The length of the business cycle is measured from peak to peak. The above picture is stylized. A genuine business cycle has a short, usually steep, decrease in the recession phase (usually lasting several months) and a long rise in the recovery and prosperity phases (usually lasting several years).

Source: Mikel Cohick

Trough: This is the point where unemployment and transfer payments are at their highest and tax collections are at their lowest. Layoffs of employees continue through this phase so total spending for goods and services is also at its lowest. The future looks bleak to both producers and consumers. This phase occurs just before the recovery begins.

Recovery/ Expansion/ Prosperity: Conditions begin to improve, and unemployment begins to slowly drop as producer's expectations grow more positive. Total spending begins to recover, and business firms' sales of goods and services begin to grow. As the recovery period continues, business expectations improve even more, and businesses begin to call employees back to work. Consumers' expectations also improve. As people get back to work, incomes grow, and spending increases. When the level of GDP increases to a level higher than the previous peak, prosperity sets in. This phase continues until the next peak.

Why Do We Have to Correct Nominal GDP for Inflation?

Nominal GDP is what we get when we add up all the numbers valuing each purchase in current year dollars. "Nominal" always means just as measured, that is, without removing the effects of inflation on prices. That poses the problem of figuring out how much of an increase in nominal GDP is due to an actual increase in the goods and services produced and how much of it is due to price increases. **Nominal**

GDP must be adjusted to remove the inflation factor. The result is **Real GDP**. "Real" always means that the effects of inflation have been removed. To find Real GDP, use the following formula:

$$\text{Real GDP} = \frac{\text{Nominal GDP}}{\text{GDP Deflator}} \times 100$$

The **GDP Deflator** is a price index used to convert Nominal GDP to Real GDP. It is constructed by taking a representative sample of goods that are included in GDP and observing price changes in this sample of goods from year to year. A base year is arbitrarily chosen, and the GDP Deflator price index for the base year is set to 100. The price of a sample of goods and services was measured in the base year, and it is measured every other year. Finding the GDP Deflator in any other year becomes a ratio problem:

$$\frac{\text{GDP Deflator in year x}}{\text{GDP Deflator in base year}} = \frac{\text{Sample price in year x}}{\text{Sample price in base year}}$$

The base year GDP Deflator is always set to 100. As an example, the sample price in year x is $306 and the sample price in the base year was $300, then the GDP deflator in year x is 102. That means that, on the average, prices of the goods and services in the sample increased 2 percent from the base year to year x.

This technique is used on Nominal GDP measurements for each year. This yields a list of Real GDP measures for those years. Once that is accomplished, what happens to Real GDP from year to year can be calculated. This is essential to identify economic growth, economic decline, and stagnation.

What Are Economic Growth, Stagnation, and Decline?

To measure growth, stagnation, and decline, we use the percent change formula:

Percent change = (the change) x 100 / (the original number)

For example, Real GDP at the end of 2017 was $18,296.69 million and Real GDP at the end of 2018 was $18,721,28 million. The change was $424.59 million. Using the percent change formula, we get (424.59) x 100 / (18,296.69), which equals 2.32 percent. Therefore, Real GDP grew at the rate of 2.32 percent in 2018.

Define **economic growth** as an increase in real GDP and is measured as a percentage change. The 100-year average for increases in Real GDP is about a 3 percent increase per year. A **growth economy** is an economy that is increasing 3 percent per year or faster. A **stagnant economy** is one where growth is less than 3 percent and a **declining economy** is one where GDP is decreasing.

Economies do decline. During the first few years of the Great Depression in the 1930's, GDP declined as much as 30 percent. The countries that don't make enough investments in capital goods to replace the capital goods that are wearing out or becoming obsolete will eventually experience a declining GDP.

The COVID-19 pandemic also caused economic decline. Real GDP declined by 3.4 percent in 2020 after growing at a rate of 2.3 percent in 2019. In 2021, real GDP then grew by 5.7 percent as the economy recovered. In the second quarter of 2020, when several state governments issued shutdown orders, there was a severe decline in real GDP by 31.2 percent. When the government rescinded these orders, real GDP grew by 33.8 percent in the third quarter of 2020.

SUMMARY

1. **Define GDP.**

   GDP is the total dollar value of all final goods and services produced in the country in one year. GDP is the principal measure of the output of the United States.

2. **Tell why Nominal GDP must be corrected for inflation.**

   GDP is measured each year in current year dollars. This is nominal GDP, that is, GDP uncorrected for inflation. Since the purpose of measuring GDP is to calculate economic growth, GDP must be compared from year to year. To do this, each year's Nominal GDP value must be corrected for the changes in the value of the dollar due to inflation. The corrected value is called Real GDP, that is, GDP with the effects of inflation removed. Real GDP for each year is expressed in the value of the dollar as it existed in the base year.

3. **Describe how economic growth is calculated.**

   The percent change formula is used. Divide the change in Real GDP from one year to the next by the original Real GDP value, and then multiply it by 100 to get a percentage. That percent change is the economic growth rate.

4. **Outline the difference between growth, stagnation, and decline.**

   Economic growth occurs when the Real GDP increases by three percent or more per year. Stagnation occurs when Real GDP grows by less than three percent per year. Decline occurs when Real GDP decreases from one year to the next.

5. **Describe the phases of the business cycle.**

   The business cycle has four phases. The peak is the highest point, where Real GDP reaches its maximum value during the cycle. After a peak, recession or contraction occurs, as Real GDP decreases. When Real GDP stops decreasing, the trough is reached. The trough is the lowest Real GDP value during the cycle. After the trough, the economy begins to turn up and recovery or expansion occurs. After the cycle recovers to a Real GDP value higher than the previous peak, we can say the economy is in prosperity. Prosperity lasts until the next peak is reached.

Homework Chapter 9

Name_____

DESCRIPTIONS

Match the key terms with the descriptions.

_____ Dollar market value of all final goods and services, produced within a nation's borders, in one year.

_____ Payments for which no goods or services were produced.

_____ Spending for goods and services by the end-user of those goods and services.

_____ Goods that are expected to last at least 3 years.

_____ Spending, primarily by businesses, for physical capital, or capital goods.

_____ When total spending on goods and services equals the capacity of the economy to produce those goods and services.

_____ When equilibrium occurs where all the capacity is not being used and we have idle factors of production (labor and capital).

_____ Funds leaving the circular flow.

_____ Funds entering the circular flow.

_____ Goods kept "in stock" and ready for sale to consumers.

_____ GDP adjusted for inflation.

_____ An increase in Real GDP.

_____ An economy increasing at least 3% a year.

_____ An economy where GDP is decreasing.

_____ What goods and services one can purchase with their money income.

KEY TERMS

1. Consumption spending
2. Declining economy
3. Durable goods
4. Economic growth
5. Gross Domestic Product (GDP)
6. Growth economy
7. Injections
8. Inventories
9. Investment spending
10. Leakages
11. Macro equilibrium
12. Real GDP
13. Real income
14. Recession
15. Transfer payments

EXERCISES

1. Describe the four phases of the business cycle.

2. Why aren't unreported transactions included in GDP?

3. How will producers change their level of production when inventories increase unexpectedly? Why?

4. What are the requirements for macro equilibrium?

5. Describe the chain of events for a recession.

10 Macroeconomic Measurements: Inflation and Unemployment

The two economic concepts most frequently making news are the inflation rate and the unemployment rate. Inflation affects all who must buy and sell and use money. In effect, that means everyone. Unemployment is a problem to those unemployed more than those who still have jobs. d by Changes in the macroeconomy affect both.

Each year, a price index is measured to keep track of how prices change. The year-to-year change in the price index is a measure of inflation. The labor force consists of those working and those who are currently not working but actively seeking work. Define this latter group as the unemployed. The percentage of the unemployed relative to the labor force is the unemployment rate.

After studying this chapter, you should be able to:

1. Identify the harmful effects of inflation.
2. Differentiate between the three types of inflation.
3. Define the unemployment rate.
4. Describe the four types of unemployment.
5. Identify which type of unemployment is of most concern to policy makers.
6. Define the full employment goal.

What Is Inflation?

Inflation is a rising average level of prices across the board, not for just one product. Not all prices rise at the same rate, and some may fall. We will examine how to measure inflation, why inflation happens, what are its effects, and who is most affected.

The primary measurement of inflation is based on the **Consumer Price Index (CPI)**. Inflation is measured by the percent change in the CPI during a year. The CPI index is constructed very much like the GDP Deflator, but the sample of goods and services used is specifically those items urban consumers typically buy. Once the CPI is calculated for each year, the inflation rate is calculated using the percent change formula, as we did for economic growth.

There are several harmful effects of inflation. The purchasing power of the dollar falls. There is a redistribution of income and wealth. The savings rate falls. Business plans must have a short time horizon. Interest rates increase.

The Purchasing Power of the Dollar Falls

Money income is the actual amount of money or income one has. Real income is what goods and services one can purchase with their money income. When average prices rise, real income falls because we can no longer buy as many goods and services with our money income. The prices of these goods and services have gone up. Inflation feeds on itself. When prices start going up, people tend to buy before the price goes up even more, increasing total spending and making inflation worse.

Income is Redistributed

If the prices of the goods and services that you normally consume are increasing and the prices of the goods and services that your neighbor normally consumes are not rising as fast or even falling, then your money income declines in value to you faster than your neighbor's income. In effect, income is redistributed from you to your neighbor. If your money income is fixed and your neighbor's money income is increasing as the price level increases, then your neighbor is gaining relative to you. Services in general and health care normally experience much faster price increases than goods. Senior citizens have fixed incomes and consume a lot of health care services, while many younger people have rising incomes and consume more goods than services, so we end up with a double redistribution from the elderly to the younger people.

Wealth is Redistributed

During periods of inflation, some assets rise in value faster than others. Real estate and other hard assets rise in value at least as fast as inflation. Fixed amount financial instruments like a savings account or savings bonds do not rise in value since their face value is fixed. If you put $1,000 in a saving account, at the end of one year you can withdraw your interest plus your original $1,000, but no more. People holding their savings in savings accounts give up value while those holding real estate (those that own their own home, for instance) gain value. During times of inflation, there is a redistribution of wealth from those owning assets like savings accounts and bonds to those owning assets like real estate.

Borrowers usually gain from inflation, because they pay their loans off with dollars that have less purchasing power than the dollars they borrowed. Lenders usually lose from inflation, since they are paid back with cheaper dollars than they loaned. Thus, during periods of inflation, wealth is redistributed from lenders to borrowers.

Reduced Savings Rate

During periods of inflation, people try to buy things before the price goes up, thus spending more than they would during periods of price stability. If savings are put into a fixed savings account, then the money that comes out has less purchasing power than the money that went in. Since savings are one of the important sources of funds that are available to finance investments in capital goods, this reduces the potential for future economic growth.

Business Plans are Risrupted

Inflation makes it difficult to forecast future revenues and costs because managers do not know the effect of inflation on future goods and services prices and resource costs. The decision to make an investment in capital goods depends on the expected future return. Forecasting is difficult enough when prices are stable and becomes next to impossible when prices are not. Thus, investments in capital goods are not made unless they become absolutely necessary, such as times when machinery and equipment break down and must be replaced. In addition to the lack of savings to finance investments in capital goods, businesses are reluctant to make these kinds of investments when future conditions are uncertain, further stifling economic growth.

Interest Rates Increase

The interest rates that we earn on saving accounts or pay on loans are nominal rates of interest. Nominal rates of interest have two component parts, the real rate of interest and expected inflation. The real interest rate compensates the lender for the use of his money during the term of the loan. The expected inflation component is there to compensate the lender for the fact that they will be paid back with dollars that have less value than the dollars they lent. When inflation increases, expected inflation also increases, which increases interest rates. Higher interest rates make it harder to finance big-ticket purchases like automobiles and homes, because the payments are higher. Higher interest rates make it more difficult to finance purchases of capital goods. Thus, the auto and housing industries suffer, as well as industries that produce capital goods.

What Are the Types of Inflation?

In general, price increases come from shortages of goods and services. When demand exceeds supply at a particular price, a shortage exists. Shortages are resolved in a market-based economic system by raising the price. Those willing and able to pay the higher price get the goods and services. Shortages allow sellers to raise prices and encourage buyers to pay the higher price, especially if prices have a history of going up and people expect this increase to continue. The shortage resulting from an excess of demand over supply can exist throughout the entire economy, resulting in an increased overall average price level.

There are three types of inflation, depending upon the cause: **monetary inflation, demand-pull inflation, and cost-push inflation**.

Monetary Inflation

We will learn in Chapter 11 how the Federal Reserve System (the Fed) controls the money supply. When the money supply grows, there is more money available for spending and credit is easier to obtain.

Usually, the Fed increases the money supply at about the same rate as growth in Real GDP. Real GDP tends to rise over time at an average of 2.5 to 3 percent a year. If the Fed lets the money supply grow at the same rate as Real GDP, monetary inflation will not be a problem. If the Fed lets the supply of money grow faster than Real GDP, monetary inflation results. There is a saying that when there are too many dollars chasing too few goods and services, prices will rise.

Demand-pull Inflation

There is an excess of demand. This type of inflation happens because total spending exceeds total production of goods and services in an overheated economy. At full employment, the economy is producing its ideal level of output and there are few, if any, idle resources. When total spending increases beyond that point, there are no idle resources to be added to produce more goods and services. Factory orders cannot be filled, and shortages occur. Again, a market-based economy rations shortages by raising the price. Those willing and able to pay the higher price get the goods.

Total spending can increase as leakages decrease or injections increase. Consumers spend more on domestically produced goods because savings, taxes, or imports (leakages) decrease. Investment, government spending, or exports (injections) can increase, causing total spending to increase.

Leakages will decrease when savings (S) fall. Savings usually fall when people expect good times are corning. Prosperity is ahead so we can afford to spend more now and save less. Another effect on saving is that when interest rates decrease, the reward for saving decreases. Why put your money in a savings account to draw 1 percent interest? Finally, when people expect higher prices in the future, there is a tendency to spend more today. Taxes (T) can decrease if governments reduce tax rates. Imports (M) can decrease when incomes decrease.

Injections may increase, which is the more probable cause of demand-pull inflation. Investment spending (I) can increase when business managers become optimistic about the future or when innovation leads to ways to increase productivity through more and/or better capital goods. Investment can also increase when interest rates are low, making investment and housing purchases easier to finance and their payments lower. A government spending (G) increase is the culprit in causing demand-pull inflation. Exports (X) usually increase when our trading partners' incomes increase.

Cost-push Inflation

This type of inflation occurs if there is a decrease in production or output, which could be caused by rising production costs because of falling productivity, rising production costs because of increasing resource prices;,increased business taxes, increased cost of complying with government regulations, and an adverse supply shock to the economy, like a natural disaster, a terrorist attack or an interruption in energy supplies.

During cost-push inflation, the economy will experience shortages, resulting in higher prices, and lower production levels. The economy can experience both high inflation and high unemployment at the same time. The press named this situation **stagflation—stagnant economic growth accompanied by inflation.**

During the 1970's, the oil-producing nations comprising the OPEC cartel severely cut production of crude oil. As a result, crude oil prices increased dramatically. This resulted in cost-push inflation and high inflation and high unemployment occurred simultaneously.

What Is Unemployment?

The U.S. Department of Labor defines the **unemployed** as those persons who are at least 16-years-old and who are not working but are actively seeking work. They define the **employed** as those who are at least 16 years old and are working.

Define the **labor force** as the unemployed and the employed, or everyone that is at least 16 years old and either working or actively seeking work. Those **not in the labor force** are either under 16 or not actively seeking work for reasons such as retirement, disability, illness, incarceration, or because they just want to live on the beach and be a bum.

In order to measure the unemployment rate, the Labor Department surveys a sample of about 60,000 households each month to find out whether or not people are working (the employed) or not working but actively seeking work (the unemployed). They also find people not working and not actively seeking work (not in the labor force). They then extrapolate the results to the entire population and calculate the rate of unemployment:

Unemployment rate (in percent) = 100 x Unemployed / Labor force.

Assume there are 1,000,000 people in the labor force and 900,000 are working and the other 100,000 are not working but actively seeking work. They are the unemployed. Then the unemployment rate is 100,000/1,000,000 or 10 percent.

What Are the Types of Unemployment?

A person out of work does not care why he or she is out of work. There are different causes of a person being unemployed. There are four types of unemployment **seasonal, cyclical, frictional, and structural**, each with a different cause.

Those **seasonally unemployed** are the people whose work depends on the season of the year. Migrant farmworkers, lifeguards, department store Santas, and employees of ski resorts are examples. Seasonal unemployment is minimal, and policymakers do not consider it to be much of a problem. Unemployment data is seasonally adjusted to disregard seasonally unemployed.

Those **cyclically unemployed** are what most people assume is the only real cause of unemployment. Cyclical unemployment is unemployment that results from changes in the business cycle. During recessions, when total spending and production decreases, business firms do not need as many workers and some are laid off or terminated, causing the rate of unemployment to increase. In recovery, the opposite happens and the rate of unemployment decreases. This is the type of unemployment that policymakers focus on.

Those **frictionally unemployed** are volunteers. People voluntarily leave jobs for one reason or another and it can take some time to find another job. During the time the person is looking for that better job, he or she is frictionally unemployed. This type of unemployment is a freedom issue. It contributes about 2 percent to the unemployment rate, but it is due to the freedom employees enjoy to voluntarily leave one job and search for a better opportunity elsewhere.

Those who are **structurally unemployed** lost their jobs due to a change in the structure of an industry. Because of this, this type of unemployment is more problematic. As we transition from an industrial manufacturing-based economy to a service technology-based economy, there is usually a mismatch between skill sets and job requirements and a geographical mismatch. Economic progress and technological change eliminate jobs in one industry or in one geographical area and create jobs in another industry or another geographical area. Picture the newly unemployed 55-year-old steelworker in West Virginia and a job opening for a medical technician in San Antonio. What are the chances the steelworker relocates and retrains? At that age and with roots in the community, early retirement is a more likely option. Structural unemployment is also a freedom issue. Employers must restructure their businesses and shift from old to new technology, even though that eliminates jobs in the process. Depending on the degree of technological innovation and the changing market conditions for products, structural unemployment can contribute 2 to 4 percent to the unemployment rate.

What Is the Full Employment Goal?

Full employment is a macroeconomic goal, defined as the rate of unemployment that exists when there is zero cyclical unemployment. Only frictional unemployment and structural unemployment exist. Those two categories of unemployment usually make up about 4 percent of the labor force. In times of industrial upheaval due to innovation, it could be about 5 or 6percent. Full employment would usually have 96 percent of the labor force employed, although it could be as low as 94 or 95 percent. Full employment occurs at a Real GDP existing at or near the peak of the business cycle.

SUMMARY

1. **Identify harmful effects of inflation.**

   The harmful effects of inflation are the decrease in the purchasing power of money, the redistribution of income, the redistribution of wealth, a reduced savings rate, disruption of business plans, and an increase in nominal interest rates.

2. **Differentiate between the three types of inflation.**

   The three types of inflation are monetary, demand-pull, and cost-push. Monetary inflation occurs when the money supply grows faster than Real GDP. Demand-pull inflation occurs when over-enthusiastic buyers try to buy more goods and services than the economy can produce, creating shortages in the product market and in the skilled labor market. Because of this, desperate buyers pull up prices by outbidding each other. Cost-push inflation occurs when the costs of producing goods and services rise for any reason. Firms, seeing their profit falling, push up their prices to cover the additional costs.

3. **Define the unemployment rate.**

   The unemployment rate is the number of unemployed divided by the number in the labor force, expressed as a percent.

4. **Describe the four types of unemployment.**

   The four types of unemployment are seasonal, cyclical, frictional, and structural. Seasonal unemployment is of least importance as it is tied to the calendar year and is easily anticipated by those who would be unemployed. Cyclical unemployment occurs as the business cycle goes into recession and, because of declining sales and declining production, business firms lay off workers. Many of those workers will be hired back when the economy recovers. Frictional unemployment occurs when employees voluntarily quit their jobs to seek better opportunities. Structural unemployment occurs when employers decide to restructure their businesses in response to changing market conditions or changing technology. Skilled workers lose their jobs, which have been eliminated.

5. **Identify which type of unemployment is of most concern to policymakers.**

   The type of unemployment that is of most concern to policymakers is cyclical unemployment. Frictional and structural unemployment have freedom issues; to reduce them, the government would have to restrict the freedom of employees to quit their jobs and the freedom of employers to restructure their businesses.

6. **Define the full employment goal.**

   The full employment goal is to have the economy operate at a Real GDP level where only frictional and structural unemployment occur. Cyclical unemployment is zero at the full employment level. Typically, the unemployment rate at the full employment level is four to six percent.

Homework Chapter 10

Name_____

DESCRIPTIONS

Match the key terms with the descriptions.

_____ Average rising prices

_____ Inflation is caused by an excess of demand oversupply.

_____ Money supply increases faster than Real GDP.

_____ Simultaneous occurrence of high inflation and high unemployment.

_____ The unemployed and the employed.

_____ Those who are at least 16-years-old and are working.

_____ Those who are at least 16-years-old, not working, and not actively seeking work.

_____ Those who are at least 16-years-old, not working, but actively seeking work.

_____ Unemployment caused by changes in the structure of the economy.

_____ Unemployment that results from the business cycle.

_____ Voluntary unemployment where people haven't found a new job yet.

_____ A natural disaster, a terrorist attack, or an interruption in energy or other inputs to production.

_____ Inflation caused by a decrease in production or output.

KEY TERMS

1. Adverse economic shock
2. Cost-push inflation
3. Cyclical unemployment
4. Demand-pull inflation
5. Frictional unemployment
6. Inflation
7. Structural unemployment
8. Stagflation
9. Monetary inflation.
10. Employed
11. Unemployed
12. Labor force
13. Not in the labor force.

EXERCISES

1. Describe the four phases of the business cycle.

2. Why aren't unreported transactions included in GDP?

3. How will producers change their level of production when inventories increase unexpectedly? Why?

4. What are the requirements for Macro equilibrium?

5. Describe the chain of events for a recession.

11

Money and the Federal Reserve

A tool is a device that makes a task easier to perform. Money is a tool. It makes the daily effort of transactions, large and small, and much easier. A country's central bank controls the money supply, which is the amount of money that is available to the public at any one time. In the United States, this task is performed by the U.S. central bank, the Federal Reserve System (the Fed). In this chapter, we shall investigate what money is and then look at the ways the Fed controls the money supply.

After studying this chapter, you should be able to:

1. Identify what is money.
2. Describe the three functions of money.
3. Tell what is included in the money supply.
4. Describe how banks create money.
5. Outline fractional reserve banking.
6. Describe how the Federal Reserve can use its four tools to manipulate the money supply.
7. Outline how the Fed conducts Open Market Operations.
8. Outline how the Fed uses its tool of paying interest on reserve balances.
9. Tell when the Fed would favor an easy money policy.
10. Tell when the Fed would favor a tight money policy.

What Is Barter and Why Is It Hard to Do?

Barter is the mutual exchange of one good for another

At one time, barter was the basis for all commerce. The problem with barter is the requirement to have a double coincidence of wants.

Consider a baseball team with a couple of extra outfielders but with a shortage of good pitchers. Now imagine another team with a couple of spare pitchers but a dearth of outfielders. One team would have to identify that the other team exists before any negotiation could begin. The trade of an outfielder for a pitcher would improve both clubs. The transaction costs, that is, the time spent scouting each team's players and negotiating the trade, are enormous. Just consider the effort required to get to an agreement between the two teams about which pitcher should be swapped for which outfielder. Imagine what an impediment to trading these kind of transaction costs would be if every time you buy groceries, clothes, gasoline, entertainment, etc., you had to locate someone who needs what you had to offer and had what you needed.

The invention of money makes transactions easier to complete and less costly in terms of time and effort. The use of money eliminates the double coincidence of wants. We work in exchange for money and then use the money to acquire the goods and services we want. Money has replaced barter in everyday life.

What Is Money and What Gives Money Value?

Is money just the coins and paper money that we carry around with us for times when we need cash? Money consists of much more than that. Most money is stored in banks, credit unions and savings associations in the form of an electronic data entry called a **deposit**.

Money is anything that is generally accepted as payment for goods and services and payment for employment. In the prison camps during World War II, prisoners received packages from the Red Cross that included soap, socks, cigarettes, and candy. The prisoners traded with each other, first by barter, but quickly they adopted the convention of using cigarettes as money. Therefore, they accepted cigarettes in exchange for other goods, not because they wanted to smoke but because they knew they could use the cigarettes as money to buy other goods. All goods were priced in cigarettes, for example, one bar of soap for three cigarettes. Therefore, they considered cigarettes to be money.

What gives money its value? Is it backed up by gold or silver? U.S. dollars used to be called Silver Certificates and were backed up by precious metals. Today, U.S. dollars are Federal Reserve Notes, which are a liability of the Federal Reserve System. The dollar's value comes from its **purchasing power**. What can be purchased by the dollar determines its value.

We trust that the Federal Reserve System will not increase the amount of dollars available for public use faster than the amount needed for transactions. This trust also gives the dollar value. If the Fed increases the supply of dollars faster than the increase in the output of goods and services, then more dollars will be available to buy the same amount of goods, and the purchasing power of each dollar decreases. Consequently, the value of the dollar decreases.

What Are the Desired Characteristics of Money?

Portable. If we used cows for money, it would be difficult to take our money with us when we go shopping or to transfer it to someone else. The dollar is easily transported—we can take cash with us or use a debit card or check or a mobile payment application on our phone to transfer our money out of our bank account and into the bank account of the supermarket, the gas station, or at a retail store. Banks transfer billions of dollars around the world electronically every day.

Durable. If we used chickens for money, they would not last very long in a purse or pants pocket, much less while being transferred from place to place. The paper U.S. dollar is durable. It is hard to tear and seems to last a long time before wearing out, even though it can change hands every day or so. Dollars that are electronically recorded in bank accounts don't experience any wear and tear. Coins are durable also.

Divisible. If we used hard metals for money, it would be difficult to break it down into smaller parts. Gold bars would not work very well in everyday life. The dollar is divisible into 100 cents, making transactions that include amounts of less than one dollar easy to do. The best the eighteenth-century pirates could do with the old gold Spanish dollar was to chop it up into eight wedges, called "pieces of eight."

Recognizable. Would you be able to tell if something made of gold or silver was authentic? The dollar is easy to recognize, and the government tries to stay ahead of the counterfeiters by changing the look and texture of the dollar quite often.

Rare. Could we use oak leaves or pebbles as money? If everyone had all the dollars they wanted, how much value would each dollar have? We depend on the Federal Reserve System to keep the supply of dollars low enough so that the currency is considered rare and valuable.

What Are the Three Functions of Money?

Medium of Exchange. When we use the money to pay for something we bought, or to loan to someone else, or to pay our taxes, money is used as a medium of exchange. Employers use money to pay their employees and to pay off their debts. Thus, we work for money, and we use the money to acquire the goods and services we want to buy. Money is the middle step, that is, the medium of exchange, and using money replaces barter.

Store of Value. We do not have to spend our money the same day we receive it. We can spread it out during the week and spend it as we need it. This is because the value of the effort that went into earning the money stays with the money during its time in storage (in our pocket or in our bank account). As our incomes grow, we can save our money for the down payment on a house or automobile, our children's education, or our own retirement.

Standard of Value. The market economy works as well as it does because we can express all prices in dollars. Each dollar is worth the same as every other dollar. We can compare the price of a good at Wal-Mart to the price of the same good at target. If prices had to be expressed in chickens or some other commodity, it would be difficult because this form of money would come in different sizes, grades, and quality. After a while, we began to evaluate things in terms of dollars. You might say "Its price is $10; I don't think it is worth that much." Or, on a very hot day, you might say "It would be worth $20 to me to have a glass of ice-cold lemonade right now."

What Is Meant by the Money Supply?

The money supply is the money that people can access and spend. The Federal Reserve System controls the size and the growth of the money supply. Growth of the money supply is limited so that it stays rare and therefore keeps its value. The Federal Reserve Bank using two primary methods to measure the money supply, depending upon the liquidity. **Liquidity of money is a measure of how easy it is to access and spend money.** The more liquid, the easier it is to spend.

The two primary measures are M1 and M2. The Fed changed their definition over the years. The Fed currently defines them as follows:

M1 is the most liquid form of money. It includes all the coins and paper money, checkable deposit accounts, and other liquid deposit accounts, such as savings deposit accounts and money market accounts. A checkable deposit account is an account you can withdraw by writing a check, using a debit card, or using a payment app. These are called demand deposit accounts, since you, the account holder, can retrieve the money on demand whenever you want. Some deposits pay interest on the balance, and you can still access whenever you want.

M2 is less liquid. It includes all M1 plus Certificates of Deposit in denominations of less than $100,000 (called small-denomination time deposit accounts). You cannot access an M2 account on demand. You must make a withdrawal to convert the M2 money into M1 money. There may be a prepayment penalty of some kind when you withdraw funds from an M2 account. Since M2 must be transformed into M1 before you can spend it, it is less liquid than M1.

There are even lesser liquid forms of money. For example, M3 adds Certificates of Deposit of $100,000 or more to M1 and M2.

What about credit cards? Are the credit cards we use to buy things considered money? In the strictest sense, no. Credit cards are a loan from the company that issued you the credit card. The actual payment for your goods does not occur until you pay your credit card bill. Debit cards are different. Debit cards are indeed a way of accessing your money in a bank account just like a check, only faster, so they act just like money.

How Do Commercial Banks Function?

Commercial banks are privately-owned, profit-seeking institutions. They primarily make a profit by taking advantage of the difference between the rate of interest they pay depositors on savings accounts and certificates of deposit and the higher rate of interest they charge for loans or earn on investments. This is called the spread. In addition, banks earn fees for providing a variety of other services to customers. The vital function of commercial banks is to redirect savings back into the economy by making loans for business investment and personal consumption.

Commercial banks create money when they make loans. The Federal Reserve System allows this by authorizing the commercial banks to loan out the money deposited with them. When you borrow money from a bank, they usually do not hand over cash equal to the amount of the loan. They simply make a bookkeeping entry increasing the borrower's deposit balance. Before the loan, there was a certain amount of money on deposit in the banking system. After the loan is made, the amount of deposits increases by the size of the loan. Therefore, the money supply increases. Money is created by the loan. When the loan is repaid, the amount of deposits decreases by the size of the loan. The money supply decreases.

> **Banks make a loan. Money supply increases. Money is created.**
>
> **Loan is paid back. Money supply decreases. Money is destroyed.**

What Are the Roles of the Federal Reserve System?

The Federal Reserve System, the Fed, is our nation's central bank. The U. S. Congress created the Fed through the Federal Reserve Act of 1913. It is designed to be relatively independent of the U. S. government and insulated from day-to-day political matters. The Fed consists of a Board of Governors located in Washington, D.C. and 12 regional Federal Reserve Banks. It acts as a banker's bank for commercial banks through twelve regional Federal Reserve Banks. The regional banks are legally organized as private not-for-profit corporations. These regional banks perform most of the same services for commercial banks as the commercial banks do for their customers. They hold reserve deposits, make loans, clear checks, and change money for their member banks.

The Fed also has an economic policy-making role in managing the size of the money supply, interest rates, and the availability of credit. They implement fractional reserve banking.

Fractional Reserve Banking. The Fed controls the money supply through the commercial banking system and the reserves commercial banks are required to keep. **All deposits made in commercial banks are called reserves.** The Fed requires commercial banks to keep a fraction of their reserves in a category from which loans cannot be made. These reserves are **required reserves.** All other reserves can be loaned out to customers. Until they are loaned out, they are **excess reserves.** The amount of required reserves is determined by the Fed by using a **reserve ratio**, which equals the required reserves divided by the total reserves on deposit. The reserve ratio is a fraction, say 1/10, or a percent, say 10 percent.

When banks loan money out of their excess reserves, no actual currency changes hands. A deposit is created in the name of the borrower and a loan account is created in the name of the borrower by a simple bookkeeping entry increasing loans and increasing deposits. The example below presents such a transaction assuming a reserve ratio of 10 percent, or 1/10, and a loan of $20,000:

	Pre-Loan	**Loan**	**Post-Loan**
Deposits (reserves)	$100,000	$20,000	$120,000
Required reserves (10%)	10,000		12,000
Sub total	90,000		108,000
Loans and investments	50,000	20,000	70,000
Excess reserves	$40,000		$38,000

This transaction increased the money supply by $20,000 and only decreased the bank's excess reserves by $2,000, or 10 percent of the increase, which is the reserve ratio.

The new $20,000 was borrowed by someone who wants to buy something. Once spent, it will wind up in the bank account of the vendor and increase that bank's reserves and their lending capability.

How much money can be eventually created out of a new deposit? The **money multiplier** is a measure of the eventual total deposit creation from a new deposit.

The money multiplier (mm) is the reciprocal of the reserve ratio (mm = 1/ reserve ratio).

For a reserve ratio of 10 percent or 1/10, the money multiplier is 10. The total excess reserves of all the commercial banks times the money multiplier gives the lending capacity of the banking system assuming money stays in the banking system and banks are fully loaned or invested. When loans are paid the reverse happens. The amount loaned out decreases and the multiplier effect works in reverse. Because of this, the money supply shrinks. For a graphic presentation of the multiplier effect, see Figure 11-1.

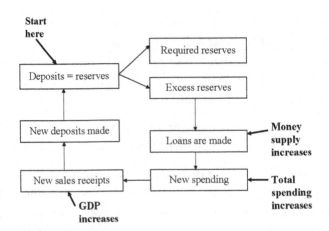

FIGURE 11-1. The Multiplier Effect

A bank receives a new deposit. It must set aside part of this deposit as Required Reserves, but it can loan out the rest, called Excess Reserves. When the loan is made, the money supply increases by the size of the loan. The borrower spends the borrowed money, increasing total spending in the economy by that amount. GDP increases, also. The seller deposits his sales receipts in his bank, which immediately sets aside Required Reserves and makes a loan on the Excess Reserves, starting the cycle again. Each time around the cycle, the amount of Excess Reserves diminishes. Each time around the cycle, the money supply grows, as does total spending and GDP.

Source: Mikel Cohick

How Does the Fed Use Its Tools to Manipulate the Money Supply?

The four tools of the Fed are changing the reserve ratio, changing the discount rate, conducting Open market Operations, and paying interest on reserve balances (required and excess reserves). These four tools allow the fed to conduct monetary policy by manipulating the money supply.

Changing the Reserve Ratio. One way that the Fed can control the money supply is to change the reserve ratio, which will change the money multiplier.

If it wishes to increase the money supply, it can lower the reserve ratio, enabling banks to loan more money. For example, lowering the reserve ratio from 10 percent to 8 percent would allow banks to increase their amount of loans from 90 percent of deposits to 92 percent of deposits. This increases the money multiplier from 10 to 12.5.

If it wishes to decrease the money supply, it can raise the reserve requirement which will reduce the amount of money that banks can loan and invest. For example, raising the reserve ratio from 10 percent to 20 percent would require banks to reduce the amount of loans from 90 percent of deposits to 80 percent of deposits, leading to a decrease in the money multiplier from 10 to 5.

As a practical matter, the Fed rarely changes the reserve requirement because the effect of a change can be disruptive, especially if the requirement is raised and banks are forced to call in loans or sell investments. Setting and changing the reserve ratio is one tool of the Fed for controlling the money supply.

In 2020, the Fed lowered the reserve requirement to 0 percent. They wanted to increase the money supply to allow member banks to loan out all of their reserve balances to boost the economy during the COVID-19 pandemic.

Changing the Discount Rate. When member banks are short of reserves, they must either sell investments or reduce their loan balances, both of which are disruptive, or they borrow excess reserves on an overnight basis. These excess reserves can be borrowed from other member banks (these loans are called Federal Funds) or from the Fed itself. The rate of interest charged by one bank to another bank for an overnight loan is the Federal Funds rate. It is determined by changes in the supply of and demand for funds in the Federal Funds market.

However, if a bank cannot obtain a loan from another bank, they turn to the Fed as the lender of last resort. The Fed loans money at the Discount Rate, which is set by the Fed at from ¼ percent to 1 percent greater than the targeted Federal Funds Rate to encourage banks to borrow from each other if possible.

Thus, to encourage lending, which increases the money supply, the Fed lowers the Discount Rate, making it less expensive to borrow money. To discourage lending, the Fed does just the opposite—it raises the Discount Rate, making it more expensive to borrow money. By changing the Discount Rate, the Fed influences the Federal Funds Rate. The Discount Rate effectively serves as the upper limit for the Federal Funds Rate.

These types of loans are used to control the money supply but are not as widely used by the Fed as compared to the next two tools described below.

Conducting Open Market Operations. When the Federal Government borrows to fund its budget deficit, The Treasury Department issues IOU's called U.S. Treasury Securities. These securities are sold through dealers and, after their initial sale to the public, trade in the open market among individual and institutional buyers, including commercial banks. The Federal Reserve owns many of these securities. The Federal Open Market Committee can change the money supply by buying and selling these securities (or by buying and selling other marketable securities), that is, by conducting Open Market Operations.

When the Fed **buys** securities, such as from commercial banks, it puts money into the banking system and takes the securities out. If a bank sells the securities to the Fed, the bank has more deposits and fewer investments, enabling the bank to make more loans and thus increase the money supply. If a non-bank investor sells the securities to the Fed, they deposit the proceeds in a bank, increasing the bank's deposits and its ability to make more loans and increase the money supply. In addition, the effect of the Fed buying the securities puts upward pressure on their price which has the effect of lowering interest rates, making it cheaper for companies and individuals to borrow the money.

When the Fed **sells** securities, such as to commercial banks, the opposite happens. The securities go into the banking system and excess reserves shrink, regardless of who buys the securities. When reserves shrink, it reduces a bank's ability to make loans. The sale of securities also puts downward pressure on the price which has the effect of increasing interest rates (bond prices and interest rates have an inverse relationship), making it more expensive to borrow money.

To summarize:

If the Fed wants to increase the money supply, that is, make more money available to the public, it buys securities in the open market. The Fed pays the seller of the securities, which increases the deposits in the buyer's account.

If the Fed wants to decrease the money supply, that is, make less money available to the public, it sells securities in the open market. The buyer pays the Fed for the securities, which decreases deposits in the buyer's account.

Open market operations used to be the Fed's favorite tool to influence and target the Federal Funds Rate it wishes to maintain. Using open market operations, the Fed manipulates the supply of Federal Funds so that the actual rate is very close to its targeted rate. The Federal Funds Rate is a benchmark rate. When the Fed increases it, banks and other lending institutions increase the interest rates they charge to their customers. The rate they charge their best customers is the Prime Rate, which is usually about 3 percent higher than the targeted Federal Funds Rate. The opposite occurs when the Fed decreases the Federal Funds Rate.

Paying interest on reserve balances. During financial crisis of the Great Recession of 2007 to 2009, and again during the COVID-19 crisis, the Fed's use of open market operations declined in importance and the new tool of paying interest on reserve balances gained importance. The Fed had reached a limit on how much it could influence the Federal Funds Rate using open market operations as interest rates dropped close to zero.

The Fed had lowered targeted Federal Funds Rate to 0 to 0.25 percent in response to the financial crisis. The Fed then increased the amount (**quantitative easing**) as well as the variety (**qualitative easing**) of the securities it held. This increased the quantity of bank reserves, which increased the loan capacity by dramatically increasing the amount that could be loaned out by banks. Managing these ample reserve balances became a monetary policy option.

The Fed manages ample reserve balances by paying interest on required and excess reserves, that is, reserve balances. In the past, the Fed did not pay banks interest on required reserves. Thus, banks preferred not to hold any excess reserves with the fed overnight because they could profit by lending them out. When the Fed started to pay interest on required and excess reserves, the result was a substantial increase in excess reserve holding of banks. Paying interest on reserve balances has become an important monetary policy of the Fed. If the Fed paid 1 percent interest, then, instead of loaning out excess reserves to another bank at, say, 0.75 percent, a bank can earn more by holding the excess reserves at the Fed. If a bank could borrow overnight from another bank at 0.75 percent and hold it at the Fed at 1 percent, it would profit overnight. This is **arbitrage**, the art of buying low and selling high. Such arbitrage action ensures that the Federal Funds Rate closely matches the Fed's interest rate on reserve balances. Thus, the interest rate on reserve balances is the lower limit for the Federal Funds Rate and the Discount Rate is its upper limit.

The Fed's long-term monetary policy relies on a banking system with ample reserves. Its interest rate on reserve balances influences the Federal funds Rate as a benchmark rate for the prime rate and other interest rates charged by lending institutions to customers.

What Are Easy Money and Tight Money Policies?

The Fed keeps a close watch on the economy and tries to steer a course between an underperforming economy having unemployment as the problem and an overheated economy having inflation as the problem. Its goal is to reach a full-employment economy.

If the economy is underperforming, the Fed will adopt an **easy money policy** (an expansionary monetary policy) to encourage lending and borrowing. The easy money policy options of the Fed to expand credit are to:

1. lower the reserve ratio.

2. lower the Discount rate.

3. buy securities in Open Market Operations,

4. lower the interest rate on reserve balances (which will decrease the targeted Federal Funds Rate).

If the economy is overheating, that is, growing too fast, the Fed will adopt a **tight money policy** (a contractionary monetary policy). The tight money policy options of the Fed to reduce credit are to:

1. raise the reserve ratio.

2. raise the Discount rate.

3. sell securities in Open Market Operations.

4. raise the interest rate on reserve balances (which will increase the targeted Federal Funds Rate).

SUMMARY

1. **Identify what is money.**

   Money is anything that is generally accepted as payment for goods and services and payment for employment,

2. **Describe the three functions of money.**

   The three functions of money are as a medium of exchange, as a store of value, and as a standard of value.

3. **Tell what is included in the money supply.**

   The money that people can access and spend is the money supply. This includes cash in the hands of the public and demand deposits, such as a checking or savings account. Thus, cash in a bank vault is not part of the money supply.

4. **Describe how banks create money.**

   Every time a bank makes a loan, a new deposit is created, and the money supply increases. The reverse is true when the loan is repaid.

5. **Outline fractional reserve banking.**

   Banks loan out their deposits. To control the amount of loans a bank can make, the Federal Reserve requires each bank to set aside a fraction of the deposits they have. These required reserves cannot be loaned out.

6. **Describe how the Federal Reserve can use its tools to manipulate the money supply.**

   To manipulate the money supply, the Fed can change the reserve ratio, change the discount rate, conduct Open Market Operations, or change the administered interest rate on reserve balances.

7. **Outline how the Fed conducts Open Market Operations.**

   If the Fed wants to increase the money supply, it will buy securities in the open market. If the Fed wants to decrease the money supply, it will sell securities in the open market.

8. **Outline how the Fed uses its new tool of paying interest on reserve balances.**

   To increase the money supply, the Fed lowers the administered interest rate on reserve balances, which lowers the Federal Funds Rate and causes increased demand for bank loans. To decrease the money supply, the Fed raises the administered interest rate on reserve balances, which raises the Federal Funds Rate and causes decreased demand for bank loans.

9. **Tell when the Fed favors an easy money policy?**

   If the economy is underperforming, that is, there is a recession, the Fed will favor an "easy money" policy by causing the money supply to grow and induce increased spending.

10. **Tell when the Fed favors a tight money policy.**

   If the economy is overheated, that is, the big problem is inflation, the Fed will favor a "tight money" policy by causing the money supply to shrink and induce decreased spending.

Homework Chapter 11

DESCRIPTIONS

Match the key terms with the descriptions.

_____ Direct trade of one item for another, without money.

_____ Anything generally accepted as payment for goods and services and for employment.

_____ A liability of the U.S. Federal Reserve System.

_____ How easily an item can be transported from one place to another.

_____ Using money to affect an employment or trade transaction between two parties.

_____ The ability to spend our money when needed rather than when received.

_____ A uniform way of setting prices on a variety of goods and services.

_____ The amount of money that people can access and spend.

_____ A measure of how easy it is to access and spend money.

_____ Coins, paper money, and savings accounts.

_____ A deposit you can withdraw by writing a check.

_____ M1 plus Certificates of Deposit <$100,000 and retail money market funds.

_____ A process of increasing the money supply by commercial banks making loans.

_____ The U.S. central bank or banker's bank for commercial banks.

_____ The amount of commercial bank reserves from which loans cannot be made.

_____ Required reserves/total reserves.

_____ A measure of the eventual deposit creation from a new deposit.

_____ The interest rate charged by banks for overnight loans to other banks short of reserves.

_____ The Fed's buying and selling of U.S. Treasury Securities in the open market to increase or decrease the money supply.

_____ Name given to Fed policy designed to encourage borrowing and lending.

_____ Name given to Fed policy designed to discourage borrowing and lending.

_____ The interest rate charged by the Fed for overnight loans to member banks short of reserves.

KEY TERMS

1. Barter
2. Checkable deposit
3. Discount rate
4. Easy Money
5. Fed funds rate
6. Federal reserve system
7. Liquidity
8. M1
9. M2
10. Medium of exchange
11. Money creation
12. Money multiplier
13. Money supply
14. Money
15. Open market operations
16. Portability
17. Required reserves
18. Reserve ratio
19. Standard of value
20. Store of value
21. The U.S. dollar
22. Tight money

EXERCISES

1. Why does "barter" make trade difficult?

2. Name and briefly describe the five characteristics of money.

3. Name and briefly describe the three functions of money.

4. Are credit card money? Why or why not? What about debit cards?

5. How is each of the Fed's tools used to enact an easy money policy?

6. How is each of the Fed's tools used to enact a tight money policy?

12

The Dynamics of the Macro Economy

The macroeconomy of a society is indeed dynamic. This is the result of the constant actions and interactions of the individual participants: the consumers, the business firms, the government, the international sector, the employees, the employers, and the resource owners. The collective goal of any society is to obtain economic growth, thereby raising the standard of living of the members of the society.

A society has a production possibilities curve (PPC) on which it has several choices of which combination of consumer goods and capital goods it may select. Due to the business cycle described in Chapter 9, society can operate under its PPC and underperform, or it can occasionally attempt to operate beyond its PPC and become overheated. How does this happen? If the economy underperforms, can it "fix" itself? If the economy overheats, can it "fix" itself? Whether it can or not, should the government step in and "fix" the economy?

After studying this chapter, you should be able to:

1. Describe what fosters long-run economic growth.

2. Tell what a society can do to get the economy to grow faster.

3. Outline what conditions could lead to long-run economic decline.

4. Tell why society's institutional PPC is at lower output levels than its physical PPC.

5. Describe the principal economic problem in an underperforming economy.

6. Describe the principal economic problem in an overheated economy,

7. Tell what the main objection is to a self-correcting economy.

How Does a Society Achieve Long-Run Economic Growth?

A society must choose where it wants to be on the production possibilities curve, just as mom did in Chapter 1, when she had to decide between making cookies and cake. As shown in **Figure 12-1**, society must decide which combination of capital goods and consumer goods best suits its current and future wants and needs. In Figure 12-1, society could choose the combination, represented by point A, which emphasizes consumer goods—satisfying more current needs—over capital goods, or the combination represented by point B, which emphasizes capital goods and promotes faster economic growth and more satisfaction of needs in the future.

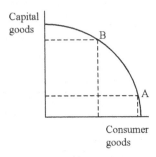

FIGURE 12-1. Society's PPC

If society chooses point A, it emphasizes consumer goods, not capital goods. If society chooses point B, it emphasizes capital goods, not consumer goods. When a society produces capital goods, it is increasing its resource base. Increased resources push the PPC outward.

Source: Mikel Cohick.

If society switched from the combination at point A to combination at point B, the trade-off would be a decreased availability of consumer goods and an increased production of capital goods. This society would be sacrificing current enjoyment for a better, more productive future. This is just like college students sacrificing current earnings (and consumer goods) to get an education (improving human capital) which will enable them to higher earnings in the future.

In Chapter 1, we described economic growth as the outward push of the production possibilities curve. Economic growth occurs when more or better resources are added or when there is technological advancement.

Figure 12-2 shows that economic growth will be greater, and standard of living will improve faster if society chooses point B, emphasizing the production of capital goods. More capital goods—a resource—are produced at point B than at point A. In either situation, some capital goods are produced, therefore, there is some economic growth no matter which point society selects. Growth will be faster at point B than at point A because more capital goods will be produced at B than at A

Can There Be Long-Run Economic Decline?

Instead of increasing the resources available or applying new technology, a society could experience the opposite. Its resource base could be destroyed by war or by a natural disaster, such as a tsunami, an earthquake, a hurricane, or a volcanic eruption. If its birthrate declines, its human resource could be

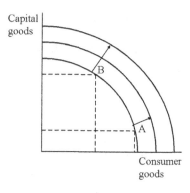

FIGURE 12-2. Economic Growth

Point A emphasizes producing a large amount of consumer goods and a small amount of capital goods. This society will grow more slowly. Point B emphasizes producing a large amount of capital goods and a small amount of consumer goods. This society will grow more rapidly.

Source: Mikel Cohick.

degraded in quantity as workers age and retire. The human resource could also be degraded in quality if the education and training systems of the society are allowed to deteriorate.

Figure 12-3 shows the PPC pushing inward. A decrease in the quantity or quality of available resources for any reason, or a decline in technology, will cause the PPC to recede inward, lowering society's standard of living.

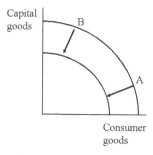

FIGURE 12-3. Economic Decline

Reduced resources, degraded human capital, or obsolete technology will cause the PPC to push inward, lowering society's standard of living.

Source: Mikel Cohick.

This society can no longer produce any of the combinations of capital goods and consumer goods that could previously be produced. Necessarily, this society's standard of living must decline. Some lesser developed countries must put most or all of their production into consumer goods in order to survive, possibly slowing their growth even more. As their populations increase, they fall into a declining standard of living spiral, which is difficult to reverse.

What Are Society's Short-Run Economic Problems?

A society can put itself on a long-run path of economic growth that is relatively steady for several decades. In the short run, however, year-to-year changes in GDP are by no means steadily increasing. In Chapter 9, the business cycle showed us that, during the recovery and prosperity phases, the economy sometimes grows at a faster rate than the long-run trend and, during the recession phase, it can grow slower or can actually shrink.

These short-run variations cause significant economic problems. To analyze these short-run variations, let us fine tune society's production possibilities curve to account for some institutional decisions that society has imposed upon itself. Our society has institutionalized, for example, the 40-hour workweek, overtime pay, child labor laws, minimum wage laws, and unemployment compensation laws. All of these reduce the number of labor hours (and increase the number of leisure hours) available.

Also, our society has decided to restrict the access to many natural resources. We prefer state and national parks, forests, and recreational areas, instead of using up the natural resources located in those places. Also, our society has decided not to use some technology readily available, such as DDT and nuclear power. All place constraints on society's ability to maximize its production, that is, being able to reach the physical limit of the PPC. Our society has chosen to do these things because we believe they improve our quality of life and therefore improve the standard of living of the people.

Why Does Society Create an Institutional PPC?

Figure 12-4 shows how the PPC that is affected by institutional constraints will exist at output levels below the physical PPC that would exist if none of the institutional constraints had been adopted. The institutional constraints imposed by society, in general, have been adopted to improve the lives of its citizens. The trade-off society is willing to accept is a loss of production of material satisfactions for an improved quality of life.

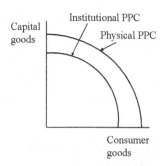

FIGURE 12-4. Institutional PPC

Every society imposes some restrictions on the use of its resources and technology. This effectively limits the productive capacity of the society. Full employment occurs at its institutional PPC, not its physical PPC.

Source: Mikel Cohick.

Thus, full employment is reached at society's institutional PPC. The institutional PPC becomes the short-run economic goal of society. Full employment, as defined in Chapter 8, is attained at any point on the institutional PPC. In **Figure 12-5**, if society is operating at point X on the institutional PPC, it has achieved full employment with little upward pressure on inflation. This is the situation near the peak of the business cycle.

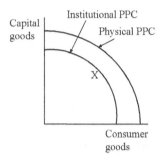

FIGURE 12-5. Full-Employment at the Peak of the Business Cycle

Full employment is attained if society operates on its institutional PPC. Exactly where depends on society's preferences and priorities at the moment. The "X" represents the economic goal of society. Point X is a typical location on the institutional PPC.

Source: Mikel Cohick.

How Does a Society Become an Underperforming Economy?

If the economy falls into a recession, it is moving away from point X near the peak inward into the area of inefficient production. This is shown as a shift toward point Y in **Figure 12-6**.

As the recession progresses, sales fall. Surpluses occur as inventory piles up. Retailers cut back on their factory orders. Salespeople and production workers are laid off. Unemployment rises. As production decreases, real GDP decreases. This process continues until production falls enough to equal sales again. Society has fallen inside its institutional PPC. See **Figure 12-7** for a step-by-step portrayal of falling into recession.

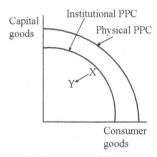

FIGURE 12-6. Going into Recession

An underperforming economy produces less output. As the recession takes place, society shifts from point X to point Y inside (under) the PPC. The farther inward point Y is, the deeper the recession. In this figure, the economy would be seriously underperforming at point Y.

Source: Mikel Cohick.

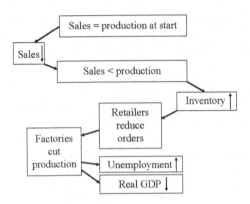

FIGURE 12-7. Going into an Underperforming Economy

At full-employment equilibrium, sales and production are equal. As the recession begins, sales decrease, and inventory rises. Retailers reduce orders, causing factories to cut back production. Workers are laid off and unemployment rises. GDP falls.

Source: Mikel Cohick.

Can a Society Self-Correct Out of an Underperforming Economy?

A dynamic market economy, however, begins to correct itself. Ultimately, the trough is reached (at point Y in Figure 12-6) and the decrease in real GDP stops. Recovery will begin. **Figure 12-8** shows the step-by-step version of the self-correction as the economy works itself out of its underperforming state back to a level of output where full employment is achieved.

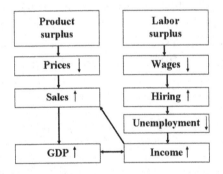

FIGURE 12-8. Self-Correction Out of an Underperforming Economy

A surplus of products leads to reduced prices, which encourages more sales. A surplus of workers leads to people accepting jobs at lower wages. At lower wages, employers are likely to increase hiring, causing unemployment to fall. Increased income spurs sales. In response, production and GDP rise.

Source: Mikel Cohick.

In the product market, high inventory levels cause sellers to mark down prices and move out the unsold goods. As sales increase, there is a need for more salespeople. Ultimately the overstock is gone, and retailers need more goods from the factories. Factory orders increase, prompting increased production and increased hiring at the factory.

Meanwhile, the labor surplus (the unemployed workers) causes a downward pressure on wages as some unemployed workers accept job offers at lower pay. Lower wages also prompt hiring increases. This process is slow, as businesses are reluctant to expand quickly or to add to their workforce rapidly. They want to make sure the upturn in business is real before committing to the expansion of either plant or workforce.

Also, during the downturn, many businesses will reorganize their method of operation and eliminate some jobs while doing so. Because of this, the unemployment rate falls very slowly at first. What decrease in unemployment occurs due to cyclical forces may get overwhelmed by the increases due to structural forces as business reorganize.

The relentless self-correction continues and ultimately the unemployment rate decreases, incomes increase, sales increase, production increases, real GDP increases, and recovery turns into prosperity as the economy marches back to full-employment at the institutional PPC. Self-correction gets the economy back to the full employment level at a lower inflation rate.

How Does a Society Become an Overheated Economy?

It is possible for the economy to overheat. When it does, inflation becomes the big problem. Society wants to buy and consume more goods and services than the institutional PPC can provide.

The overheated economy is shown in **Figure 12-9**, where society wants a combination of goods that lies outside the institutional PPC (but still inside the physical PPC). The economy tries to produce more than can be done at the institutional PPC. As it moves outward from point X to point Z, the economy overheats, and inflation becomes the problem. Unemployment is abnormally low, below the full-employment level.

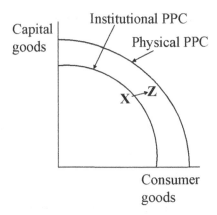

FIGURE 12-9. The Economy Overheats

An overheated economy attempts to produce more output than is acceptable at the institutional PPC. Society tries to operate at point Z.

Source: Mikel Cohick.

As the economy tries to push beyond full employment into the overheated area, sales orders rise and shortages develop as inventory is depleted. Producers try to expand to fill the backlogged orders but are constrained by their maximum capacity to produce, by shortages in raw materials, and by shortages in skilled-labor markets. See **Figure 12-10** for a step-by-step portrayal of the economy as it moves into an overheated state. The shortages in the product market and the shortages in the labor and raw materials markets trigger inflation as more and more buyers bid up the prices.

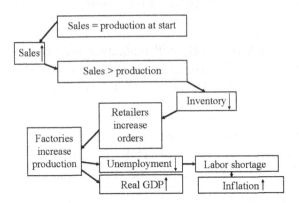

FIGURE 12-10. Going into an Overheated Economy

At full employment equilibrium, sales and production are equal. As overheating begins, sales requests outstrip production capacity, and inventory falls. Retailers increase orders, which the factories have difficulty filling. Shortages in raw materials and skilled workers arise, leading to rising costs, rising prices, and inflation. Unemployment becomes abnormally low.

Source: Mikel Cohick.

Can a Society Self-Correct Out of an Overheated Economy?

A dynamic market economy begins to correct itself. The shortages in labor and raw materials cause their costs to rise. Profits are squeezed. Firms begin to cut back on production. Product prices rise. Previously eager buyers begin to have second thoughts about buying and sales decrease.

Figure 12-11 shows the step-by-step version of the self-correction as the economy works itself out of its overheated state back to full employment at the institutional PPC. In the product market, shortages cause prices to rise which depresses sales. In the raw materials and labor markets, prices (wages) also increase, which suppresses the firms' desire to acquire them. Hiring decreases.

The abnormally low unemployment rate begins to rise on its way back to the full-employment level. As the ardor of the buying public wears off, the upward pressure on prices wanes as the economy returns to the full-employment level at the institutional PPC. Self-correction gets the economy back to the full employment level but at a higher inflation rate.

Is There an Economic Role for Government?

The problem with the self-correcting efforts in a dynamic market economy is that they take a substantial amount of time to complete the correction. Recall the lengthy period of time the business cycle took in the recovery/prosperity phase of the business cycle. The problem of an underperforming economy can persist longer when business firms learn how to operate with fewer employees because they have restructured. Then even when sales increase, firms still don't increase hiring very fast and we experience what is called a jobless recovery.

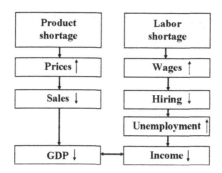

FIGURE 12-11. Self-correction out of an Overheated Economy

A shortage of products leads to increased prices which puts a damper on sales. A shortage of skilled workers leads to rising wages as employers outbid each other for the workers. Decreasing sales and rising wages cause some employers to stop hiring. Unemployment, abnormally low, rises back up to the full-employment level.

Source: Mikel Cohick.

Modern society easily becomes impatient and wants results now. This impatience usually overflows into the political arena, especially as the time for an election nears. The Government, as the agent of society (and politicians eager to show the electorate they can deliver a better economy than their opponents), are then called upon to step in and "fix" the problem. Government action may be implemented to hurry the correction along. There are several policy options that the government can choose in its effort to speed up the correction back to full employment. This is the subject of Chapter 14, where policy options are discussed.

Before we discuss policy options that are available to the government, in the next chapter, we shall create a basic macro model to describe what is happening in the nation's economy as well as the long-run and short-run changes that affect the economy. We develop the macro model, based on the trade-off between unemployment and inflation that occurs in the short run.

SUMMARY

1. **Describe what fosters long-run economic growth.**

   Economic growth occurs when more or better resources are added or when there is technological advancement.

2. **Tell what a society can do to get the economy to grow faster.**

   Society can get its economy to grow faster if it chooses to produce a combination of its PPC that increases the production of capital goods and decreases the production of consumer goods. Capital goods are resources, so adding more capital goods will increase the rate of economic growth.

3. **Outline what conditions could lead to long-run economic decline?**

   War or a natural disaster could destroy resources and productive capacity. The quantity of the workforce could decrease if it ages and is not replaced. If the quality of education and training deteriorates, then the quality of the workforce could also decline.

4. **Tell why society's institutional PPC is at lower output levels than its physical PPC.**

   Society imposes several restrictions upon itself that precludes it from completely using its resources. It does this to advance a better quality of life for its citizens. With a reduction in available resources, society must necessarily operate on a PPC that consists of a smaller set of combinations of consumer goods and capital goods.

5. **Describe the principal economic problem in an underperforming economy.**

   The principal economic problem in an underperforming economy is unemployment. Unemployment rises as sales fall short of production.

6. **Describe the principal economic problem in an overheated economy.**

   The principal economic problem in an overheated economy is inflation. Inflation rises as sales outstrip the capability to produce.

7. **Tell what the main objection is to a self-correcting economy.**

   Its progress toward the full-employment goal is slow, perhaps too slow for an impatient public. Consequently, members of society call upon the agent of society—government—to step in and "fix" the problem.

Homework Chapter 12

Name_____

DESCRIPTIONS

Match the key terms with the descriptions.

_____ Forty-hour work week, child labor laws, overtime pay, minimum wage laws and unemployment compensation.

_____ Unemployed workers.

_____ Name was given to the process, whereby the economy if, left alone, will eventually return to a place on the Institutional PPC.

_____ The PPC without the institutional constraints.

_____ Problems caused by short-run variations in the business cycle.

_____ High levels of unsold goods.

_____ When society wants to buy more goods and services than the institutional PPC can provide.

_____ More and/or better resources or technological advances.

_____ Decrease in available resources or a decline in technology.

_____ PPC with institutional constraints in place.

KEY TERMS

1. Causes of economic decline
2. Inflation and recession
3. Institutional constraints
4. Institutional PPC
5. Labor surplus
6. Overheated economy
7. Overstock
8. Physical PPC
9. Requirements for economic growth
10. Self-correction

EXERCISES

1. Explain why the production of capital goods instead of consumer goods will result in faster future economic growth.

2. What would be the causes of a decline in resources that resulted in long-run economic decline or shrinking PPC?

3. Why does a society impose institutional constraints on its capacity to produce?

4. Describe the self-correction process in an underperforming economy.

5. Describe the self-correction process in an overheated economy.

6. Why is government often called in to "fix" an economic problem?

7. Why do we consider full employment to occur at the Institutional PPC and not at the Physical PPC?

13 The Macro Model

When the economy is overheated, inflation is the major problem. When the economy is underperforming, unemployment is the major problem. At times, and particularly in short-run situations, these two problems are trade-offs, that is, as the inflation rate increases, the unemployment rate decreases, and vice versa. At other times, in long-run situations where significant changes are occurring in the economy, both can increase and decrease at the same time. In this chapter, we describe each of these situations. Then we create a basic macro model. We will then use the model to describe what is happening in the nation's economy. We will use historical examples to do this. Finally, we will describe how long-run and short-run changes affect the economy.

After studying this chapter, you should be able to:

1. Describe the trade-off inherent in the Phillips Curve.

2. Using the macro model, tell what causes a movement upward and to the right, leading to higher employment and higher inflation.

3. Using the macro model, tell what causes a movement downward and to the left, leading to lower employment and lower inflation.

4. Using the macro model, tell what causes a movement downward and to the right, leading to higher employment and lower inflation.

5. Using the macro model, tell what causes a movement upward and to the left, leading to lower employment and higher inflation.

6. Describe the macroeconomic goal.

What Is the Trade-Off between Unemployment and Inflation?

In the short run, any change begins to affect the economy rather quickly. In the long run, a change usually takes a significant amount of time to begin to affect the economy and a large amount of time to complete its effect. If there are no significant long-run changes, the economy's capacity, and incentive to produce is relatively stable.

In the 1960's, economists noted that, in periods of economic stability, there seemed to be a trade-off, an inverse relationship, between a change in the inflation rate and a change in the unemployment rate. The Phillips Curve shows this.

The Phillips Curve is a graphical representation of the short-run trade-off between a change in the inflation rate and an opposite change in the unemployment rate. This trade-off occurs when there are changes in total spending in an otherwise unchanging economy. Since the two variables move in opposite directions, the Phillips Curve is downward sloping curve on a graph that has the inflation rate on the vertical axis and the unemployment rate on the horizontal axis. This is a short-run phenomenon, where there is a net increase or decrease in total spending in the nation's economy.

The position of the Phillips Curve at any one point in time is determined by the capability and the incentive of the economy to produce. These do not change much in the short run. However, in the long run, the nation indeed can and will increase or decrease its capability to produce as well as increase or decrease its incentive to produce.

Figure 13-1 shows a typical Phillips Curve, a short-run movement along the Phillips Curve as total spending increases, and a long-run shift in the Phillips Curve as the nation's incentive in its capability to produce or its incentive to produce increases.

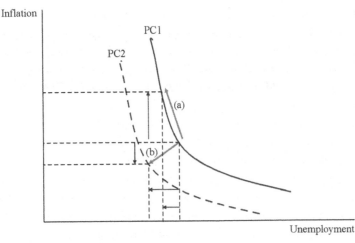

a. Movement along the Phillips Curve as spending increases (inflation rises, unemployment falls)

b. Movement to a new Phillips Curve as the capability and/or incentive to produce increases (inflation falls, unemployment falls)

c. Vice versa applies in both cases

FIGURE 13-1. The Phillips Curve

The location of the Phillips Curve is determined by the capacity and the incentive of the economy to produce. It shows a trade-off between unemployment and inflation.

Source: Mikel Cohick.

What Does the Macro Model Look Like?

From the Phillips Curve, we can proceed to build a model of the economy. To build the model we shall focus on the **employment rate**, instead of the unemployment rate.

Define the employment rate to be 100 percent minus the unemployment rate.

Once we do that, the resulting Phillips Curve would appear as a mirror image to the one shown in **Figure 13-1**. In either case, the location of the Phillips Curve at any one time is fixed by the by the capability and the incentive of the economy to produce.

Short run changes in total spending in the nation's economy cause a movement along this Phillips Curve. Since the location of this Phillips Curve is determined by the nation's capability and incentive to produce, it traces out the nation's supply-side. Economists renamed this line the **aggregate supply (AS) curve,** the mirror image of the Phillips Curve.

We show the nation's desire to spend by a downward sloping line that crosses the AS line at the point indicated by the current measurements of the inflation rate and the employment rate. This line is the **aggregate demand (AD) curve.** This line slopes downward and to the right because the nation can and will want to buy larger quantities of goods and services at lower inflation rates and smaller quantities at higher inflation rates. It follows that for the nation to buy more, then more must be produced, and more employment will be needed.

Figure 13-2 shows this model in the short run, where the nation's capability and incentive to produce do not change. The intersection of AD and AS occurs at the current measurements of the inflation rate and the employment rate.

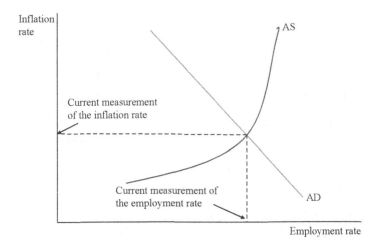

FIGURE 13-2. The Macro Model

The intersection of aggregate demand (AD) and aggregate supply (AS) occurs at the current measurements of the inflation rate and the employment rate.

Source: Mikel Cohick.

We desire this model to not only be understandable, but also to describe, in a timely manner, the current conditions and trends in the economy. There are three interrelated variables of concern to macroeconomics: changes in the inflation rate, changes in the unemployment rate, and changes in real gross domestic product (real GDP).

Of these three variables, two (inflation rate and unemployment rate) for a particular month are reported in final form during the following month. One (real GDP) is reported quarterly. It is reported in preliminary form at the end of the month following that quarter. The real GDP report is updated twice with added information and the final report of real GDP is not made public until the end of the quarter following the quarter reported upon. For example, consider the data report for December 2020 (end of fourth-quarter 2020). During January 2021, final reports of the unemployment rate and the inflation rate became available. At the end of January 2021, a preliminary report of real GDP for the fourth-quarter 2020 became available. This report was modified twice before the final report of real GDP for the fourth-quarter 2020, which was reported at the end of March 2021, 3 months after the end of the quarter of interest.

Since the inflation rate and the unemployment rate are quickly available, we use those variables on the axes of the model instead of Real GDP. To be able to track movements in the economy with reliable new data as soon as possible, this model relies on the inflation rate as the variable on the y-axis and the employment rate as the variable on the x-axis. We choose the employment rate, instead of the unemployment rate, so that improvements in employment are shown as movements to the right, which parallels improvements in real GDP.

What Causes Movement in the Macro Model?

There are four types of movements in this model.

Two are short-run phenomena caused by changes in total spending. **Figure 13-3** shows these movements.

When an increase in total spending occurs, AD shifts to the right along the stationary AS curve, and the employment rate rises (unemployment falls) and the inflation rate rises.

When a decrease in total spending occurs, AD shifts to the left along the stationary AS curve, and the employment rate falls (unemployment rises) and the inflation rate falls.

The other two are long-run phenomena caused by changes in the capability and/or incentive of the nation to produce. **Figure 13-3** also shows these movements.

When an increase in the capacity and/or the incentive to produce occurs, AS shifts to the right along the stationary AD curve, and the employment rate rises (unemployment falls) and inflation rate falls.

When a decrease in the capacity and/or the incentive to produce occurs, AS shifts to the left along the stationary AD curve, and the employment rate falls (unemployment rises) and inflation rate rises.

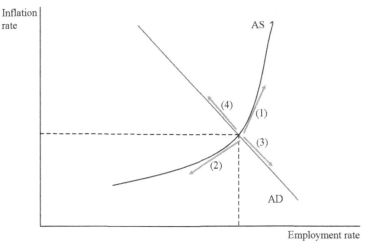

1. Total spending increases (AD shifts right)

2. Total spending decreases (AD shifts left)

3. The capacity and/or incentive of the nation to produce increases (AS shifts right)

4. The capacity and/or incentive of the nation to produce decreases (AS shifts left)

FIGURE 13-3. Movements in the Macro Model

There are four movements. Two, indicated by (1) and (2), happen because there is a net change in total spending and AD shifts in the short run. Two, indicated by (3) and (4), happen when there is a change in the nation's capability to produce or a change in the nation's incentive to produce, and AS shifts in the long run.

Source: Mikel

Cohick.

Of the four movements above, the short-run movements, labeled (1) and (2), occur when there is no change in the capability or the incentive for the economy to produce, but there is a change in the total spending of the economic participants.

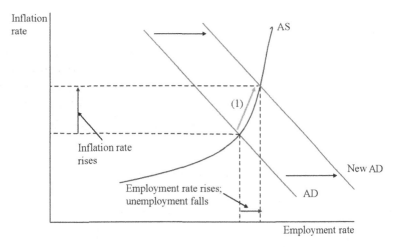

FIGURE 13-4. Results Due to an Increase in Total Spending

An increase in net spending results in a shift in AD to the right. This movement, labeled (1), results in rising inflation, lowering unemployment and increased employment.

Source: Mikel Cohick.

An increase in total spending will cause a movement upward and to the right in the model, labeled (1), causing the inflation rate to rise, the unemployment rate to fall and the employment rate to rise. **Figure 13-4** shows this trade-off.

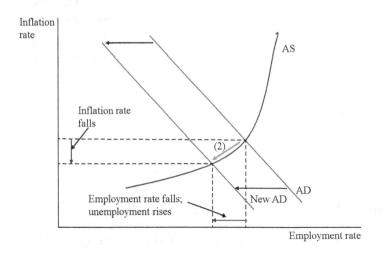

FIGURE 13-5. Results Due to a Decrease in Total Spending

A decrease in net spending results in a shift in AD to the left. This movement, labeled (2), results in decreasing inflation, rising unemployment and lowering employment.

Source: Mikel Cohick.

Conversely, a decrease in total spending will cause a movement downward and to the left in the model, labeled (2), causing the inflation rate to fall, the unemployment rate to rise and the employment rate to fall. **Figure 13-5** shows this trade-off.

Shifts in the AS curve, labeled (3) and (4), are long-run changes. They take more time to implement and have a longer-lasting impact on the economy.

If anything occurs that either lowers production costs (reduced business taxes, decreased costs of complying with government regulations, or lower input costs) or increases productivity (improved human capital, innovation, implementation of new technology, increased incentive to work more or harder, lower personal taxes on work), then the capability or the incentive of the economy to produce increases. This causes a shift of the AS curve to the right along the stationary AD curve in the model, labeled (3). Both the unemployment rate and the inflation rate will decrease and the employment rate will increase. **Figure 13-6** shows this.

If anything occurs that raises production costs (higher business taxes, increased costs of complying with government regulations, or higher input costs) or decreases productivity (degraded human capital, technological obsolescence, decreased incentive to work more hours or harder, higher personal taxes on work) then the capability or the incentive of the economy to produce decreases. This causes a shift of the AS curve to the left along the stationary AD curve in the model, labeled (4). Both the unemployment rate and the inflation rate will increase and the employment rate will decrease. **Figure 13-7** shows this.

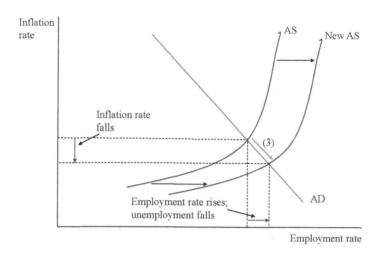

FIGURE 13-6. Results of an Increase in the Capacity/Incentive to Produce

An increase in either the capacity or the incentive to produce results in a shift of AS to the right. This shift, labeled (3), results in decreasing inflation, rising employment, and lowering unemployment.

Source: Mikel Cohick.

What Are Some Real-World Examples Using the Macro Model?

AD shifts right

The AD curve will move to the right in the macro model when total spending in the economy increases.

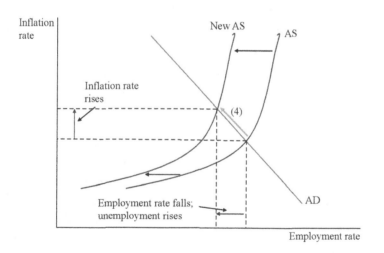

FIGURE 13-7. Results of a Decrease in the Capacity/Incentive to Produce

A decrease in either the capacity or the incentive to produce results in a shift of AS to the left. This shift, labeled (4), results in increasing inflation, decreasing employment and increasing unemployment.

Source: Mikel Cohick.

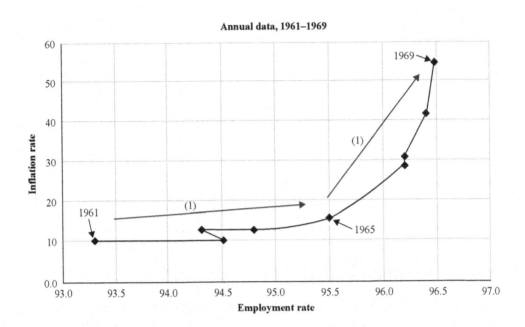

FIGURE 13-8. The 1960's

In the 1960's, there was an increase in total spending, especially in government spending, as President Lyndon Johnson initiated the War on Poverty and expanded the War in Vietnam. After 1965, this accelerated the economy into the overheated region where the inflation rate rose rapidly.

Source: Mikel Cohick.

A good example of this occurred in the mid to late 1960's as government spending increased rapidly in response to funding the escalation of the War in Vietnam and the increased government spending for the Great Society and the War on Poverty. This movement, labeled (1), is shown in **Figure 13-8**.

Note: In Figure 13-8 through Figure 13-12, the data points represent the intersections of AD and AS on the dates indicated. Thus, each graph shows how the economy moved from one time to the next.

AD shifts left

The AD curve will move to the left when total spending in the economy decreases. A good example of this occurred during the onset of the Great Depression from 1929 to 1932. The following adverse actions occurred: high tariffs implemented in 1929 decreased exports; a tight money policy by the Federal Reserve, coming on top of bank failures due to bad loans, decreased credit spending by both businesses and consumers; the stock market crash diminished wealth and decreased consumer spending; and the government, trying to balance its budget in the face of falling tax revenues, decreased government spending, and increased tax collections. Thus, total spending decreased. As a result, unemployment soared to 24 percent by 1932. The shift was so drastic that inflation rates were all negative, that is, deflation occurred. This movement, labeled (2), is shown in **Figure 13-9**.

A similar, but not so drastic, event occurred during the Great Recession of 2008-2009. A housing bubble grew when the Federal Reserve held interest rates abnormally low, causing more people to become home buyers, enticed by low mortgage rates. At the same time, Congress urged lenders to offer mortgages to

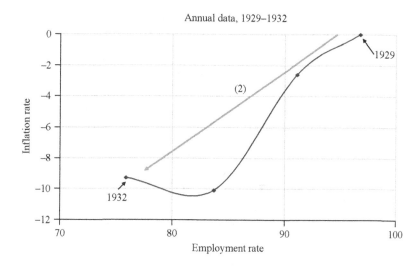

FIGURE 13-9. The Great Depression

The worldwide economic downturn, known as the Great Depression, saw a significant decrease in total spending as huge numbers of people were thrown out of work. Note that the unemployment rate climbed to 24 percent (employment at 76 percent). Deflation occurred as the inflation rate turned negative.

Source: Mikel Cohick.

people who ordinarily would not qualify for such a loan. Mortgages were offered at a low starter interest payment which would "balloon" after a couple of years. Semi-government agencies—Fannie Mae and Freddie Mac—were charged with "backing" these riskier loans.

To service these loans, mortgage firms repackaged the individual mortgages into financial instruments, called mortgage-backed securities (MBS), with varying degrees of risk of non-payment. All of this caused an increase in the demand for housing and housing prices skyrocketed in parts of the country.

When the housing bubble popped and overvalued houses were dumped onto the market, prices fell dramatically. Many mortgage payers found that they were "underwater," that is, they owed more than the house could sell for. When payments of interest and on the principle came due, other mortgage payers found that they could no longer pay their mortgages.

Holders of the risky mortgage-backed securities began to see their assets devalue rapidly and they needed a bail out by the Federal government. All of this caused a significant slowdown in the economy, with large parts of society decreasing their spending and opting to pay down debt instead of spending. Companies failed and layoffs occurred.

This led to the Federal government bailing out other companies, for example, in the automobile industry. The result was a large decrease in total spending in the economy. **Figure 13-10** shows this decrease in spending and a movement, labeled (2), in the macro model. Vast increases in government spending could not offset this trend.

The examples above represent short-run movements in the model. Next, we identify examples of long-run movements as the nation changes its capacity and incentive to produce.

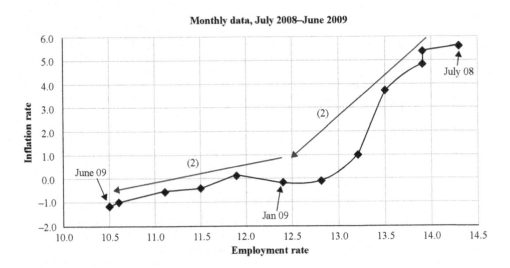

FIGURE 13-10. The Great Recession

During the economic downturn in 2008 and 2009, called The Great Recession by some, many saw their wealth decrease rapidly as their assets, such as houses and stocks, lost value and many lost their jobs as firms cut back or went bankrupt. Thus, there was a huge decrease in net spending, shown as a movement, labeled (2). The implementation of three government stimulus plans failed to reverse this trend.

Source: Mikel Cohick.

AS shifts left

Rising input costs will cause a movement in the model to the left which leads to higher unemployment, higher inflation, and lower employment. Increases in the price of crude oil on the worldwide market were the cause of "supply shocks" in 1973–1974, in 1979–1980 and, to a lesser extent, in 2002–2003. A negative "**supply shock**" occurs when input prices rise and the producers using those inputs are faced with rising costs of producing their products.

In 1973–1974, the price of a barrel of crude oil tripled, caused by the nationalization of the oil fields by oil-producing countries and the embargo on shipments of oil, imposed by Arab oil producers in response to the West backing Israel against the Arabs in a war. The input costs of producing energy products and subsequently of producing nearly every product rose rapidly. The 1973–1974 movement on the model, labeled (4), is shown in **Figure 13-11**.

This situation occurred again in 1979–1980 when the price of a barrel of crude oil doubled, caused by the revolution in Iran. The revolutionaries cut off shipments of oil to the west. Again, input costs rose rapidly and the result in the economy was like the 1973–1974 situation. In 2002–2003, impending war in Iraq led to expectations of higher oil prices, which were realized. Again, input costs rose and the subsequent increases in inflation and unemployment occurred just as before.

AS shifts right

In 1982-83, 1984-86, 1992-94, and 1996-97, enormous productivity gains due to the implementation of new technology, deregulation, and decreasing business and individual tax rates caused a movement to

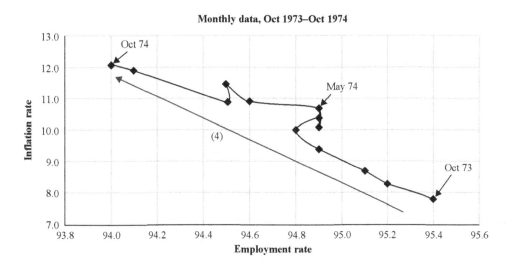

FIGURE 13-11. Supply Shock

The "supply shock" that occurred when the price of oil tripled in 1973 and 1974 caused a movement, labeled (4), as AS shifted left, with significantly rising inflation and increased unemployment (decreased employment).

Source: Mikel Cohick.

the right, labeled (3), in the macro model. In each situation, this led to a lower inflation rates, a lower unemployment rate, and a higher employment rate. Data from 1996–1997 showing this can be seen in **Figure 13-12**. Graphs of the other periods would appear similar.

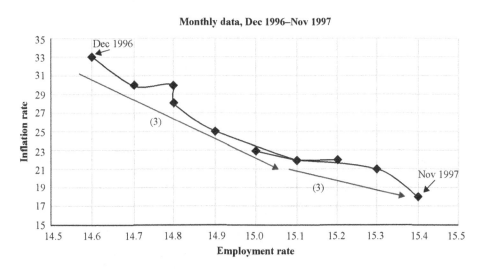

FIGURE 13-12. Favorable Supply-Side Shift

AS shifted right several times in the mid-1980's and 1990's due to lowered tax rates, which increased the incentive to produce, and significant improvements in technology, which also increased the capability to produce. This led to a movement, labeled (3), with lowered inflation rates, rising employment, and decreasing unemployment. This is shown using events of 1996–1997 as an example.

Source: Mikel Cohick.

Can AD and AS Shift at the Same Time?

The macroeconomy is dynamic in that there is change occurring all the time. AD and AS can shift independently of each other. Therefore, they can shift at the same time.

Prior to the COVID-19 pandemic, the economy had been in macro equilibrium from the autumn of 2016 to March 2020. The unemployment rate hovered around 3.8 percent and the inflation rate stayed between 2 and 3 percent. In 2017, legislation reduced tax rates for businesses and individuals and decreased governmental regulation of businesses. In response, both AD and AS shifted to the right. The unemployment rate stayed at or below the full-employment rate while the effects of inflation seen in a type (1) AD shift and a type (3) AS shift canceled each other out.

Figure 13-13 shows changes in employment and inflation during the COVID-19 induced recession and recovery. In the spring of 2020, the COVID-19 pandemic hit the economy. In response, the government ordered a lockdown of major parts of the economy. Consumer and business spending decreased significantly, causing AD to shift left. Businesses were forced to close their doors, lay off workers, and decrease production, causing AS to shift left. As shown on **Figure 13-13**, both contributed to a huge increase in the unemployment rate, but again the effect of these shifts on inflation canceled out.

Massive increases in government spending in response to COVID-19 stimulated demand and caused AD to shift right (AD was also reacting to large increases in the money supply by the Fed). AS began to shift right in response to the rising demand for goods and services, but continued restrictions imposed by government slowed its progress. Also contributing to the slowness of the rightward shift

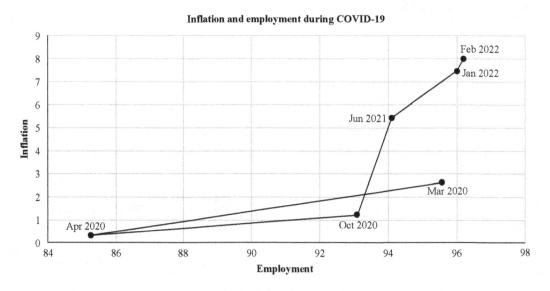

FIGURE 13-13. Inflation and Unemployment During COVID-19.

AD and AS both shifted sharply left due to the lockdowns combatting COVID-19 in the Spring of 2020, resulting in a substantial increase in unemployment. Massive government spending turned this around beginning in April 2020 as AD shifted to the right and AS followed. Excessive increased government spending and excessive increase in the money supply after October 2020 led to rising inflation thereafter.

Source: Mikel Cohick.

of AS were supply chain bottlenecks for many items such as computer chips, paper products, and finished consumer goods, and government disincentives for people to return to the workplace, where government payments to unemployed people were higher than the wages they might receive if they went back to work.

Since AD shifted right faster than AS, the net result was a significant rise in inflation in 2021 and 2022 to levels not seen since the early 1980s.

What Is the Macroeconomic Goal?

Recall from Chapter 10, that there is an unemployment rate, called full employment, which includes only frictional and structural unemployment, but no cyclical unemployment. **The goal of macroeconomic policy is to reach full employment.** At this point, the economy is on its institutional production possibilities curve.

The full employment rate has several names. It is called by some the natural rate of unemployment, indicating that the economy, left to its own devices, will ultimately adjust to reach this rate of unemployment, via self-correction in a vibrant market economy, was discussed earlier.

Economists also call this rate the "non-accelerating inflation rate of unemployment." This term implies that if the unemployment rate drops below the full-employment rate, inflation will accelerate upward. We show this point on the macro model as a vertical line, and name it the Long-Run Aggregate Supply (LRAS) curve. In the long run, after all adjustments have been made to accommodate changes in spending, capacity, and incentive, the economy will rest on this line. In the long run, then any changes in inflation will not affect the full-employment rate.

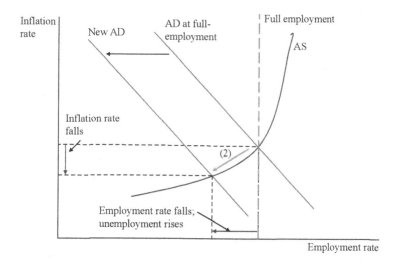

FIGURE 13-14. From Full Employment to an Underperforming Economy

The full-employment line crosses the AS at the point where the trade-off between unemployment and inflation changes. The economy can move from full-employment to the left of the full-employment line, into an underperforming economy. This usually occurs with movement, labeled (2). Then unemployment becomes the major problem.

Source: Mikel Cohick.

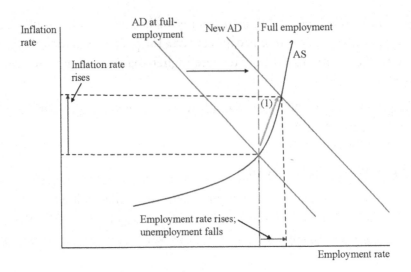

FIGURE 13-15. From Full Employment to an Overheated Economy

The full employment line crosses the AS at the point where the trade-off between unemployment and inflation changes. The economy can move from full employment to the right of the full-employment line, into an overheated economy. This usually occurs with the movement labeled (1). The inflation becomes the major problem.

Source: Mikel Cohick.

Figure 13-14 shows LRAS, the full-employment line, as a vertical dashed line. This shows up in the macro model where the AS curve suddenly climbs upward faster than before. We can identify the region on the model that lies to the left of this point the **underperforming region**, when unemployment is too high, and inflation rises as a slow rate. We can identify the region on the model that lies to the right of this point the **overheated region**, when unemployment is too low, and inflation rises as a rapid, accelerating rate.

Figure 13-15 also shows the full-employment line as a vertical dashed line. To its right, the economy is overheated and inflation is the major problem; employment is too high, and unemployment is abnormally low. A large increase in inflation accompanies a small rise in employment (and decrease in unemployment), and vice versa.

In Chapter 10, full employment was identified as an unemployment rate of about 4 percent, which corresponds to an employment rate of about 96 percent. The location of the full-employment rate can change as institutional impediments to hiring and production change. Also, location of the full-employment rate can change as frictional and structural unemployment changes. If there are more impediments or if either frictional or structural unemployment increases, full employment will occur at a higher rate of unemployment (a lower employment rate). If there are fewer impediments or if either frictional or structural unemployment decreases, full employment will occur at a lower rate of unemployment (a higher employment rate).

What Is Next?

We see how the economy changes. It is quite dynamic. Eighter the AD curve or the AS curve or both are in motion most of the time. The status of the economy can be in one of three configurations:

The economy can be underperforming, that is, operating inside its institutional PPC (see Chapter 10) and to the left of the full-employment line (see above). Unemployment is the major problem. The decisions of over 300 million economic players will tend to cause the economy to self-correct back to the institutional PPC and full employment.

The economy can be overheated, that is, operating outside the institutional PPC and to the right of the full-employment line. Inflation is the major problem. The decisions of those 300 million economic players will tend to cause the economy to self-correct back to the institutional PPC and full employment.

The economy can be performing exactly at the institutional PPC and on the full-employment line. Neither inflation nor unemployment is a problem. This is the **macroeconomic policy goal**.

Since achieving this goal, coming from either an underperforming economy or an overheated economy, takes quite a long time, our impatient society will call on its agent – government – to do something to speed up the process. To do this, government policies have to be formed, enacted, and implemented. We will study these policies in the next chapter.

SUMMARY

1. **Describe the trade-off inherent in the Phillips Curve.**

   The Phillips Curve demonstrates the trade-off between unemployment and inflation. As the economy moves along its Phillips Curve upward and to the left, the unemployment rate decreases and the inflation rate increases. As the economy moves along its Phillips Curve downward and to the right, the unemployment rate increases and the inflation rate decreases.

2. **Using the macro model, tell what causes a movement upward and to the right, leading to higher employment and higher inflation.**

   Increased spending by any or all of the economic participants—consumers, business investments, government, or exports—will cause a movement upward and to the right in the macro model. This leads to higher employment (lower unemployment rates) and rising inflation rates.

3. **Using the macro model, tell what causes a movement downward and to the left, leading to lower employment and lower inflation.**

   Decreased spending by any or all of the economic participants – consumers, business investments, government, or exports—will cause a movement downward and to the left in the macro model. This leads to lower employment (higher unemployment rates) and decreasing inflation rates.

4. **Using the macro model, tell what causes a movement downward and to the right, leading to higher employment and lower inflation.**

   Anything that increases the capability of the nation to produce or that increases the incentive of the nation to produce will cause a movement downward and to the right, leading to higher employment (lower unemployment rates) and lower inflation rates. There is increased capability and/or incentive of the nation to produce when costs are lowered (production costs, input costs, business taxes, and compliance with government regulations), when new technology is implemented, or when personal taxes on work are lowered.

5. **Using the macro model, tell what causes a movement upward and to the left, leading to lower employment and higher inflation.**

   Anything that decreases the capability of the nation to produce or that decreases the incentive of the nation to produce will cause a movement upward and to the left), leading to lower employment (higher unemployment rates) and higher inflation rates. There is decreased capability and/or incentive of the nation to produce when costs are increased (production costs, input costs, business taxes, and compliance with government regulations), when technology becomes obsolete, or when personal taxes on work are raised.

6. Describe the macroeconomic goal.

Congress declared that, as an agent of society, the government shall take necessary action to achieve full employment. This is the economic goal. Recall that full employment means that there exists only frictional unemployment and structural unemployment. No cyclical unemployment exists at the full-employment level. The economy would be at its institutional PPC. On the macro model, full employment occurs when the trade-off between unemployment and inflation changes character. In an underperforming economy, the unemployment rate can drop rapidly with only a small trade-off in the inflation rate. In an overheated economy, further reductions in the unemployment rate would come at large increases in the inflation rate. Inflation is accelerating. The full-employment point in the macro model occurs where this transition in the unemployment-inflation trade-off takes place.

Homework Chapter 13

Name _____

DESCRIPTIONS

Match the key terms with the descriptions.

_____ Shows the short-run trade-off between a change in the inflation rate and a change in the unemployment rate.

_____ Improved human capital, innovation, implementation of new technology, increased incentive to work more, or harder.

_____ Degraded human capital, technological obsolescence, decreased incentive to work more, or harder.

_____ Lower business taxes, decreased regulatory costs, and lower input costs.

_____ Higher business taxes, increased regulatory costs, and higher input costs.

_____ Government programs were initiated as part of the "War on Poverty."

_____ High tariffs, a tight money policy, stock market crash, decreased government spending, and decreased credit spending.

_____ Embargo of oil shipments, causing the price to triple.

_____ Total of frictional and structural, but not cyclical, unemployment.

_____ Economy operates inside its institutional PPC with cyclical unemployment.

_____ Economy operates outside its institutional PPC with inflation.

_____ Both employment rate and inflation rate fall.

_____ Both employment rate and inflation rate rise.

_____ Employment rate falls, inflation rate rises

_____ Employment rate rises, inflation rate falls.

KEY TERMS

1. Actions that made the Great Depression worse.
2. Events that decrease production costs
3. Events that increase production costs
4. Full employment or the natural rate of unemployment
5. Overheated economy
6. AD shifts right
7. AD shifts left
8. AS shifts right
9. AS shifts left
10. Supply side shock
11. The Great Society.
12. The Phillips Curve
13. Things that decrease productivity
14. Things that increase productivity
15. Underperforming economy

1. What determines the position of the Phillips Curve and the Aggregate Supply (AS) Curve?

2. What will cause the economy to experience (a) a shift of AD to the right; (b) a shift of AD to the left?

3. What will cause the economy to experience (a) a shift of AS to the right; (b) a shift of AS to the left?

4. What shift must occur so you would expect the economy to experience (a) a decrease in inflation and an increase in unemployment; (b) an increase in inflation and a decrease in unemployment?

5. What sift must occur so you would expect the economy to experience (a) an increase in inflation and an increase in unemployment; (b) a decrease in inflation and a decrease in unemployment/

6. Why isn't full employment a zero rate of unemployment?

7. Why is LRAS a vertical line in the macro model?

14 Macroeconomic Policies

A policy is a plan of action taken to resolve a problem. The government implements a macroeconomic policy to achieve full employment with stable prices. The macroeconomic problems to be addressed are substantial unemployment and accelerating inflation rates. They are not acceptable as policy goals. In Chapter 13, we added the full-employment line to the macro model at a point where the trade-off between a **decreasing** unemployment rate and an increasing inflation rate became much worse.

It might be useful for the reader to review **Figures 13-14 and 13-15**.

To the left of the full-employment line, the economy is underperforming, and unemployment is the main problem. To "fix" this problem, the government could implement a short-run policy that promotes increased total spending. Such a policy can increase GDP, increase employment, and decrease unemployment at a cost of modestly increasing inflation, while the economy returns to the full-employment state.

To the right of the full-employment line, the economy is overheated, and the main problem is inflation. Increased total spending will aggravate the problem as it will cause inflation to increase more rapidly. To "fix" this problem, the government could implement a short-run policy that promotes decreased total spending. Such a policy will reduce GDP and reduce inflation at a cost of increasing unemployment, while the economy returns to the full-employment state.

Alternatively, the government could implement a long-run policy to address the problem.

What policies are available that the government can choose to "fix" the economy? We will explore government policies, both short-run and long-run, in this chapter.

When you are finished studying this chapter, you should be able to:

1. Identify the three macroeconomic policy options available to the government.
2. Describe who conducts fiscal policy and how it is done.
3. Tell how increasing the Federal budget deficit could lead to "crowding out."
4. Describe the connection between the Federal budget deficit and the national debt.
5. Tell what type of fiscal policy should be implemented in an underperforming economy,
6. Tell what type of fiscal policy should be implemented in an overheated economy.

7. Identify existing laws counteract the movement in the economy and thereby automatically stabilize the business cycle,

8. Describe who conducts monetary policy and how it is done.

9. Tell what type of monetary policy should be implemented in an underperforming economy.

10. Tell what type of monetary policy should be implemented in an overheated economy.

11. Outline how the implementation of supply-side policy differs from the implementation of either fiscal or monetary policy.

12. Tell why supply-side policy should focus only on causing a rightward shift of AS on the macro model (but not a leftward shift of AS).

What Economic Policies Are Available to the Government?

In Chapter 12, we described how an economy experiencing unacceptable amounts of either inflation or unemployment will self-correct, but the long period of time it takes to do this might not be acceptable to members of society. Society will call upon government, as its agent, to speed up the process. This chapter explores three policy options available to the government:

Fiscal policy, in which Congress and the President would manipulate Federal government spending and tax laws to solve the macroeconomic problem.

Monetary policy, in which the Federal Reserve would manipulate the money supply and interest rates to solve the macroeconomic problem.

Supply-side policy, in which Congress and the President would manipulate government regulations, incentive programs, and tax laws to expand production capability and provide individuals and businesses motivations to increase the nation's capability to produce and to have an incentive to become more productive and more innovative.

Both fiscal and monetary policies operate by changing total spending and shifting AD on the macro model. Supply-side policy shifts AS to the right on the macro model as well as invigorating long-run economic growth. No government policy should intentionally strive to shift AS to the left on the macro model, because employment decreases and both unemployment and inflation increase in this stagnation scenario. A shift of AS to the left on the model is usually caused by either an outside event, a "supply shock," or by the unintended consequences of government actions designed to confront other, non-economic issues.

What Is Fiscal Policy?

The term "fiscal" refers to the Federal budget. To conduct fiscal policy, the Congress and the President manipulate the Federal budget for the purpose of moving the economy toward the goal of full employment with stable prices.

The budget is created by a series of laws—appropriations bills and tax bills—that are enacted to change the amount of dollars coming into the government's treasury, that is, tax revenues (T), and the amount of dollars going out of the treasury, that is, government spending (G). Obviously, these laws are enacted principally to enable the government to conduct its functions as agent of society and to be able to collect funds to pay the obligations of the government. Making changes to these appropriations and tax bills also can be used to speed up the self-correcting tendencies of the economy when it is underperforming or when it is overheated.

When government spending exceeds tax receipts (G > T), there is a **budget deficit,** and the government must borrow funds to finish paying its obligations. Borrowing by the government increases the demand for funds in the credit market and generates an upward pressure on interest rates. Thus, all borrowers will find borrowing to be more costly. Also, in the short run, since at any time, the supply of funds available to borrow is fixed, increased borrowing by government may lead to fewer loans granted to individuals and business firms in the private sector. This situation is **crowding out**.

The government knows that they will be able to borrow what they need to cover their budget deficit. This is because they will offer to pay a higher interest rate to the lender than the private sector is offering and the risk of loss on government bonds is lower than on corporate bonds. Therefore, increased deficit spending by the government can dampen spending in the private sector, crowding them out of the picture.

All additional borrowing to fund deficit spending adds to the already substantial national debt. The funds that are used to pay the interest on the national debt make up about ten percent of government expenditures. Continued deficit spending and/or an increase in interest rates will cause this portion of government expenditures to rise. Tax dollars used to pay interest on the national debt cannot fund other government expenditures.

Any increase in government spending (G) or decrease in tax revenues (T) will shift AD to the right on the macro model, regardless of intention. Any decrease in government spending (G) or increase in tax revenues (T) will shift AD to the left on the macro model, regardless of intention. For this reason, any change in government spending or tax laws influences the state of the nation's economy, whether there was any intention by Congress or the President to create such an effect.

Any change in G or T can generate a multiplier effect. All added spending, either directly by increased G or indirectly by decreased T (and therefore increased C or I), becomes new income to the producers of the items purchased. They partition their new income into more spending and some saving (the saving leaks out of the circular flow in the short run). More spending becomes someone else's new income, and the cycle continues to repeat, but with smaller additions to income each time.

This multiplier effect is stronger when initiated by government spending than when initiated by a reduction in tax revenues. For the multiplier to be fully effective, there cannot be significant reductions in the spending-income-spending cycle, say, due to sudden excessive saving.

The multiplier effect indicates that the government needs only to get the cycle started to move the economy toward full employment and the natural workings of the economy will do the rest. For this reason, it is said that the government "jump starts" the economy.

What Is Fiscal Policy for an Underperforming Economy?

Unemployment is the big problem. To get the economy moving toward full employment, the Congress and the President can choose to increase G or decrease T. Both will shift AD to the right on the macro model and will trigger the multiplier effect. **Figure 14-1** shows this movement. Both will cause an increase in the budget deficit, and both may lead to higher interest rates and "crowding out." Policy makers must be careful not to increase G or decrease T too much, because the economy could shoot right past the full-employment goal and result in an overheated economy.

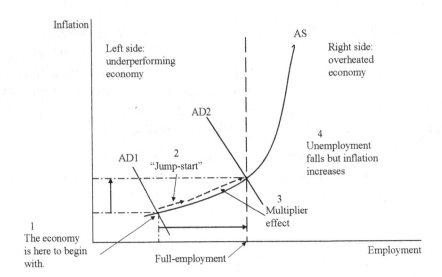

FIGURE 14-1. Fiscal Policy for an Underperforming Economy

Fiscal policy "jumpstarts" the economy to move from an underperforming economy toward full employment. The increased spending is the jumpstart (step 2). Then the multiplier effect takes over (step 3).

Source: Mikel Cohick.

What Is Fiscal Policy for an Overheated Economy?

Inflation is the big problem. To get the economy moving toward full employment, the Congress and the President can choose to decrease G or increase T. Both will shift AD to the left on the macro model and will trigger the multiplier effect. **Figure 14-2** shows this movement. Both will cause a decrease in the budget deficit, and both may lead to lower interest rates and provide some relief for "crowding out." Policymakers must be careful not to decrease G or increase T too much, because the economy could shoot right past the full-employment goal and result in an underperforming economy.

What Are Some Problems with Using Fiscal Policy?

There are time lags in the fiscal policy process. If the Congress and the President are responding to a recession, it usually takes over six months for a recession to be declared officially. The official definition of a recession is an economic downturn that has lasted at least two consecutive quarters.

Many politicians want to expand the role of government, so they would prefer to increase G to fight a recession and increase T to fight inflation. Other politicians think government is already too big and too intrusive in the affairs of the people, so they would prefer to decrease T to fight a recession and decrease G to fight inflation. The ensuing debate might last for several months.

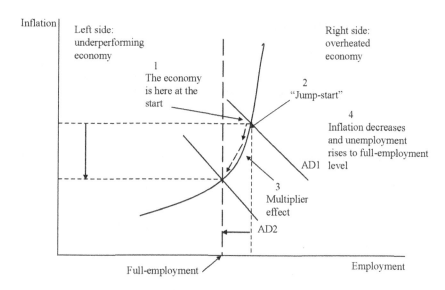

FIGURE 14-2. Fiscal Policy for an Overheated Economy

Fiscal policy "jumpstarts" the economy to move from an overheated economy toward full employment. The decreased spending is the jumpstart (step 2). Then the multiplier effect takes over (step 3).

Source: Mikel Cohick.

When legislation is passed, it takes time for the jumpstart and the multiplier effect to become fully effective. Therefore, the impact of a fiscal policy move may not occur for almost a year after the onset of the problem.

Also, decreasing G and increasing T, for any reason, are politically unpopular decisions.

What Are Automatic Stabilizers?

There are two existing laws that go into effect immediately without Congressional action and that counteract an adverse movement in the economy. They are the laws that authorize **income tax withholding** and **unemployment compensation.**

When a recession begins and people become unemployed, they no longer have income tax withheld from their now non-existent paycheck, so T decreases. Also, they become eligible to receive unemployment compensation, so G increases. The deeper the recession, the stronger these actions become. Reducing T and increasing G are the countermeasures for a recession.

Similarly, when recovery begins and previously unemployed people go back to work, unemployment compensation payments stop, and G decreases. Their first paycheck has income tax withheld, so T increases. The deeper into the recovery and prosperity, the stronger these actions become. Decreasing G and increasing T are the countermeasures for inflation.

These two laws, therefore, stabilize the economy. Their counteraction tends to reduce the depth of a recession and to dampen the exuberance that leads to inflation. The amplitude of the business cycle is less extreme because of these laws.

How Is Monetary Policy Conducted?

To conduct monetary policy, the Federal Reserve will employ one or more of its tools to change the size of the money supply and change interest rates. Those tools, described in Chapter 11, are changing the required reserve ratio, changing the discount rate, Open Market Operations, and paying interest on reserve balances.

What Is Monetary Policy for an Underperforming Economy?

Unemployment is the major problem and inflation is not a problem. The Federal Reserve would conduct an **"easy money" policy (expansionary money policy)**, by either lowering the required reserve ratio, lowering the discount rate, by buying government securities in the open market, or by lowering the administered interest rate on reserve balances.

Lowering the required reserve ratio allows banks to make more loans, as excess reserves grow and required reserves shrink. Lowering the discount rate makes it less expensive for a bank to borrow money from the Fed, and it signals that all interest rates will begin to decrease. Buying government securities in the open market will move money into checking accounts of the sellers of the securities. Thus, the money supply increases, deposits increase, and loan making should increase. Lowering the interest rate paid on reserve balances will lower the Federal Funds rate which leads to lower interest rates across the board, incentivizing more loan making.

The initial action by the Fed will trigger an increase in spending much like the "jumpstart" in fiscal policy. Then the multiplier effect will expand total spending to cause a shift of AD to the right on the macro model toward full employment. **Figure 14-3** shows this movement.

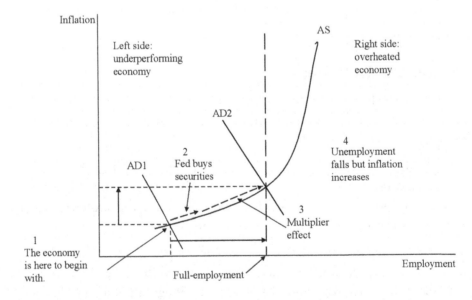

FIGURE 14-3. Monetary Policy for an Underperforming Economy

An easy monetary policy "jumpstarts" the economy to move from an underperforming economy toward full employment. The increased spending is the jumpstart (step 2). Then the multiplier effect takes over (step 3).

Source: Mikel Cohick.

An excessive amount of an "easy money" policy could move the economy out of an underperforming situation and into an overheated situation, moving from unemployment as the main problem to inflation as the main problem.

What Is Monetary Policy for an Overheated Economy?

Inflation is the major problem and unemployment is not a problem. The Federal Reserve would conduct a **"tight money" policy (contractionary money policy)**, by either raising the required reserve ratio, raising the discount rate, by selling government securities in the open market, or by raising the administered interest rate paid on reserve balances. Raising the required reserve ratio forces banks to make fewer loans, as excess reserves shrink and required reserves grow. Raising the discount rate makes it more expensive for a bank to borrow money from the Fed to make more loans, and it signals t that all interest rates will begin to increase. Selling government securities in the open market will move money out of checking accounts of the buyers of the securities. Thus, the money supply decreases, deposits decrease, and loan making will decrease. Raising the interest rate paid on reserve balances will raise the Federal Funds rate which leads to higher interest rates across the board, disincentivizing loan making.

The initial action by the Fed will trigger a decrease in spending much like the "jumpstart" in fiscal policy. Then the multiplier effect will further decrease spending to shift AD to the left on the macro model toward full employment. This movement is shown in **Figure 14-4**.

An excessive amount of a "tight money" policy could move the economy out of an overheated situation and into an underperforming situation, moving from inflation as the main problem to unemployment as the main problem. Many recessions during the past fifty years were preceded by a period of "tight money" policy.

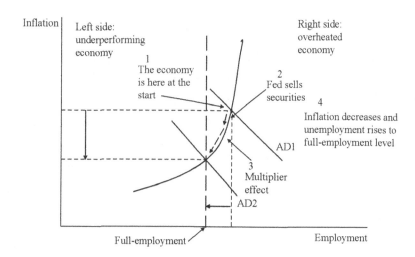

FIGURE 14-4. Monetary Policy for an Overheated Economy

A tight monetary policy "jumpstarts" the economy to move from an overheated economy toward full employment. The decreased spending is the jumpstart (step 2). Then the multiplier effect takes over (step 3).

Source: Mikel Cohick.

What Is Supply-Side Policy?

The purpose of supply-side policy is to increase the capability and incentive of the nation to produce and to shift AS to the right on the macro model. This will lower both the inflation rate and the unemployment rate and raise the employment rate, while at the same time promoting long-run economic growth. **Figure 14-5** shows this movement.

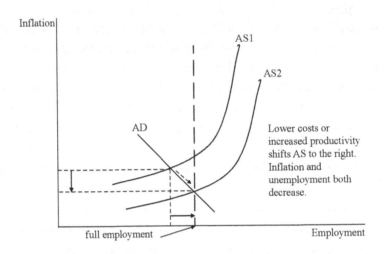

FIGURE 14-5. Supply-Side Policy

Supply-side policy is designed to shift the AS Curve. Government should only adopt a policy that shifts the AS curve to the right, as shown in this figure, causing a triple good: increased GDP, lower inflation, and lower unemployment. Government should never consciously adopt a policy that shifts the AS curve to the left, causing a triple "bad": lower GDP, rising inflation, and increased unemployment.

Source: Mikel Cohick.

At no time should a government policy intentionally strive to shift AS to the left on the macro model. This would be an **adverse supply-side shift**. This is **stagflation**, the simultaneous occurrence of rising unemployment rates, rising inflation rates, and stagnating economic growth.

An example of this "triple bad" occurred in the 1970s as a result of adverse outside influences, such as the two major oil shocks, and the unintended consequences of government policies designed to remedy other problems, such as the implementation of government regulations designed to remedy major pollution problems, to remedy unsafe workplaces, and increased payroll taxes designed to bail out a failing Social Security system. All these influences contributed, along with the increase in resource (especially crude oil) prices, to a shift of AS to the left on the macro model, resulting in stagflation.

A deliberate government policy to shift AS to the right on the macro model would be a **favorable supply-side shift,** and will result in a lower inflation rate, a lower unemployment rate, and, at the same time, promote long-run economic growth.

Government policies aimed at lowering production costs include reducing business taxes and decreasing the costs of complying with government regulations. Government policies aimed at increasing productivity include providing an incentive for individuals to work more or harder, providing incentives to improve human capital, and encouraging firms and individuals to innovate and to implement new technology. All of these will either lower the costs of production, or expand the capability to produce, or both.

What Are the Effects of Changing the Tax Laws?

Creating a greater reward for effort is of significant importance to increase the incentive to work more or harder and to increase the incentive for individuals to innovate. Lowering the tax rates provides this incentive. Earners get to keep more of their income.

When President Kennedy came to office in 1961, the marginal tax rate in the top tax bracket was 91% percent and the tax rates in all other tax brackets were proportionately high. A worker in the top tax bracket, if offered an opportunity to work extra hours with an added payment of $1,000, would end up paying $910 in added tax and get to keep just $90 as his reward for the added work. President Kennedy started action that resulted in getting lower tax rates for all tax brackets, with the top tax bracket falling to 70 percent. Now, that worker would pay only $700 in tax and keep $300. His reward for the same effort tripled, changing the decision to do the work from no to yes.

Later, in the 1980s, President Reagan initiated action to again lower the tax rates for all tax brackets. This time, the top rate dropped to 28 percent during his last year in office. Now that worker would pay $280 in tax and keep $720, more than doubling his reward for that effort. Lowering tax rates enables earners to keep more of what they earn and gives them incentive to work more and harder, to innovate, and to invest in new technology.

It is safe to assume that most high-income earners do not wish to pay higher taxes. They employ tax accountants and tax lawyers to find ways of legally sheltering their income from the tax collector. They lobby Congress to provide them special tax breaks. All this tax avoidance activity is a costly use of resources that could be used to produce desired goods and services. However, if at lower tax rates, the reduction on their tax bill exceeds the cost of avoiding taxes, it becomes cost-beneficial for those taxpayers to simply pay their taxes instead of trying to avoid paying them. The higher the tax rates, more of this tax-avoidance activity will occur.

As a result, lowering tax rates on high-income earners may increase the tax revenues collected from this group by the government. Additionally, if the reward for effort is greater, these highly productive earners will produce more and, therefore, earn a higher income, which is subject to tax. So, they may pay more taxes. For the high-income brackets, decreasing the tax rates ultimately could generate higher tax revenue receipts for the government. This is the essence of the **Laffer Curve,** named after economist Arthur Laffer, shown in **Figure 14-6**, which posits that lower tax rates on high-income earners will yield higher tax revenues, and vice versa.

For low- and middle-income earners, there is no possibility they could afford to acquire the tax avoidance schemes available to high-income earners. Therefore, at higher tax rates, these earners simply pay more in tax revenue and at lower tax rates, they pay less. In the 1980s, lowering tax rates resulted in high-income earners paying more taxes, a 51 percent increase in tax revenues from them by the end of the decade, and low- and middle-income earners paying less taxes, an 8.5 percent decrease in tax revenues from them by the end of the decade. This is also shown on the Laffer Curve, which posits that lower tax rates on low-income earners will yield lower tax revenues, and vice versa.

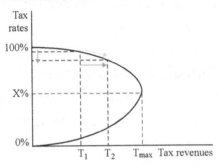

FIGURE 14-6. Laffer Curve

Laffer Curve.

Source: Mikel Cohick.

At 100 percent tax rate, earners hide their income and pay no tax. At 0 percent tax rate, the government collects no tax. Lower the rate from 100 percent or raise the rate up from 0 percent, and government collects some tax. This will continue until the tax rate is X% (exactly what percent that is, is up to conjecture), where the government collects the maximum tax revenue. There was evidence in the 1980s that X percent was in the vicinity of 35 percent. This figure shows a lowering of the tax rate and its subsequent increase in tax revenue.

The political objection to lowering tax rates, especially on the high-income earner, is that the government will receive fewer tax dollars and run a larger budget deficit. In the short run, this is true. In the long run, however, it is possible, as it was in the 1980s, that tax revenues could increase as the economy grows.

Politicians think only in the short run and look only at the short-run response to the tax cut. They can see only that a tax rate reduction reduces tax revenues and expands the budget deficit. They conclude that what is needed to reduce a budget deficit is a tax rate increase. Again, this is true, but it is a disincentive for the nation to produce and its effect will be short-lived. The long-run effect of a tax increase slows down economic growth and generates a shift to the left of both the AD curve and the AS curve.

The Laffer Curve is an example of dynamic tax analysis. People who are taxed react to tax changes. For example, an income earner who thinks the tax increase is too high may engage in tax avoidance schemes and evade paying taxes, or may work less, or invest less. Alternatively, an income earner who is satisfied with a tax rate decrease may reduce or stop using tax avoidance schemes, or work more, or invest more. The potential positive or negative consequences on economic growth depend on where society is on the Laffer Curve. The difficulty is to find the optimum tax rate (the X percent on Figure 14-6).

SUMMARY

1. **Identify the three macroeconomic policy options available to the government,**

   The three macroeconomic policy options available to the government are fiscal policy, monetary policy, and supply-side policy.

2. **Describe who conducts fiscal policy and how it is done.**

   The Congress and the President conduct fiscal policy by changing Federal tax and government spending laws.

3. **Tell how increasing the Federal budget deficit could lead to crowding out.**

   Increasing the Federal budget deficit, by either increasing G or decreasing T, will require the U.S. Treasury Department to borrow more funds from the credit market. Since, at any one time, there is a finite amount of funds available to borrow in the credit market, added borrowing by government may deplete the funds so that private sector borrowing by consumers and businesses may not be able to acquire the funds they need. In effect, they are "crowded out" of the credit market.

4. **Describe the connection between the Federal budget deficit and the national debt.**

   When the Federal government runs a budget deficit, additional borrowing is required. This adds to the already substantial national debt. The most significant impact of increasing the national debt is the need to allocate more tax revenue to the interest payments that go to the holders of the national debt.

5. **Tell what type of fiscal policy should be implemented in an underperforming economy.**

   In order to increase spending in the economy, the appropriate fiscal policy would be to increase G or decrease T. Both will jumpstart the economy in the right direction and then the multiplier effect will go into action.

6. **Tell what type of fiscal policy should be implemented in an overheated economy.**

   In order to decrease spending in the economy, the appropriate fiscal policy would be to decrease G or increase T. Both will jumpstart the economy in the right direction and then the multiplier effect will go into action.

7. **Identify existing laws that counteract the movement in the economy and thereby automatically stabilize the business cycle.**

   The income tax withholding law and the unemployment compensation law go into effect immediately as workers are laid off in a recession. These laws increase G and decrease T in small amounts for each worker laid off and thereby counteract the economic downturn. When recovery begins, for each worker hired back, these laws decrease G and increase T in small amounts, again counteracting the economic upward movement. Because of these laws the peaks and troughs of the business cycle are muted and the cycle's amplification is smaller.

8. Describe who conducts monetary policy and how it is done.

The Federal Reserve System conducts monetary policy by manipulating the size and growth of the money supply, using one of three tools: changing the required reserve ratio, changing the discount rate, or conducting Open Market Operations.

9. Tell what type of monetary policy should be implemented in an underperforming economy.

In an underperforming economy, the Fed would increase the money supply (and thereby induce increased total spending), by lowering the required reserve ratio, lowering the discount rate, or buying securities on the open market.

10. Tell what type of monetary policy should be implemented in an overheated economy.

In an overheated economy, the Fed would decrease the money supply (and thereby induce decreased total spending), by raising the required reserve ratio, raising the discount rate, or selling securities on the open market.

11. Outline how the implementation of supply-side policy differs from the implementation of either fiscal or monetary policy.

Fiscal policy and monetary policy each shift the AD curve along a stationary AS curve toward the macroeconomic goal of full employment. Supply-side policy, in contrast, is designed to shift the AS curve to the right along a stationary AD curve, thereby lowering both the inflation rate and the unemployment rate. While fiscal policy and monetary policy are concerned with short-run growth only, supply-side policy has the added advantage of generating long-run economic growth also.

12. Tell why supply-side policy should focus only on generating a rightward shift of AS on the macro model?

Shifting the AS curve to the right will result in a triple good: lower inflation rates, lower unemployment rates, and long-run economic growth. Shifting the AS curve to the left will result in a triple bad: higher inflation rates, higher unemployment rates, and long-run economic stagnation or decline.

Homework Chapter 14

Name_____

DESCRIPTIONS

Match the key terms with the descriptions.

_____ Congress and the President manipulate Federal government taxes and spending to attempt to solve macroeconomic problems.

_____ Federal Reserve manipulates the money supply and interest rates to solve macroeconomic problems.

_____ Congress and the President manipulate regulations, incentive programs, and tax laws to expand production capability.

_____ Government spending > tax revenues.

_____ Government spending < tax revenues.

_____ When increased government borrowing leads to fewer loans granted to individuals and business firms.

_____ Follow-on economic activity increases the effect on total spending than the original change had.

_____ The decrease in tax collections and increase in unemployment compensation during a downturn with the opposite in a recovery that tends to stabilize the economy.

_____ Deliberate government policy that will generate a shift of AS to the left on the macro model, resulting in increases in both unemployment and inflation.

_____ The tax rates on all income within a certain tax bracket.

_____ The minimum and maximum range of income that is taxed at a one tax rate.

_____ Raising tax rates on producers and production.

_____ The simultaneous occurrence of rising unemployment rates, rising inflation rates, and stagnating economic growth.

_____ Dynamic tax analysis.

KEY TERMS

1. Automatic stabilizers
2. Budget deficit
3. Budget surplus
4. Crowding out effect
5. Fiscal policy
6. Disincentive to produce
7. Marginal tax rates
8. Monetary policy
9. Multiplier effect
10. Stagflation
11. Favorable supply-side policy
12. Adverse supply-side policy
13. Tax bracket
14. Laffer curve

EXERCISES

1. Describe the appropriate fiscal policy for an underperforming economy.

2. Describe the appropriate fiscal policy for an overheated economy.

3. What are the problems with using fiscal policy to stabilize the economy?

4. Describe the appropriate monetary policy for an underperforming economy.

5. Describe the appropriate monetary policy for an overheated economy.

6. Describe the appropriate supply-side policy to counteract stagflation.

15 Economic Growth and Productivity

Economic growth, increased productivity of resources, and an increased standard of living go hand in hand. It should be obvious that several things that contribute to one's standard of living cannot be quantified. They would include experiences, memories, interactions, and the like. Many satisfactions do not require material goods and services. Economic measurements are concerned primarily with the material standard of living. However, without the satisfaction of basic wants and needs, few can aspire to the satisfaction of higher-order, more qualitative wants and needs.

In Chapters 1 and 12, we showed economic growth as an outward movement of the Production Possibilities Curve (PPC). This occurs when a society expands or improves its resource base (including the quality and the quantity of its labor resource) or adopts new or better technology. In this chapter, we discuss how a society can initiate or enhance such an outward movement in its PPC.

After studying this chapter, you should be able:

1. Define the standard of living and tell how it is measured.

2. Describe how the standard of living can be raised.

3. Tell what might lower the standard of living.

4. Describe productivity and tell why it is important.

5. Describe how specialization leads to efficiency.

6. Tell what is necessary for specialization.

7. Define innovation and tell how it increases productivity.

How Is the Standard of Living Determined?

We use standard of living as an indication of our economic well-being. We measure it by computing how much of our total output each person would be able to consume, assuming that the output was divided equally. The total output of the country is its Real Gross Domestic Product (GDP). Real GDP is divided by the population to get a material measure of the standard of living:

$$\text{Standard of Living} = \frac{\text{Total Output (Real GDP)}}{\text{Population}}$$

This measure ignores the distribution of GDP or who gets to consume the output. Like any average, half of the population are above average, enjoying a higher standard of living than those who are below average, having to be satisfied with a lower standard of living.

The average, however, is an effective way to judge the economic well-being of a country. As average output rises, the goods and services produced also rises, and our satisfaction from consuming those goods and services also rises. Fewer wants and needs go unsatisfied, although there will always be scarcity of resources as our wants and needs rise with the passage of time.

The economic goal of about every society is to maximize the output of goods and services that satisfy the wants and needs of its members. This is the same as saying that society wants to improve its standard of living. One of the objectives of government should be to maximize social welfare. One way to increase a society's social welfare is to increase its standard of living. As with many things, the government can best achieve this by increasing the economic freedom of its citizens: protecting private property rights and reducing taxes, regulations, and other restrictions on trade.

Look at the formula above. The standard of living can increase by either a reduction in the population or an increase in the output. While techniques to reduce the population are loaded down with moral problems, few should have a problem with increasing the output in relation to the population. Most countries have a growing population, so a worthy economic goal would be to increase the level of output faster than the population grows.

How Can We Raise the Standard of Living?

If we step back and look at what would make our output grow, we can return to the thinking about the discussion of production possibilities in Chapter 12. A nation's production possibilities are the capacity of its economy for production of goods and services assuming a given level of resources, technology, and economic freedoms. To increase the productive capacity of an economy, we need to increase either the level of resources or the efficiency of using those resources through better technology or more economic freedoms.

To see how increasing the level of resources can raise the standard of living, we need to look at each of the four resource categories: land, labor, capital, and entrepreneurship.

Land is a good example of a resource that is finite. However, increasing the level of technology can improve our ability to extract things from the land. New technology has enabled increased oil extraction from abandoned oil fields that were declared to be depleted. This has increased proven attainable oil reserves more rapidly than the world's current consumption of oil. By using advanced geological techniques, new oil fields were discovered by independent oil producers by drilling much deeper exploratory wells than those previously drilled. The use of hydraulic fracturing (fracking) and horizontal drilling have increased oil and natural gas production in the United States.

The **labor** resource can be increased in several ways. The quantity of labor has increased by immigration, raising the retirement age, and an increase in the number of women entering the workforce. The ability to keep more of one's wages, instead of giving them up in the form of taxes, makes one more likely to want to increase the number of hours worked in a primary job or to take a second job. The quality of labor is increased by education, training, and experience, all of which help improve the output from labor resources.

Investment in new **capital goods** depends upon business managers' expectations about future economic activity but it also must be funded. Higher interest rates make it harder to finance capital expenditures because the overall cost of capital will be higher, requiring higher returns on investment. This procedure was outlined in Chapter 8.

Three sources of funding for capital investments are: (1) households foregoing present consumption and saving their money, (2) the undistributed earnings of businesses, and (3) direct foreign investment in the United States.

While the present savings rate of households (excluding the increase in one's retirement fund and any growth in equity of one's home) is low, both American and foreign corporations have amassed dollar-denominated undistributed earnings. Thus, both American and foreign corporations become sources of funding for a capital investment in the United States. A favorable climate for investment must be maintained to keep these investment funds in, or flowing into, the United States. If a more favorable investing climate exists elsewhere, these funds will flow there instead of the United States. In addition to expectations about future economic growth, the tax and regulatory environment of the U.S. needs to be friendly to business firms considering a capital investment.

A friendly tax and regulatory environment also encourage **entrepreneurial activity**. The easier it is for an entrepreneur to start up a business, the more likely it will happen and the more likely that spark of innovation will be able to blossom and grow into the next Apple, Microsoft, or Google. Who wants to start a business and must deal with excessive government regulation or excessive taxes on their earnings? Several entrepreneurs are immigrants who came to the United States because its economic freedoms were better than in their home country.

How Can We Increase the Level of Technology?

The same economic freedom and environment that encourages entrepreneurship also encourage technology development. Many inventions and innovations come from hungry entrepreneurial companies, who can read the signals the market is sending and can quickly respond. As companies grow ever larger, they become less flexible and more bureaucratic, and thus they are less able to be innovative.

Recall, however, from Chapter 4, that innovation generates clones, competition, and fosters expansion. During this expansion, the successful, low-cost providers of the innovative product flourish and grow while others stumble and fall by the wayside. This failure must also be allowed to happen, because it frees up resources so that the successful firms can grow. The ultimate result is industry maturity dominated by a few large corporations. The situation is then ripe for another innovation to come along. This will only occur in an environment where the government does not protect the mature industries.

How Could the Standard of Living Decline?

A nation can experience a decline in its standard of living if it decreases the availability of its resources, falls behind in technology, or restricts the economic freedom of its citizens to exploit their talents and energy.

One way to decrease resources is to engage in destructive practices, such as war and civil insurrections. As other countries modernize technologically, a country that fails to keep up falls further behind. Stifling bureaucracies and widespread corruption, coupled with poorly defined property rights, make it almost impossible for potential entrepreneurs to get started. Onerous taxes also inhibit the desire of entrepreneurs to operate legally. In countries where these events occur, entrepreneurial, innovative, and productive people flee as fast as they can to other, more favorable climates for business.

What Is Productivity?

Productivity is the key to raising the standard of living. Productivity is measured by comparing output to input, with labor hours as a proxy for input. We define **productivity as output per labor hour worked.**

$$\text{Productivity} = \frac{\text{Output}}{\text{Labor hours}}$$

You are familiar with many productivity measurements: for your car, miles per gallon and miles per hour; for a runner, speed, that is, distance covered per unit of time; for a typist, words per minute; for a football quarterback, passing yards per game; for a student, grade points per credit hour (grade point average); for a dietician, calories per serving.

How can we improve productivity? Three basic ways are: (1) through the reduction of waste, (2) improved efficiency through specialization, and (3) by innovation.

Reducing waste allows more production from the same input of resources. Inefficient processes create waste products in addition to the desired goods. As resources become more expensive, there is more incentive to reduce the waste output and increase the desired goods output. For example, in the past, sawmills produced both boards and sawdust from their input, logs. Sawdust was a waste product, which, if improperly disposed of, polluted rivers. Mill owners innovated by recycling sawdust as an input to a new process and produced particleboard, another profit-making product.

There is an interesting juxtaposition between the agriculture industry and the real estate industry. When land was plentiful, soil conservation was not a priority. As population increased, land became less plentiful relative to the population, so soil conservation became necessary. This and other innovations in agriculture led to a transformation in labor use from one-half of the labor force working in agriculture in 1900 to <2 percent of the labor force currently working in agriculture. Their productivity has increased a hundred-fold. Those no longer destined to work in the agricultural field entered other, newer, more technical fields.

Meanwhile, an increase in population meant that we require more housing, and land use switched from agriculture to residential housing. As the population grew, housing became harder to find depending upon the location and the land for housing became more valuable. One house per sixty acres became one house per five acres, then one house per acre, then four houses per acre, and then eight houses per acre. Finally, multi-family housing was necessary and eventually high-rise multifamily housing became necessary in the larger cities. Land once used for agriculture became housing developments.

How Does Specialization Lead to Efficiency?

There is an old saying: "A jack-of-all-trades is a master of none." This certainly applies to production. As we specialize in one task, we improve the skills necessary to complete the task. Just as athletes and musicians get better with practice so do production workers. The **division of labor—splitting up a job into its component tasks and assigning each task to a separate worker—allows for specialization.** As we concentrate on one particular task, we are focused enough to be able to invent new or better tools or processes specialized for that task. The result is more production per hour, that is, an increase in productivity. On a countrywide basis, as a nation's efficiency increases, productivity increases, and output increases, thus increasing its standard of living.

In what occupation should a worker specialize? What good or service should a business firm or even a whole country specialize in producing? People should seek to find the task at which they have the **comparative advantage** over somebody else. Also, the producer should seek the product where they have a comparative advantage.

Having a comparative advantage means that you can complete the task or produce the product at a lower opportunity cost compared to others. We looked at this concept in an international setting in Chapter 7.

Opportunity cost is what you must give up producing something. Should Stephen King, a famous author, mow his own lawn? Or should he hire a local teenager to mow it? Let us look at the opportunity cost of each, that is, what would each be doing if they were not spending 2 hours mowing grass on King's estate. King's opportunity cost is 2 hours of writing on the next multimillion-dollar bestseller. The teen's opportunity cost is 2 hours of hanging out with his friends. Which one has the lower opportunity cost?

Should the United States manufacture clothing? What is our opportunity cost of producing clothes? We would take the resources out of the production of more valuable products such as aircraft, high-end computer chips, or high-end telecommunications switching equipment. Factories in Asia or Central America manufacture most clothing sold in the United States. The opportunity cost of their clothing workers is giving up subsistence farming, a very inefficient kind of agriculture in small plots of land. The teenager has the comparative advantage over Stephen King in lawn mowing and other countries the comparative advantage over the United States in clothes manufacturing.

As individuals, business firms, or nations, when we specialize in what we do best and become more productive, we gain the financial resources to acquire other things that other individuals, business firms, or nations specialize in producing. We make more of our product than we need and, assuming no governmental restrictions on trade, can trade the excess for other things produced by those that have a comparative advantage in those products. We produce the things in which we have a comparative advantage and buy everything else from someone who has a comparative advantage in those goods and services.

Specialization allows us to use resources that are most suited to produce those goods and thus have a lower opportunity cost. This leads to overall gains for society because more goods are produced at a lower cost of resources. The production is more efficient because it is using fewer resources, which leads to a gain in productivity. As productivity increases, individual producers can increase their earnings while the standard of living of society increases.

What Is Innovation?

Innovation involves the use of technology—the application of knowledge—either to improve a production process or to improve the tools (capital goods) used in the process. Following are examples of how innovation can improve efficiency and result in an increase in productivity.

One way is to **reorganize the production process**. In the early days of the auto industry, all production was done on a "batch mode" basis. Autos were built one at a time. Each auto had a particular place on the factory floor and was built there without any division of labor.

Henry Ford wanted to build an auto so inexpensive that the workers in his factory could afford to buy one knowing that, if his workers could afford to buy a car, then more workers in other trades could as well. Ford reorganized his factory into an assembly line to do this. With the assembly line, the autos were sent through the factory on a conveyer belt and each part was installed by a worker who specialized in that one part, such as an axle, a windshield, or a fender. As workers specialized, they became more proficient and their productivity increased. Autos were completed faster and at a lower unit cost. The workers became more valuable to the firm. Ford recognized this and raised their wages to the highest in the industry at that time.

Another example of a productivity increase due to process reorganization occurred early in World War II. The United States was desperate to rapidly expand its Navy. Henry J. Kaiser, a West Coast shipbuilder, completely reorganized how a ship was built by switching from batch mode to assembly line technology and reduced the time from start to finish from 8 months per ship to 6 weeks per ship.

Another way is to **switch resource inputs.** A firm can lower costs, improve productivity, and reduce pollution by switching its energy source from, say, coal to natural gas.

Repetitive tasks can be accomplished by automating the factory with robotics. This means using machinery and equipment that can be preprogramed to accomplish a number of tasks as part of a production process. In early adoptions of robotics, equipment was programmed using numerical control language, which was fairly time-consuming to accomplish.

Later, computers replaced people to do the programming. The later programs used a simplified programming language which required responses to a series of questions about what the equipment was to accomplish. Then, computer numerical control equipment did the work, which was much easier and less time-consuming. Replacing labor with capital equipment, especially computer-driven capital equipment, was much more efficient. It increased productivity and lowered costs.

A third way is to begin **mass production.** Economies of scale are the benefits a producer gets from larger and larger production runs. A large production run allows a producer to spread the fixed cost of setting up a production line over a larger number of units produced, resulting in lower-than-average cost per unit. Here is an example:

Fixed Costs:	$10,000,000			
Quantity Produced per time period	10,000	100,000	1,000,000	10,000,000
Average Fixed Cost	$1,000	$100	$10	$1

The firm must sell the product for a price that covers the costs of making it, including the fixed cost. At low production rates, the sales price must be quite high and only the very wealthy could afford it. The higher the quantity produced, the lower the price can be, and lower-income people can afford to buy it to satisfy their wants. Also, the firm can compete more favorably in its market.

Most materials and components used in a production process are sold in a manner to encourage large quantity purchases. Component manufacturers incur costs to set up a production line and would like to spread those costs over a long production run and experience economies of scale themselves.

The key benefit of achieving economies of scale is to lower unit production costs. If the buyer of materials or components can buy in large quantities, they and the seller can share the benefits of the seller's economies of scale.

Large firms that mass produce usually have a backlog of orders. They can produce continuously and are able to reduce production downtimes by scheduling production more efficiently. Smaller firms may not have the backlog of orders to support continuous production. Downtimes are costly to both the producer and their idled workforce.

If a producer has multiple product lines, there is an opportunity to improve efficiency and lower costs by standardizing components and subassemblies. For example, if General Motors can use the same frame for several of its brands of vehicles, then they can acquire a larger number of frames from a frame supplier at one time and get the benefit of quantity purchase discounts.

Mass production also allows the producer to use specialized equipment in their factories. The larger the company, the more likely that a highly specialized piece of equipment can be put to beneficial use over an extended period of time. Also, there is less chance that a piece of equipment will become useless to the company if it has multiple functions in the manufacturing process.

Finally, mass production allows more specialization of workers into a particular task. The small factory may have five employees, all of whom must perform several diverse kinds of tasks. As the production grows and more workers are added, then each worker can better concentrate and focus on doing one function in the production process and become more productive.

A fourth way is to introduce **mechanization.** As tasks become more repetitive, machines replace lower-skilled workers, which results in more uniformity of results. Using labor is a better option than mechanizing if rapid changes are needed or if the same part is not produced repeatedly. However, where long production runs are common, using capital (machinery and equipment) results in faster production of better quality products.

The replacement of labor with capital (factory automation) means that low-skill and low-paying jobs usually disappear because machines replace those workers. However, factory automation also results in the creation of more high-skill and higher-paying jobs.

With reduced costs of production, product prices fall as well because of competition among producers. Lower product prices mean that those products that were previously not affordable to the masses are now more affordable so firms will produce more of them to meet the expanding demand. This will result in a greater need for high-skill workers. In summary, while factory automation does change the mix of jobs from low skill to high skill—brawn to brain — it does not reduce the number of jobs in total.

Finally, **mass markets** are created, both domestically and internationally. Selling into a larger market gives producers an opportunity to experience economies of scale and other advantages of mass production. The advantages get passed on to consumers in the form of lower prices. Products become more affordable to more people. A system of distribution that is global in scope allows firms to take advantage of economies of scale and increases the quality of production through standardization. For example, Toyota produces autos for sale in several markets and enjoys the benefits of mass production and mass markets, and has an excellent reputation for quality products that consumers can enjoy at affordable prices. If Toyota could only sell their autos in Japan, then they would not be able to offer the high-quality vehicles at reasonable prices because they would not get the benefits of mass production for mass markets. Selling in markets around the world generates a benefit to consumers everywhere by increasing competition. Increased competition leads to lower prices and improved quality, and by increasing the variety of products from which the consumer can choose.

To recap, reorganizing the production process, switching resource inputs, mass production, mechanization, and mass markets all lead to a gain in efficiency, productivity, and in a nation's standard of living.

Not everything can be mass-produced. Services must be individualized to the customer. Because of this, prices for services increase in lockstep with wages of service workers, while prices for many goods have been decreasing. This may change as innovative use of artificial intelligence robotics are created to perform service tasks. Products in widely scattered markets and products for only a few customers will be custom produced. Arts and crafts are custom made. However, anything that is custom-made will be higher priced than products that are mass- produced.

What Are the Causes of Economic Growth?

The following are causes of economic growth:

- Increased resources
- Expanded capital goods base
- Increased or improved technology
- Increased productivity
- Protection of individual property rights
- Economic freedom
- Improved infrastructure
- Peace and stability
- Low or no political corruption
- A favorable tax climate
- A favorable regulatory climate

Reverse each of the above and you have causes of economic decline.

What Are the Results of Economic Growth?

The results of economic growth are:

- More satisfaction of wants and needs by more people
- Higher standard of living
- Reduced poverty rates

- Improved working conditions
- More leisure time
- Greater concern for the environment
- Greater ability to deal with poverty and environmental problems

Reverse each of the above and you have the results of economic decline.

SUMMARY

1. **Describe the standard of living and tell how it is measured.**

   A society's standard of living is determined by how many satisfactions of wants and needs, material and nonmaterial, its citizens enjoy on average. Economists measure a society's material standard of living by dividing total output (GDP) by population.

2. **Describe how the standard of living can be raised.**

   The standard of living can be raised by increasing the growth of GDP faster than the rate of increase of population. This can be done by increasing the level and quality of resources and increasing the level and quality of technology.

3. **Tell what might lower the standard of living.**

   A nation's standard of living will decrease if its resource base shrinks, if it falls behind in technology, or if it restricts the economic freedom of its citizens.

4. **Define productivity and tell why it is important.**

   Productivity, measured by output per labor hour worked, is the key to raising the standard of living. Increased productivity means that each worker is producing more satisfactions of wants and needs per hour worked.

5. **Describe how specialization leads to efficiency.**

   Specialization—concentrating on one task—causes the worker to improve skills with practice and with innovation. The worker generates less waste, more precision, and new or better processes and tools. All of these lead to a more efficient use of input resources.

6. **Tell what is necessary for specialization.**

   One must identify the task in which he or she has a comparative advantage. This would be a task that he or she can accomplish at a lower opportunity cost than others. The worker should specialize in that task, produce more than he or she needs for personal use, and make trades to exchange the rest to acquire products for which he or she does not have a comparative advantage.

7. **Define innovation and tell how it increases productivity.**

   Innovation is the application of knowledge—technology—to create new methods of production or new tools to use in production. Switching from a batch mode of operation to an assembly line process is one example. Switching from a high-cost input to a lower-cost input is another. Mechanizing the process, standardizing the production unit, and catering to a mass market are other examples.

Homework Chapter 15

Name_____

DESCRIPTIONS

Match the key terms with the descriptions.

_____ Expanding the output of goods and services through increasing the resources used in production, improving the level of technology, and increasing the amount of economic freedoms.

_____ Freedom from excessive taxes, government regulations, and trade restrictions.

_____ Automating the more routine steps in the production process or replacing workers with machines.

_____ Average total costs.

_____ A pool of unfilled orders from which to draw from for continuous production.

_____ Computer-driven and directed capital equipment.

_____ Very large production runs without any downtime.

_____ Using technology – the application of knowledge – either to improve a production process or to improve the tools used in the process.

_____ Building a particular product one at a time, rather than with as assembly line.

_____ Being able to complete a task or produce a product while incurring less opportunity cost.

_____ Increases in efficiency, productivity, and output, thus increasing the standard of living.

_____ Rotating crops to keep good topsoil intact.

_____ Splitting up a job into its component tasks and assigning each task to a separate worker.

_____ Output per unit of input, using labor hours as a proxy for input.

_____ The risk-taking function of recognizing which new products or services have a better chance of commercial success, organizing the production process, and attaining commercial success.

_____ Immigration, raising the retirement age, and increasing the number of people in the labor force.

_____ Household savings, retained earnings of business firms, and direct foreign investment in capital goods.

_____ Output of a nation (GDP) divided by its population or output per person.

KEY TERMS

1. Advantages of specialization
2. Backlog of orders
3. Batch production
4. Comparative advantage
5. Division of labor
6. Economic freedoms
7. Economic growth
8. Entrepreneurship
9. Innovation
10. Mass production
11. Mechanization
12. Productivity
13. Robotics
14. Soil conversation
15. Sources of funding for capital investments
16. Sources of increased labor resources
17. Standard of living
18. Unit production costs

EXERCISES

1. How might a nation's standard of living be raised?

2. What might cause a nation to experience a decline in its standard of living?

3. How can productivity be improved?

4. What is required for specialization and what are its benefits?

5. How do we (an individual or a nation) decide what to specialize in producing?

6. What are the benefits of mass production?

7. What are the benefits of mechanization?

16 Personal Financial Literacy

In the last resort, each of us ends up being responsible for our own actions. So far in this book, the goal was to make you aware of the tools you have available to make decisions to improve your life. Along the way, we informed you on how different elements and institutions of our economy work, how decisions are made in these institutions, and how you can keep informed and maintain awareness of the changes in the economy that engulfs your life.

In this chapter, we introduce you to several institutions and situations that affect you daily and that you will have to deal with, if you are not already doing so, in your personal life. One of the activities many aspire to accomplish is to start up and operate a business. We start with a general overview of business organization, the rights and responsibilities of business operation, and the sources of funds. Then we investigate personal savings and borrowing, how financial markets operate, and how to manage your finances.

After studying this chapter, you should be able to:

1. Describe the rights and responsibilities of starting a business.
2. Describe the role of financial institutions in saving, borrowing, and capital formation.
3. Outline how you can become a wise investor.
4. Tell how you can initiate and maintain a savings program and a checking account.
5. Describe the responsibilities and obligations of borrowing money.
6. Describe how you should manage credit card debt.
7. Describe how you should manage personal bankruptcy, insurance needs, and charitable giving.
8. Describe how you should manage a personal budget.
9. Describe how you should decide whether to rent or to buy a home.
10. Identify what options are available to pay for postsecondary education and training.

What Are the Different Types of Business Ownership?

It is highly likely you will have some connection with a business in your life. At the very least, you will work for a business. It is also possible that you may want to start up your own business. This section outlines the forms of business organizations that exist, along with their characteristics and how they get started.

The two basic questions to answer when selecting the form of business organization will determine which type of business organization is appropriate:

1. Does the owner desire to have taxable earnings passed through to the owner or have those earnings taxed at the business level?

2. Does the owner desire to spend the extra effort and funds to avoid personal responsibility for the firm's liabilities?

Sole proprietorships and general partnerships pass through any taxable income or loss directly to the owner to avoid double taxation but do not protect the owner from personal responsibility for the liabilities of the firm.

Sole proprietorships are one-owner small businesses where the owner is the business. The owner owns the assets of the business and is directly responsible for its liabilities. Sole proprietorships are usually small, have limited access to funds, and the talents and skills available are limited to those of the owner and whomever the owner can hire.

General partnerships have the same characteristics as sole proprietorships except that there are two or more owners with an agreement between them regarding each ones' responsibilities, obligations, and shares of profits and losses. One thing to remember when organizing a partnership is to make sure from the beginning there are provisions to wind down the operation, liquidate the assets and pay the liabilities of the partnership should the partners no longer desire to be in business together. Those provisions should be determined before operations begin while the partners are still on good terms with each other.

Corporations, unless they make provisions otherwise, pay taxes on their taxable income and then the after-tax income is taxed again when distributed to the owners (known as "double taxation"). The owners of a corporation do not have personal responsibility for the corporation's liabilities unless they consent to that responsibility (which may be necessary for a new corporation to obtain a loan). The corporation is a legal entity which directly owns its assets and is directly responsible for its liabilities. The owners of a corporation own shares of the corporation, commonly called stock.

Some organizations are hybrids. The organizations described above represent the main forms of business organization that have existed for hundreds of years. Two new forms of organization are limited partnerships and limited liability companies.

A **limited partnership** includes one or more general partners that have responsibility for management and liabilities of the limited partnerships. Many have limited partners who are only investors that do not participate in management or share any responsibility for the liabilities. Limited partnerships are used to finance real estate acquisition and development and oil and gas exploration and production.

A **limited liability company** shields all the owners from responsibility for liabilities and are managed pursuant to an agreement among the owners (called members). Both limited partnerships and limited liability companies avoid double taxation by passing taxable income and losses directly to the owners and investors.

What Are the Economic Rights and Responsibilities of a Business?

Subject to certain governmental imposed limitations, such as franchise and licensing requirements, businesses have economic rights. The most basic economic right is what kind of business activity to conduct and where to conduct it. Other rights would include what employees to hire and fire (subject to certain child labor and anti-discrimination laws), how much to pay employees (subject to minimum wage laws), and how to conduct their business operationally (subject to Occupational Safety and Health Association (OSHA) and other federal and state regulations).

On the local level, every business start-up has the responsibility to determine if their proposed business is legal, requires licensing, and is legal in the location of their choice. Most cities have regulations that prohibit certain kinds of business conducted close to residential neighborhoods or schools. In addition, cities have provisions in their zoning codes that prohibit businesses from being conducted on land unless that land is specifically zoned for that purpose.

On the state level, the business owner needs to determine if sales taxes must be collected and remitted to the state. The State of Texas requires tax returns to be filed for all businesses other than sole proprietorships. Even if sales volumes are under the minimum required to pay taxes, the returns must still be filed. States also require filings and payments for unemployment taxes and workman's compensation insurance.

On the federal level, a tax return must be filed for every corporation, partnership, and limited liability company, even if no tax payments are due. Sole proprietorships report their taxable income and losses as part of the owner's personal tax return. Occasionally, small businesses get in trouble with the Internal Revenue Service by not fulfilling their responsibilities to withhold income, social security, and Medicare payroll taxes from their employee's paychecks and remit those taxes to the Internal Revenue Service along with the proper forms. In addition, once a year each business must make a federal unemployment tax payment.

How Do Corporations Raise Money?

Corporations have three sources of funding: (1) income earned but not paid out to shareholders, called retained earnings, (2) increasing debt, and/or (3) increasing ownership equity.

While the first source, income earned is the most preferable, sometimes it is inadequate, especially for new fast-growing companies.

Increasing debt is the next best option and is done in two ways, depending upon the size and the creditworthiness of the company. Small to mid-sized businesses can usually borrow directly from banks or nonbank commercial finance companies. Short-term money can be obtained by using receivables (what customers owe them) and inventory as collateral. The loans are based on a percentage of the carrying value of the collateral (usually 80 percent for receivables and 50 percent for inventory). If the collateral is in place and the lender's auditors approve of it, the loans can be renewed. Long-term money can be obtained by using fixed assets such as real estate, machinery, and equipment as collateral. The loans are usually paid down monthly, much like a home mortgage loan.

Large companies can bypass the banks and obtain short-term funds in the money markets and long-term funds in the capital markets. Money-market funds lend investor money to the U.S. government by buying Treasury Bills and to large corporations and banks by buying Commercial Paper. The Treasury Bills and Commercial Paper matures in 1-year or less. One advantage of the money market is that these securities do not require a costly registration process with the U.S. Securities and Exchange Commission (SEC). Another advantage is that all other things being equal, the shorter the loan, the lower the interest rate.

Long-term funds are available to corporations by issuing notes and bonds in the capital markets. These securities must be registered with the SEC before they can be sold unless they are sold privately to qualified financial institutions. The SEC's registration process focuses primarily on making sure that all the disclosures have been made by the company selling the securities so investors can make an informed decision about whether to buy the bonds.

An offering of any securities to the buying public of individual and institutional investors begins with the filing of an information document, called a registration statement, with the SEC. While the SEC is reviewing the document to determine if the disclosures are adequate, an underwriting firm will (a) conduct an examination of the company, called a due diligence review, (b) put together a syndicate of other underwriters and selling dealers for the bonds, (c) print some preliminary copies of certain parts of the document, called a preliminary prospectus, and (d) make inquiries as to their customers' level of interest in the securities. Once the SEC has completed their review and any corrections made in the document, the offering will be priced, and an interest rate will be set. The underwriting firm will buy the securities from the company at a discount and then resell them to their customers, preferably at full value.

If an underwriting firm sells the bonds privately to its institutional customers, a disclosure document like the registration statement is prepared but not filed with the SEC. The underwriting firm has the same responsibility for checking the document but usually acts as an agent for the company and sells the bonds for a commission rather than buying the bonds from the company and then reselling them to customers. In both the public sale and the private sale, the money raised goes directly into the company and the bonds are issued to the investors who buy them.

The least desirable option to raise money for a company is the sale of stock. Although there are a few very large private companies and a few very small publicly owned companies, these are exceptions. Most small to mid-sized businesses are privately owned and most large businesses are publicly owned. For small to mid-sized businesses, most owners do not wish to take on additional partners. Stock in business firms of this size is very difficult to sell and usually must be discounted because there is little or no resale value and a minority shareholder in a private company has little or no authority. In addition, there is a great deal of risk on the part of the owner of a private company selling stock. If something goes bad in the company, then the investors usually want their money back with a claim that not all the disclosures were made or that they were not made aware of the risks.

When large, publicly owned companies need money they can raise it by selling stock. Usually, the stock must be discounted from its quoted market value; otherwise, investors would just buy existing stock that trades in the market every day. In addition, when large companies sell stock, rather than bonds, investors believe that management thinks the stock is overpriced in the market. If it were underpriced, management would have the company buy it back from the market. Thus, when an announcement is made that a large company is offering additional shares of stock the market price goes down as people sell the stock. The process is like that of selling bonds but different from the process of a small company selling stock in a public offering.

Finally, a desirable option. Picture a small, rapidly growing company in a "hot" industry sector. For example, in 2012–2015, social media companies were the hot item in which many investors wanted to own shares. Other sectors that have been hot were biotech, internet, telecom, software, medical devices, pharmaceuticals, and energy. The Initial Public Offering (IPO) starts with selecting an underwriter to backstop the offering. Major underwriters have familiar names: Goldman Sachs, Morgan Stanley, Bank of America Merrill Lynch, J.P. Morgan Chase, and Citibank. The company, along with its lawyers and accountants, puts together a disclosure document containing everything that an investor would deem important in making their decision to invest. That document is filed with the SEC for review and comment.

While waiting for the SEC, a preliminary disclosure document is printed and used to promote the offering. The underwriters and senior management of the company then go from city to city, meeting with large investors and stock analysts and talking about the company. At the same time, the underwriters put together syndicates of other underwriters and selling dealers to spread the risk and help sell the stock. Customers are shown the preliminary document and asked for "indications of interest" in the new offering.

Once the SEC review is complete and all questions are answered and all corrections are made, the management and the underwriters meet the night before the offering is to begin and negotiate the offering price, based on the responses obtained from the underwriting group's customers. The next morning, stock is sold, and trading begins. The business hope that demand is strong for the stock, and it sells out the first day. As is the case with bonds, the underwriting group buys the stock from the company at an agreed-upon discount and then resells it to the investing public.

What Is the Role of Financial Institutions in Saving, Borrowing, And Capital Formation?

Functions of Financial Institutions

Households save for college expenses, down payments on a home, rainy day emergencies, and retirement. Households forego current consumption to save, expecting to earn income on their savings. We will use interest as a proxy for the earnings on savings, although earnings could include interest, dividends on stocks, rent on real estate, and capital gains on most assets in which households invest.

While businesses have some funds available from retained earnings for investment in capital goods and expansions, many have to either borrow more funds or sell ownership shares (stock) to investors. Capital investments are long-term assets and in most cases are too costly for a company to buy out of current income.

Imagine the difficulty and inefficiency of households searching for businesses in which to invest and businesses searching for households to lend them money or buy their stock. When this process actually works, it is called direct finance— households lending directly to or investing directly in business firms.

Financial institutions play a key role in channeling funds from household savings to business firms. They borrow from households and lend to business firms. This is financial intermediation. Here is a summary of the functions performed by financial institutions in this process.

Aggregation—financial institutions gather money from households in small amounts and make large loans to and investments in business firms.

Matching—investors know to put their savings in financial institutions. Businesses know to go to financial institutions to borrow. That is where the money is!

Underwriting—whether buying stocks or bonds, the financial institutions perform a great deal of examination and due diligence on businesses they lend to or invest in.

Risk assumption—financial institutions guarantee depositors will be able to get their money back whether the business pays off a loan or not.

Liquidity for households and long-term financing for business firms—households need to access their savings when they need to spend it arises: college tuition is due, the house acquisition is ready to close, or the emergency medical treatment bill must be paid. Business firms buy long-term illiquid assets with funds that should be paid back on a long-term basis.

The basis of capital formation

Two things are necessary for capital formation. First, the resources have to be available to produce the capital goods. Second, the funds must be available to purchase the capital goods. These two things are closely related. Both are related to actions are taken, or not taken, by households. When households forgo present consumption and save, these savings get recycled through financial institutions. These savings become the funds available for loans and investments in businesses to pay for capital goods. When this happens, some resources are withdrawn from the production of consumer goods and placed in the production of capital goods.

Countries that have a high degree of saving usually will have a high degree of resources devoted to production of capital goods. The supply of savings is high, so loans are inexpensive. Thus, large amounts of resources available for capital goods are inexpensive. For those two reasons, there is a large degree of capital formation and as a result, production is more efficient in those countries than in others. Japan would be a good example of a country with a high rate of savings and a very intense use of capital goods in production. Recall from Chapter 1 that shifting along with the PPC from producing consumer goods to producing capital goods will increase economic growth.

The interest rates that we pay or receive consist of three parts:

There is the **real interest rate** that includes a provision for risk-free time value of money, essentially the payment to use another's funds.

There is a provision for **expected inflation** that compensates the lenders because loans are paid back with money that has less value because of inflation. The higher the expected rate of inflation, the higher the interest rate.

There is a **provision for risk** that the loan may not be repaid, which is the risk of default. The higher the risk of default is, the higher the interest rate.

These add up to the nominal interest rate, which is what the borrower must pay:

Nominal Interest Rate = Real Interest Rate + Expected Rate of Inflation + Risk of Default

There is a wide range of interest rates paid by business firms. Large, well-established firms can borrow at low rates because their risk is lower. The problem for large firms is that they are not able to make investments that yield a high rate of return. Small growing firms are much riskier. They are new, their management can be inexperienced, they do not have much of a margin for error and in many cases, there is little or no knowledge in the field they have chosen because of its newness. For these reasons small firms, if they can borrow at all, must pay much higher rates of interest. However, because small firms are more agile and more creative, it is possible they can invest and earn a higher rate of return.

Financial intermediaries have a responsibility to evaluate potential lending and investing opportunities and evaluate the risk involved in each. The better job they do with that evaluation, the more efficient the allocation of capital.

If financial intermediaries are too cautious, good potential opportunities do not get funded, which puts a damper on invention and innovation.

If financial intermediaries are too cavalier about approving funding for potential opportunities, capital gets wasted, and "bubbles" can result.

Bubbles are phenomena that result when too much money is thrown at a specific opportunity and investors get caught up in the frenzy. The Greater Fool Theory can drive it: It does not matter what I pay for this asset as long as I can sell it to a greater fool than I am and make a profit. In the last half of the 1990s, start-up internet companies experienced such a bubble. During the mid to late 2000's, single family housing experienced a bubble, the bursting of which caused a financial crisis and a deep recession.

What Types of Accounts Are Available at Financial Institutions?

There is a wide array of choices for accounts at financial institutions. The risks, costs, and benefits of the most widely used accounts are described below.

Checking accounts at banks and savings and loan associations. The Federal Deposit Insurance Corporation (FDIC) guarantees them up to $250,000 for each individual or business firm, so the risk would only be a delay in receiving funds from the FDIC should the bank be liquidated. Benefits include liquidity, that is, being able to withdraw your funds without penalty; convenience of being able to withdraw funds from an automatic teller machine (ATM); and the record created by checks and account statements. The cost of these accounts varies with the amounts held in deposit—the larger the balances the lower the fee. Banks make a profit from offering checking accounts by charging monthly service fees.

Savings accounts at banks and savings and loan associations. These have the same guarantee from the FDIC as checking accounts and the risk of delay in payment or actual losses for accounts that exceed the FDIC guarantee should the bank be liquidated. Benefits include earning interest on the accounts, but the rates would depend upon the overall level of short-term interest rates. Some savings accounts are checkable, that is, you can withdraw funds by writing a check. Other savings accounts are less convenient, requiring the depositor to travel the financial institution when it is open for business and personally withdraw the funds.

Money market funds. While some of these are checkable, some are not. Banks and securities firms offer money market funds and pay higher rates of interest than savings accounts. Most are less liquid in that it will take longer for you to get access to your funds that are in a money-market.

Certificates of Deposit (CDs) from banks and savings and loan associations. These pay a higher rate of interest than savings accounts but have a penalty for early withdrawal. The larger the CD is and the longer is its maturity, the greater the interest rate and the greater the penalty for early withdrawal. CDs are clearly less liquid.

Credit Unions. These are non-profit institutions that can pay savers a slightly higher rate of interest with fewer fees. They charge borrowers a slightly lower rate of interest. Credit unions have been in existence since at least the mid-nineteenth century but are growing in popularity. Depositors "join" the credit union and become members. Many credit unions are open to the general public. Deposits in credit unions are insured up to $250,000 by the National Credit Union Administration (NCUA). So, deposits bear only the risk of delay in being reimbursed to the saver. Deposits of more than $250,000 are at risk of loss in liquidation.

What is the Role of the Individual in Financial Markets?

Be a wise investor. Wise investors have risk awareness. Most investors severely underestimate risk, most often in the following: stocks of rapidly growing companies, bonds with maturities of many years in the future, stock options, commodity futures, small businesses, start-up businesses, small-scale oil and gas drilling firms, marketing new inventions, and emerging market companies.

Wise investors do not put all their eggs in one basket. There are two kinds of risks with securities. The first is the **asset-specific risk** of the company itself, for example, the risk of a labor stoppage, the risk of a product recall, the risk that a new product will not have success as planned. The second is **market risk,** which is a risk to all firms, such as inflation and economic recessions. You can minimize the first kind of risk by diversification, that is, by buying securities in different firms in different industries. To diversify, a wise investor buys mutual funds.

Wise investors consider their time horizons. How long will it be before you need your money out of a savings or investment program? A down payment on a house, money to help pay your (or your children's) college education, or retirement. Most experts would agree that you need at least a 10-year time horizon to invest in stocks or mutual funds that own stocks.

When saving for and investing in the future, consider the effects of inflation. Whatever you are saving for may well go up in price, depending on the amount of time involved. Housing usually increases in value with inflation. Mortgage loans either could be easy to obtain with a small down payment or could be more difficult to obtain and require a large down payment. It will depend on the status of credit markets and governments involvement with mortgage loans. College tuition tends to increase every year or so. The amount of monthly income you believe you may need to live on when you retire will have to increase to keep up with inflation.

Begin a savings program. The earlier in life that you begin a savings program the better off you will be. It is never, never, never too late to start—you will just have to put more away if you wait too long. A painless way to begin is to have your employer make payroll deductions. That way you never see the money and do not consider spending it. If your employer does not make payroll deductions, then set up an automatic transfer each month from your checking to a savings account.

If you have an emergency and need to use part of your savings, it may be better to borrow against your saved funds and have a legal obligation to repay the loan. A loan is more likely to be repaid than if you take money from your savings account and fail to replace it later. It is important to develop the personal discipline necessary to begin and continue a savings program.

Create a personal retirement plan. The principal option available for investing in a personal retirement plan is a **mutual fund**. Mutual funds are investment companies that buy and hold securities—stocks and bonds—in other companies. They can be managed by an investment manager or passively managed by simply buying and holding the same securities that are present in one of the broad market indexes such as the S&P 500 or the Dow Jones Industrial Average. Passively managed funds have much lower overall costs than actively managed funds.

Many mutual funds specialize in certain categories of investments, such as short, intermediate, or long-term bonds, small companies, mid-size companies or large companies. Most mutual funds are "open end," so that investors can buy into the funds or redeem their investment in the funds on an ongoing basis. These transactions occur at net asset value, that is, the value of all the assets in the funds less any liabilities divided by the number of shares outstanding. Many mutual funds charge a commission to get in, some charge only when redeemed and that charge decreases the longer one owns the fund. Most charge their investors a 12-b-1 fee to pay for the marketing.

Another option that has become popular in recent years is the **Exchange Traded Fund (ETF)**. ETFs are closed-in investment companies. This means that investors do not buy in from the fund or sell out to the fund but can buy or sell the fund just like any individual stock. ETFs can be diversified like a mutual fund, can track a stock index, can invest in bonds, or can specialize in an industry, a country or part of the world, or any other degree of specialization that creative professionals can devise. A wise investor must be careful to know exactly what an ETF consists of, because some borrow a lot of money to make investments, and some buy a lot of exotic investments that are not only very high risk but difficult for even investment professionals to understand.

Individual stocks and bonds might not be practical for an individual investor. You need to have a large enough portfolio to be able to buy enough stock in individual companies and individual industries to achieve diversification and it is much more costly to buy less than 100 shares (an odd lot) because of commission rate structures. Also, individual company bonds are not a worthwhile investment choice for the small investor. Bonds usually have denominations of a minimum of $1,000 and lesser amounts of bonds are difficult to find.

Real estate is an asset class available to individual investors. Other than their personal residence, acquisitions of real estate as an investment is best left to specialists in real estate investing. Real estate is illiquid, that is, difficult to sell. Its value can fluctuate dramatically as the country realized in the crash of 2008. A small investor can use real estate as a diversifier by investing in funds that invest in real estate.

Maintain a checking account. When you open a checking account, keep a record of the deposits made, checks written, and the resulting balance. The goal is to prevent you from writing checks without funds in the bank to cover the check. Also, it will help you to spot errors and overcharges made by the bank. When you order checks, a register comes with the checks that look something like this:

CHECK REGISTER				
Date	**Payee**	**Checks**	**Deposits**	**Balance**

Record all checks written and deposits made, with the balance recalculated after each transaction. A minimum of once each month, when you receive the bank statement by mail or online, reconcile any difference between the ending balance on the bank statement and the balance in the check register.

The classic reconciliation is from bank balance to book balance and looks like this:

Balance per bank statement $4,000.00

Subtract outstanding checks:

Check number	Amount	
130	300.00	
131	400.00	
132	50.00	
Total	750.00	(750.00)

Add deposits in transit:

Date	Amount	
4/2/XX	150.00	150.00
Actual balance		$3,400.00

Outstanding checks have not yet been paid by the bank. An effective way of tracing these would be to check off each check in the register that appears on the bank statement. Those not checked off should be included in the outstanding check list.

Manage deposits the same way. Check off each deposit that is in the check register to see if they appear on the bank statement. The deposits that are "in transit" should be those that could have been mailed to the bank toward the end of the period covered by the bank statement or those that may have been made at the bank on the last day but were make after the afternoon cut-off and recorded on the next day.

If the balance does not reconcile, look for items on the bank statement but not on the check book. You could have failed to record something. Another thing to look for might be a monthly fee charged by the bank.

Bank customers can use the bank's electronic access to see their account activity at the bank every day or so, to keep a closer watch. Your bank may have an app so you can do this from your phone.

What Are the Responsibilities and Obligations of Borrowing Money?

There are several types of loans available to consumers. The cost of the loan depends upon the credit rating of the individual borrower and the collateral for a loan. A home mortgage, secured by a first lien on a borrower-occupied personal residence, is the least costly loan. A mortgage on a single-family residence occupied by a tenant would be slightly higher in cost. Loans secured by a new automobile or pickup truck would be higher still, followed by loans on a second-hand vehicle, and unsecured loans, like a credit card balance, would have a still higher interest rate.

Borrowing money, buying items on credit, and living above one's means, can be intoxicating, at least in the short run. Besides the moral obligation to pay back the loan or pay off the credit card bill, lenders and financing sources expect to be paid. All lending agreements have provisions on behalf of the lender to charge the borrower with steep fees for non-payment or for a past due payment. These fees and added interest changes can compound the obligations of the borrower and quickly render the situation from enjoyment of living beyond one's means to drowning in debt. The borrower's credit rating is lowered and any new loans, if available at all, come with a much higher price. Vehicle repossessions, home foreclosures, and/or bankruptcy may not be far behind.

You should want to be a "low-risk borrower." Low-risk borrowers pay less in borrowing costs. Becoming a low-risk borrower is a matter of having a good credit score. Good credit scores depend upon a good borrowing and payment history. The first step is establishing credit. Most college students get offered "starter" credit cards with a low credit limit to test how well they pay their obligations. You should use these cards to establish an unblemished payment history and rating.

Once you establish credit, you should pay bills as they come due and, if carrying a debt, pay more than the minimum required. Keep total purchases well within the credit limit set by the lenders. Do not apply for credit often. Pushing up against one's limit or applying for credit rapidly in succession are both red flags, as are paying late or non-payment at all. If the issuing agent sets a higher limit for you, do not immediately run up your balance to the higher limit. Obtaining copies of personal credit scores and reports and disputing any errors found therein is also important.

How Do You Apply Critical Thinking Skills to Personal Financial Decisions?

Avoid and eliminate credit card debt. Credit card debt is expensive. If you abuse the use of credit cards, you can be financially overwhelmed, demoralized, and harassed by collection agents. Abuse means only paying the minimum amount each month and continuing to charge more than one makes in the form of payments. You should avoid credit card debt by not charging more than one can pay off at each month. You should get into the habit of paying off the balance each month. Eliminating credit card debt means cutting up credit cards, controlling ones spending habits, and paying as much of the balance each month as possible.

Analyze the costs and benefits of declaring personal bankruptcy. Avoid personal bankruptcy if possible. The cost of such an event would include legal fees, which could range from as low as $5,000 up to six digits. The costs would not only include legal fees. You will ruin your personal credit for a number of years. Also, most employers are reluctant to employ someone who has declared personal bankruptcy.

The benefits would include debt relief, or relief from pending litigation. However, if one has reached the point of considering personal bankruptcy, you can negotiate much of the same relief without going into bankruptcy.

Analyze the costs and benefits of buying insurance. In general, we do not like uncertainty. Fortunately, uncertainty can be measured. The measure is risk. If you can estimate the probability of a negative event, then you can insure against the risk of it happening. A hedge is the act of buying or selling something that will pay off if the event happens to offset the loss of the negative event. Insurance is the same thing – the act of buying protection against the negative event's cost.

You should approach the cost-benefit decision this way. Cost: How much of a loss will you suffer should the event happen? How likely is it to happen? Does the state require insurance (liability insurance for drivers)? Does the lender for your car or home mortgage require insurance? The answer to those questions is usually "Yes," so you must buy insurance.

Insurance is cheap for those who need it the least and more expensive for those who need it the most. One thing to always remember—yes, the insurance company makes money when they sell you insurance. Their profits comes from what they know—it is their business or profession to know about the risk they are taking. We the insured usually do not have the tools to estimate the probability of a negative event. The insurance companies do. They can also spread the risk over a large population of insured people and assets. An individual cannot do that. They will either suffer the consequences of a negative event or not. If they do not, then it costs them nothing. But if they do, it can cost a lot.

Analyze the costs and benefits of charitable giving. In the past, non-profit institutions, charities, and religious institutions provided most social services or helped people in need. People gave money (and volunteer time) to these institutions and got the benefit of knowing how their money, time, and effort went for a worthy cause, and they got some benefit on their tax returns. Today, many of these functions have been taken over by government and now our tax dollars pay so that a government bureaucracy does this work.

The benefits of giving and volunteering to charities are still the same. The benefit of knowing how your donation or your time and effort helped other people exists but is hard to measure. There is a possibility of a tax deduction. When donating to a charity, it is always a good idea to inquire about how much of your contribution actually goes to helping people in need, how much simply pay to raise more funds, and how much pay the senior management.

How Do You Figure Out Where to Live?

You should always budget. Budgeting means identifying your income (dollar inflow) and your spending (dollar outflow) each month. Once you do that, then you can create a discipline to keep monthly spending lower than monthly income. This may require you to eliminate some spending to balance your budget. As you get used to budgeting, you can then add a routine monthly addition to your savings account as an outflow of money, to build up your net worth. Living within your means is a highly desirable attribute to have. Building up savings will enable you to have plans that become feasible.

Analyze the costs and benefits of renting a home. You have finally been "launched" and are moving away from home for the first time. Early in life, the flexibility of being able to pack up and move when a lease is up to a different location, closer to a new job, friends, or a significant other can be beneficial. Homeownership has benefits, but flexibility of location has benefits as well. While there are jobs available that pay moving expenses, including any loss on a quick sale of a house, most do not. Being flexible enough to move gives the job seeker or potential job changer a real advantage.

In addition to the flexibility of a quick move, things that go wrong with the apartment, duplex, or house you rent are usually the responsibility of the landlord/owner, not the renter. Maintenance of the premises, as well as the structure, are also the landlord's responsibility. Renting allows one to enjoy their leisure time, rather than spending it moving, edging, painting, and other normal maintenance of a property.

There are the usual costs of renting that one hears about in commercials for home mortgage lenders. Primarily, your rent payment goes to the property owner, and you get no tax benefits from it. Any appreciation of the property goes to the property owner, not the tenant.

Analyze the costs and benefits of buying a home. Many of the costs of homeownership are described in the section above as benefits of leasing. A homeowner has less flexibility to change locations for new job or other opportunities. The owner is responsible for maintenance and repairs. Depending upon interest rates, a house payment can be more expensive for the same property as a rent amount.

When you alone or as a couple are ready to settle down in one place, then you can realize the benefits of homeownership. Primarily, appreciation in the value of a home accrues to the owner. In times of inflation, single-family homes usually appreciate at least as fast as the rate of inflation. The cost of occupancy, other than taxes and insurance, is fixed, unlike renters, who are subject to increased rent as the property owner tries to make up for inflation.

Other benefits include a tax deduction to the extent that the house payment includes taxes and interest. In the early years of a home mortgage, most of one's house payment is interest, which is tax-deductible if you itemize your deductions rather than taking the standard deduction on your personal tax return.

Finally, there is that intangible, hard-to-measure benefit of entering your own home and knowing that it is yours, as long as you pay the house payment.

Analyze the transition from renting to home ownership. What about the transition of renting to homeownership? There is usually a down payment of as much as 20 percent of the purchase price. Accumulating the funds for the down payment usually requires a disciplined savings program. If you have a habit of saving that started when you got your first job, then you might be able to cover the down payment. If you need to start a savings program to be able to make a down payment on a house later in life, keep in mind that it is never too late to start.

How Can You Pay for College and Other Postsecondary Education And Training?

There are several ways to pay for college—scholarships from state governments, schools, employers, individuals, private companies, non-profits, and professional organizations. You should research and explore every scholarship opportunity. Many scholarships have ongoing requirements for maintaining grade point average. This is good for students because it helps keep them disciplined and focused on their work. Unlike loans, scholarships do not have to be paid back.

Work-study programs are another way of paying for college. These involve classroom education for a semester or a year and on-the-job training in the field one wants to pursue for a semester or a year. The funds earned in workstudy program can go a long way toward paying tuition and other costs of education.

Many grant opportunities are also available, so explore each with vigor. The Free Application for Federal Student Aid (FAFSA) has been made simpler, shorter, and more user friendly. It is explained in a video, along with many tips for applying for student aid, on the U.S. Department of Education website.

You should also explore any other available non-conventional routes to college. In any event, make every effort to minimize any student loans. Working while going to college may not have the greatest appeal to all students, but once finished, the graduate has a smaller, or no college loan to pay back, has the credibility of being able to finish college while working to pay for it, and considerable work experience to show a prospective employer. Some employers offer tuition reimbursement.

Finally, community colleges provide a low-cost way to get the basics of the first two years out of the way and many have seamless transfer routes to four-year universities. State colleges and universities are less expensive than private and/or for-profit colleges.

SUMMARY

1. **Describe the rights and responsibilities of starting a business.**

   Subject to many government-imposed regulations, the business owner has the right to decide what business to conduct and where to conduct it. Other rights would include what employees to hire and fire, how much to pay employees, and how to conduct their business operationally.

   Every business start-up has the responsibility to determine if their proposed business is legal, requires licensing and is permitted in the location of their choice. The business owner needs to determine if sales taxes are required to be collected on sales and remitted to the state. Numerous federal tax returns must be filed for every corporation, partnership, and limited liability company, even if no tax payments are due.

2. **Describe the role of financial institutions in saving, borrowing, and capital formation.**

   Financial institutions such as banks, insurance companies, and securities firms are financial intermediaries, giving savers a place to invest their savings and borrowers a place to obtain loans. These firms perform a capital allocation function – they decide which borrowers are worthy of backing and allocate funding to the most deserving borrowers. Their roles include aggregating small amounts of savings into larger loans, matching savers and borrowers, underwriting, risk assumption, and giving savers the ability to withdraw their funds when needed and borrowers the option of a long-term loan.

3. **Outline how you can become a wise investor.**

   Become aware of risks and do not take foolish risks trying to bet on the latest trendy investment, diversify your investments—just as you don't want all your eggs in one basket you also don't want all your investments in one place, industry, or fund. Consider your time horizon, buying stocks or funds that hold stocks requires a 10-year time horizon. Consider inflation. Do not be greedy. Remember, bulls make money, bears make money, but hogs get slaughtered.

4. **Tell me how you can initiate and maintain a savings program and a checking account?**

   One of the painless ways of beginning a savings program is to have your employer make payroll deductions from your paychecks. That way you never see the money and do not consider spending it. If your employer cannot or will not make the periodic payroll check deduction, then set up an automatic transfer each month from your checking to a savings account. If you have an emergency and need to use part of your savings, it may be better to borrow against your saved funds and have a legal obligation to repay the loan. A loan is more likely to be repaid than if you take money from your savings account and they try to restore it later.

   When you open a checking account, it is highly recommended that you keep a record of the deposits made, checks written, and the resulting balance. This is to prevent writing checks without funds in the bank to cover the check and will help people to be able to spot errors and overcharges made by the bank.

   Many bank customers also use the bank's electronic access to see their account activity at the bank every day or so, to keep a closer watch.

5. Describe the responsibilities and obligations of borrowing money.

Borrowing money, buying items on credit, and living above one's means, can be intoxicating, at least in the short run. Besides the moral obligation to pay back the loan or pay off the credit card bill a borrower takes on, lenders and financing sources like to be paid and expect to be paid. Paying and paying on time avoids steep fees, credit rating downgrades, vehicle repossessions, home foreclosures, and/or potential bankruptcy.

6. Describe how you should manage credit card debt.

If you abuse credit cards, they can become financially overwhelming and leave you, the borrower, demoralized and harassed by collection agents. Avoiding credit card debt means not charging more than you can pay off at each month. You achieve this by paying off the balance each month when the bill is received. One sure way to guard against credit card abuse is cutting up credit cards.

7. Describe how you should manage personal bankruptcy, insurance needs, and charitable giving.

Radio commercials for bankruptcy lawyers make it sound so easy and simple, but the after-effects are great. In addition to the legal fees, your personal credit is ruined for a number of years, and many employers are reluctant to employ someone who has declared personal bankruptcy.

Insurance is buying protection against the negative event's cost. Insurance is cheap for those who need it the least and relatively more expensive for those who need it the most. The insurance company makes money when they sell you insurance. Their profits come from taking risks that they understand and know how to measure. The insured usually do not have the tools to evaluate the risks.

The benefit of knowing how your donation to a charity or your time and effort helped other people is hard to measure. The possibility of a limited tax deduction is also available for charitable donations. When donating to a charity, it is always a good idea to inquire about how many of your dollars go for helping people in need and how many simply stay with the organization that raises the funds.

8. Describe how you should manage a personal budget?

This simply means analyzing the money you have been spending in the past, prioritizing that spending monthly into categories and deciding which are required and which are optional, and then ranking the spending by how important it is. Saving should be one of the important categories. Then fit the categories into the total monthly income available and eliminate those categories that exceed your monthly income.

9. Describe how you should decide whether to rent or to buy a home.

Until you are certain where you want to work and live, renting allows you to maintain more flexibility to get up and move.

When you alone or as a couple are ready to settle down in one place, then you can begin to realize the benefits of home ownership. Primarily, appreciation in the value of a home accrues to the owner. The cost of occupancy, other than taxes and insurance, is fixed. Other benefits include a tax deduction for the taxes and interest included in the house payment. Finally, there is that intangible, hard to measure benefit of entering your own home and knowing that it's yours, as long as you pay the house payment.

10. Identify what options are available to pay for postsecondary education and training.

There are many ways to pay for college—scholarships from state governments, schools, employers, individuals, private companies, non-profits, and professional organizations. You should research and explore every scholarship opportunity. Work-study programs are another way of paying for college. Many grant opportunities are also available.

You should also explore any other non-conventional routes to college that are available, including working. In any event, make every effort to minimize any student loans. Community colleges provide a low-cost way to get the basics of the first two years out of the way and many have seamless transfer routes to four-year universities.

Homework Chapter 16

Name_____

DESCRIPTIONS

Match the key terms with the descriptions.

_____ Legal entities that directly own their assets and are directly responsible for their liabilities.

_____ Obligations if the U.S. Treasury is due and payable in 1-year or less.

_____ A company that raises money for other companies by selling their stocks and bonds to its customers.

_____ Meetings with large investors and stock analysts to pitch a company's prospects.

_____ A study and examination of a company's past results and prospects.

_____ Interest rates that are adjusted for inflation.

_____ Interest rates that we pay or receive without any adjustments.

_____ The process of devoting resources to the production and acquisition of physical and human capital goods.

_____ Phenomena that results when too much money is thrown at a specific opportunity and investors get caught up in the frenzy.

_____ The government-sponsored institution that guarantees bank deposits up to a certain amount.

_____ Accounts where funds can be withdrawn remotely by writing a check.

_____ Non-profit institutions that pay savers a higher rate of interest and charge borrowers a lower rate of interest than banks.

_____ The process of spreading investments across many different companies in different industries (not putting all of one's eggs in one basket).

_____ The length of time before one needs the money, primarily for retirement.

_____ Investment companies that buy and hold securities in other companies.

_____ Checks which have been written and mailed or given to others but have yet to be presented for payment.

_____ A loan provision giving the lender the first right to foreclose or repossess a home, auto, or another asset.

_____ The act of buying protection against the cost of a negative event.

_____ Combination of classroom education and job training in the field.

_____ Bank savings programs that pay the saver a higher rate of interest but charge fees if cashed in before maturity.

KEY TERMS

1. Bubbles.
2. Capital formation.
3. Certificates of deposit.
4. Checkable accounts.
5. Corporations
6. Credit unions.
7. Diversification.
8. Due Diligence.
9. Federal Deposit Insurance Corporation (FDIC).
10. First lien.
11. Insurance.
12. Mutual funds.
13. Nominal interest rates.
14. Outstanding checks.
15. Real interest rates.
16. Roadshow.
17. Time horizon.
18. Treasury bills.
19. Underwriting firm.
20. Work-study programs.

EXERCISES

1. List and briefly describe the three types of business ownership.

2. Describe the role that financial institutions play in channeling savings from households to business firms.

3. Describe the relationship between households saving (forgoing consumption) and capital formulation.

4. What are credit unions and what role do they play in the financial markets?

5. Identify the characteristics of wise investors.

6. Describe a painless way to begin a savings program.

7. How does one avoid or eliminate credit card debt?

8. Describe the costs and benefits of owning your own home.